WINE BUSINESS
CASE STUDIES

Thirteen Cases
From the Real World of
Wine Business Management

PIERRE MORA

WINE
BUSINESS
CASE STUDIES

PIERRE MORA

THE WINE APPRECIATION GUILD
SAN FRANCISCO

Wine Business Case Studies
Thirteen cases from the real world of wine business management

Published by
The Wine Appreciation Guild
360 Swift Avenue
South San Francisco, CA 94080
(650) 866-3020
wineappreciation.com

Text copyright © 2013 Pierre Mora

Managing Editor: Bryan Imelli
Assistant Editors: Claude Garrabos and Corrine Cheung
Book Design: Diane Spencer Hume

Contents

Contributing Authors

Huia Vineyards: Sustainability as a Path to Success for a New Zealand Winery

Sharon L. Forbes is a Senior Lecturer of Marketing at Lincoln University in Christchurch, New Zealand. Her Ph.D. was completed in 2009 and examined the factors influencing the purchase behavior of wine consumers in New Zealand, Australia, the United Kingdom and the United States. Her wine-related research is predominantly focused on consumer behavior, as well as supply chain strategies, taste preferences, brand name perceptions, and the marketing of "sustainable" wines.

Stella di Campalto Winery: The Biodynamic Pioneer in Montalcino

Dr. Cristina Santini is Researcher at Università Telematica San Raffaele, Italy, where she lectures on Management and International Management. She earned her Ph.D. in Economics and Management of Enterprises and Local Systems at the University of Florence in 2008, and has been visiting scholar at Sonoma State University in California. Her research interests are Entrepreneurship and Strategic Management. She currently consults in research projects with the Italian Centre for Sensory Analysis in Matelica (Macerata).

Dr. Armand Gilinsky, Jr. (Corresponding author) is Professor of Business at Sonoma State University, where he has taught Strategy and Entrepreneurship since 1998. In recent years he has served as Director of SSU's Entrepreneurship Center, Wine Business Program, and Small Business Institute.

Dr. Alessandro Cavicchi is Senior Researcher at the University of Macerata, Italy, where he lectures on Marketing and Tourism.

Grandes Vinos y Viñedos: Wine Cooperatives Join Forces to Reach International Markets

Dr. Luis Miguel Albisu has a Ph.D. in Agricultural Economics from Cornell University (United States) as well as a doctorate in Agricultural Engineering from the Polytechnic University of Madrid (Spain). He also has a M.Sc. in Agro-Food Marketing from Newcastle (UK). He heads the Department of Agro-Food Economics at the CITA (Agro-Food

Research and Technological Centre of Aragon, Spain). He has been doing research on wine markets for more than 25 years. He has served on the Spanish Delegation at the OIV working group on Markets for eight years. He has published many articles in European journals and is the author and/or editor of more than ten books. His main research interests lie in food marketing, especially consumer behavior, the agro-food industries and the agro-food supply.

Winzergenossenschaft Westhofen: A German Wine Cooperative Evaluates Strategic Positioning

Prof. Dr. Marc Dressler, MBA, is professor for business administration and entrepreneurship at University of Ludwigshafen and heads the program of viticulture and enology. His scientific focus is on strategy, organization, and innovation.

Marc Dressler started his professional career in financial services followed by employ¬ments at well reputed management consultancies. He then established his own consultancy and founded Corporate Value Associates (CVA) Germany to become one of the four global senior partners leading the top-management consulting boutique CVA. He thereby successfully established longstanding client relationships with a rich portfolio of projects for globally leading companies in different industries.
Marc´s academic background is in business administration. Initial studies at the University of Nuremberg were followed by a Master of Business Administration at the University of Vermont and a PhD at the Wirtschaftsuniversität Wien, both with engagements as teaching assistant. Later he lectured at diverse universities.

Anika Kost works as an assistant for the professors of business administration and marketing in the BSc program of viticulture and enology, the first dual university program of viticulture and oenology in Germany. Before joining the university Anika supported wineries in their sales, events and direct marketing as a consultant working for marketing agencies specialized in the wine industry. Anika initially started in the food industry becoming managing director for a brand flagship store in the city of Frankfurt for an important brand of the Nestlé group. Anika holds a diploma as nutritionist.

Recovering from Bankruptcy: Towards a New Marketing Strategy for Mont Tauch Cooperative

Hervé Remaud is a Senior Professor of marketing at KEDGE Business School, France.. He is also an Adjunct Senior Research Associate at the Ehrenberg Bass Institute for Marketing Science (uniSA, Adelaide). Professor Remaud is the Academic Head of the Wine and Spirits MBA, a fully accredited MBA program dedicated to the wine and spirits industries. His research interest focuses on wine and spirits consumers' behavior and its impact on marketing strategy of the wine and spirits businesses.

Philippe Dunoguier has been working in the wine industry since 1997, starting as Area Export Manager for one of the leading wine merchants in Bordeaux in creating, launching and managing the Bordeaux City Bond with the Chamber of Commerce and Industry of Bordeaux. Since 2011, he has set up his own agency, Vidi Vini Vidum, as a consultant on sales and management issues. He is also a part-time lecturer at BEM_KEDGE BS and also at the IPC Vins (Marketing and International Trade).

Marketing Chilean Wine Domestically: Comparing Wine Sales at Supermarkets and Specialty Wine Shops

Marcos Mora G. is an Agricultural Engineer and Doctor in agricultural business. His main research is foods marketing and agribusiness management. Since 1997 he has been an assistant professor at the University of Chile, an institution which offers the wine marketing course to master's students in enology and viticulture. He has advised major vineyards of central Chile, Wine of Chile and the Chilean Association Oenologists, and also belongs to the research staff of the Wine Consortium (VINNOVA and TECNOVID) in the area of benchmarking. He has written numerous articles on the Chilean wine industry, primarily in marketing and business development strategies for wine industry.

Rodrigo Escobedo is an Agricultural Engineer and Master in viticulture and oenology at the University of Chile. His main job is marketing wine, an area in he which has investigated consumer behavior toward Chilean wine. He is currently working in the vineyard Caliterra.

Cristian Adasme is an Agricultural Engineer and MA in International Agribusiness Management. His main research is foods marketing. Since 2005 he is assistant professor at the Catholic University of Maule. He has worked in marketing food and wine in general, mainly organic. He has been a board member of the Center for Processed Food Maule, under the National Commission on Science and Technology of Chile.

Brunello di Montalcino Wine Farms: Remaining Competitive Through Full-Cost Accounting

Silvio Menghini, Ph.D. in Economics and Agricultural Policy, is Full Professor at GESAAF, Department of Agricultural, Food and Forestry Systems, University of Florence, Italy and currently he holds the course in "Agro-food and wine marketing"; he is Editor in-Chief of the Journal of "Wine economics and policy" and he is Member of the Scientific Committees of Ph.D. in "Viticulture Economics and Rural Development" and in the Master of "Wine Management and Marketing" at the University of Florence. His main research fields are rural development, economics and marketing, with a specific attention on local products, wine and oil, accounting.

Enrico Marone, Ph.D. in Forest Economics and Planning, is an Associated Professor at GESAAF, Department of Agricultural, Food and Forestry Systems, University of Florence, Italy and currently he holds the courses of "Viticulture and Enology Economics," "Marketing," and "Ecological economics evaluation." He is Member of the Scientific Committees of the Ph.D. in "Viticulture Economics and Rural Development" and in the Master of "Wine Management and Marketing" at the University of Florence. His main research fields are wine economics and marketing and accounting.

Veronica Alampi Sottini holds a Ph.D. in "Economics, Forestry Planning and Wood Sciences." Her specific scientific and research activities are: wine and oil economics and policy, environmental economics and land planning, rural development and rural tourism, CAP and national agricultural policies. Currently, she is Assistant to Research on "Multifunctional agriculture and competitiveness of the olive oil and wine Tuscan farms" at the GESAAF, Department of Agricultural, Food and Forestry Systems, University of Florence, Italy.

Nicola Marinelli is a Lecturer in "Rural Economics and Appraisal" at GESAAF, Department of Agricultural, Food and Forestry Systems, University of Florence, Italy. He holds a bachelor degree in Economics and a Ph.D. in Economics of Food Resources and the Environment. His main research fields are related to food marketing and consumer behaviour, with a particular focus on typical products and wine, economics and regulation of food safety, rural development, environmental economics and policy.

Marco Bertocci is a Ph.D. student in "Wine Economics and Rural Development", at the Ph.D. School of Agricultural Research at the University of Florence, Italy. He holds a bachelor degree in Quality Management of Food Products. He collaborates with UniCeSV (Centre for the Strategic Development of the Italian Wine Sector, University of Florence) and his main research fields are related to production costs in the wine sector, with a particular focus on Tuscan DOCG and DOC wines.

Dominio del Plata Winery: Keeping Competitive in a Rapidly Growing Wine Market

Javier Merino has a degree in Industrial Engineering granted by Universidad Nacional de Cuyo and Magister in Economy and Project Assessment at Pontificia Universidad Católica de Chile. Javier Merino is a Consultant for international organizations and Director of Área del Vino, an Argentinean company specializing in wine business communication, training and consultancy. He is also Professor in Business Economics at Universidad de Mendoza and at the Master's in Wine Business Program at Universidad Maza.

The Great Cork Debate 2012: Cork Stages a Comeback

Dr. Thomas Atkin is Professor of Operations and Supply Chain Management at Sonoma State University where he teaches in the Wine Business Program. He received his PhD in Supply Chain Management from Michigan State University in 2001 after a 25 year career in management. His research interests include customer-supplier relationships, sustainable business practice, and wine consumer preferences. He has published in International Journal of Wine Business Research, Negotiation Journal, and Journal of Business Logistics.

Dr. Duane Dove is Professor of Management at Sonoma State University.

Dark Horse Ranch Vineyard: A Mendocino County, California, Biodynamic Winemaker Explores Future Directions

Liz Thach, Ph.D., MW (pronounced "tosh") is a management and wine business professor at Sonoma State University in the Wine Business Institute, where she teaches in both the undergraduate and Wine MBA programs. Liz's passion is wine, and she has visited most of the major wine regions of the world and more than 35 countries. In addition, she is an award-winning author who has published over 100 articles and fivewine textbooks, including *Wine—A Global Business* and *Wine Marketing & Sales*. A fifth generation Californian, Liz finished her Ph.D. at Texas A&M and now lives on Sonoma Mountain where she tends a small hobby vineyard and makes garagiste wine. She also works as a wine judge in various competitions, and has served on many non-profit wine boards. Liz obtained the distinction of Master of Wine (MW) in May of 2011

A Cru Bourgeois-Médoc: Will Joining a Wine Alliance Improve Quality and Sales?

Tatiana Bouzdine-Chameeva is a Senior Professor of Operations Management and Information Systems at KEDGE Business School, France. She holds a Ph.D. in applied mathematics from Moscow State University, Russia. She is a leader of the Wine and Spirits Management Academy research team at BEM. Her current studies are on decision analysis and decision-making applied to the wine sector. She publishes in top journals such as Decision Sciences and European Journal of Operational Research, Journal of Retailing and Supply Chain Forum. She is the editor of the International Business Management Journal (IBMJ).

Philippe Barbe holds a Ph.D. in economics from Bordeaux University. He teaches macroeconomics and international finance at KEDGE Business School, France. He is the head of the Risk Management Institute, a specialized program in risk management. His research interests concern financial markets, wine economics and risk management.

Mouton Cadet: A Branded Wine in the Universe of First Great Growths

Jacques-Olivier Pesme has completed doctoral studies in France and in the U.S.A. Formerly in charge of BEM's 'Wine & Spirits Management Academy', he is currently International Development Director at KEDGE Business school, France. He's currently BEM Associate Dean, Bordeaux Management School, in charge of the 'Wine & Spirits Management Academy. Researcher for the CNRS (National Center for Scientific Research) and ISVV member (Institute of Vine and Wine Sciences), he has published several articles on wine sector strategy in collaboration with national and international organizations. He is Vice-President of the Bordeaux Wine & Business Club. An Oenovation Prize winner in 2003, he was awarded in 2004 by the French Prime Minister for the best technological innovation in the wine business sector.

BONNET-GAPENNE: A BORDEAUX WINE MERCHANT EVALUATES FUTURE POSITIONING

Pierre Mora is a Marketing Professor at KEDGE Business School, France. He is in charge of marketing courses at the Wine and Spirits MBA, a fully accredited MBA program dedicated to the wine and spirits industries and also at the Master Vins et Spiritueux. His research interest focuses on wineries' and merchants' strategic behavior, wine branding and strategic marketing. He has published many books on wine business, case studies and "The French Paradox—wine business game" which was awarded at the European Academic Software Awards.

Foreword

"In theory there is no difference between theory and practice. In practice there is."

—Yogi Berra

The world of marketing is full of experts who have theories to explain even the most delicate nuances of brand development and consumer behavior. The theories make fascinating reading because they offer so many different ways to explore every level of a marketing problem. *Excuse me,* an opportunity. In marketing theory, there are no problems, only opportunities. At least, that's the theory. Entire books have been written about how to approach (and solve) virtually every element of marketing. Those who graduate with advanced degrees in marketing should feel as if they prepared to attack any brand position, and take leadership in any category.

And yet they quickly find that there are many questions still to be answered—questions that arise because the world of theories is beautiful and pure. And perfect.

We do not live in a perfect world. And when it comes to marketing wine, we don't even come close. Between the wildly different cultural associations of wine and the Byzantine regulations around the world, wine marketers would happily settle for a logical world. Which is a world they will not see in our lifetimes. Instead, every market research project discovers at least one kernel of pure truth: that there were other questions that should have been asked, and there are important questions that only became apparent once the initial responses were evaluated. In theory, it is possible to create the perfect market study. In practice....

Every product roll-out is faced with any number of unforeseen circumstances that challenge the campaign and force the managers to stop and think. Usually, what they are thinking is: "The theories said this would work..."

What Pierre Mora has done in this book is collect a series of very practical case studies from those who have done more than just theorize. They have tried to put those theories into practice. And they have discovered that some theories don't work. They have discovered that things do not always go according to plan. Yvonne Chouinard famously said that "It's not an adventure until something goes wrong."

Exactly. And what the authors have shared in these chapters is true gold. Sure, many of these case studies are excellent examples of how a marketing theory holds truth. But even more importantly, they show us where those theories run up against the stone wall of reality, and what can be done about it. It is not always pretty, but it is always educational.

Welcome to tales of the adventures of marketing, brought to you by those who have lived to tell the tale.

—Paul Wagner
Balzac Communications and Marketing
Napa, California
December 3, 2013

Introduction

The originality of this book on the world of wine resides in the fact that for the first time, authors have come together from the four corners of the world to write a series of case studies that each express a specific identity, set of issues and plans. Above and beyond their local particularities, many of these cases also possess an international dimension—if only because the world market is generally growing more quickly than the domestic markets where the companies under study here originate.

The global market for wine is peculiar. At one level, three producer countries (Italy, Spain and France) clearly dominate, accounting for 50% of total output. Domestically, however, these three markets are stagnating and even in decline. There is wide product variety, ranging from Grand Cru elite vintages to mass wines. Plus new countries now lead the race in both production and consumption terms: starting with United States, characterised by a young and educated market enjoying strong purchasing power; but also, on the other side of the world, China, where a new elite of more than 100 million potential consumers is also starting to take an interest in wine.

Wine producers continue to invest in new technological, geographical and commercial fields, influenced by the effects of global warming and by an intensely competitive market whose rules are constantly changing. Hence this collection's broad range of strategic choices that sometimes contradict one another. Innovation—whether in relation to vineyard management, vinification or wine ageing—is also viewed as a factor of differentiation. This is because each region has its own codes, with consumers who differ in terms of expectations and behaviour. Similarly, it is sometimes difficult to compare governance modes and performance criteria between cooperatives, chateaus or groups from one and the same appellation.

All of which explains why it is so hard yet exciting to manage a company in this sector, whether you are a producer working out of a chateau, a merchant operating in a market space or an importer bringing wines to a big urban area. The question here is how unique strategies might be combined with universal factors of success. The range of possible business models is infinite.

Hence the present book's decision to rely on a variety of approaches that can only receive the airing they deserve in a collection of this kind. Far from arguing a particular doctrine or trying to establish general rules, the case study method that is used here allows readers to immerse themselves in a story and discover the underlying problems, before justifying why certain decisions had to be made. Authors also express their opinion following each case study, translating their personal sensitivities and, sometimes, the kinds of management tools that they want to apply.

A quick overview of the cases found in this book starts with New Zealand's Huia vineyards, where the emphasis is on sustainable development. Not dissimilar to this is the Stella di Campalto winery in Italy, which focuses on the power of commercial differentiation that comes with biodynamic production. Spain's Grandes Vinos y Vinedos case study revolves around export issues, whereas the German Winzergenossenschaft Westhofen wine cooperative shows the strategic specificities associated with this kind of company. Another cooperative from the south of France—Mont Tauch—involves a strategy where the goal is to improve upon today's fragile positioning. Further downstream, the Supermercados Jumbo y Lider case study illustrates the distribution problems that companies face in Chile. Back in Italy, Brallo di Montalcino mainly focuses on management control and cost analysis issues. As for Argentina's Dominio of the Plata, here the case focuses on the competitive advantages of New World players. Then, in the USA, Rodney Strong Vineyards lends itself to a discussion about the use of corks. Another Californian wine grower, Dark Horse Vineyards, is analysed in terms of its biodynamics positioning. Lastly, three French case studies complete the collection. The first looks at the Alliance des Crus Bourgeois du Médoc, highlighting the appellations system and new forms of accreditation and quality certification that have developed in this region. Mouton Cadet provide an opportunity to look at a French way of modeling brand development. Lastly, the Bonnet Gapenne case study enhances understanding of the specificities of the Bordeaux marketplace and the role that merchants play there.

Following this review of our collection, one clear thing is that few studies tardy over the "stars" in this field, players that tend to be over-capitalised and are therefore frequently objects of speculation and hyper-publicity. Instead of this, we have chosen to focus on the "simple reality" of the global wine industry, a business where actors must cope with natural and market uncertainty and innovate to build business models that are in tune with what their consumers want. This reflects our opinion that these kinds of case studies are more instructive and of greater use to the reader.

In short, the book is aimed at anyone with an interest in wine markets all across the world; in the behaviour of consumers, producers and merchants; and in all of the parties operating up and down the branch's value chain. The case study methodology teaches students to work with available real data but does not stop them from bringing their own ideas to the table and comparing what they see with practices that are familiar to them. Hence the particular recommendation that this book be used as part of an international executive education programme. At the same time, it is also invaluable to students with a technological background in oenology and winegrowing, and who may be looking to improve their understanding of the kinds of contemporary issues that they will face in the marketplace.

The project is deeply indebted to Anisya and Lynn Fritz, owners of Lynmar Estate Winery, who organised a wine business education meeting that brought together most of the case studies' authors. Our sincere thanks goes out to them. We are also grateful to

Bruno Boidron, Managing Director at Bordeaux publisher Féret and someone who was very effective in helping the Wine Appreciation Guild team in San Francisco to edit the book. Lastly, our deepest thanks goes out to Claude Garrabos, Head of Publications at KEDGE-BEM, Business School. Claude worked tirelessly for more than a year to ensure the smooth running of this project.

The idea for this book was born in the New World—specifically, in California's Sonoma Valley. It came to fruition in the Old World, on the doorstep of the Bordeaux vineyard. It is this itinerary that allows it to communicate all of the wonderful and exciting things that are happening in the world of wine. Few rival books can say the same.

—Pierre Mora
Professor
KEDGE Business School
France

CASE

1

Huia Vineyards

Sustainability as a Path to Success for a New Zealand Winery

Sharon L. Forbes
Faculty of Commerce, Lincoln University, Christchurch, New Zealand

Summary

Sustainable business practices and the quest to achieve the triple bottom line have affected how vineyards operate in the wine industry. Huia Vineyards is one of New Zealand's earliest examples of a winery that follows sustainable business practices. Its success and economic growth are in large part due to its commitment to its employees and to developing a vineyard that has a reduced environmental impact. Additionally, Huia's long-term pledge to these principles enabled them to better weather the 2008 global economic crisis.

Introduction

Huia Vineyards Limited is a small, wine-producing company located in the Marlborough region of New Zealand (see figure 1). Marlborough is the largest of New Zealand's wine regions and is best known for its distinctive Sauvignon Blanc wines. The Marlborough wine region is centered on the town of Blenheim and lies toward the north of New Zealand's South Island (as indicated by the dotted circle on the map of New Zealand in figure 1).

Figure 1. New Zealand with Marlborough wine region circled.

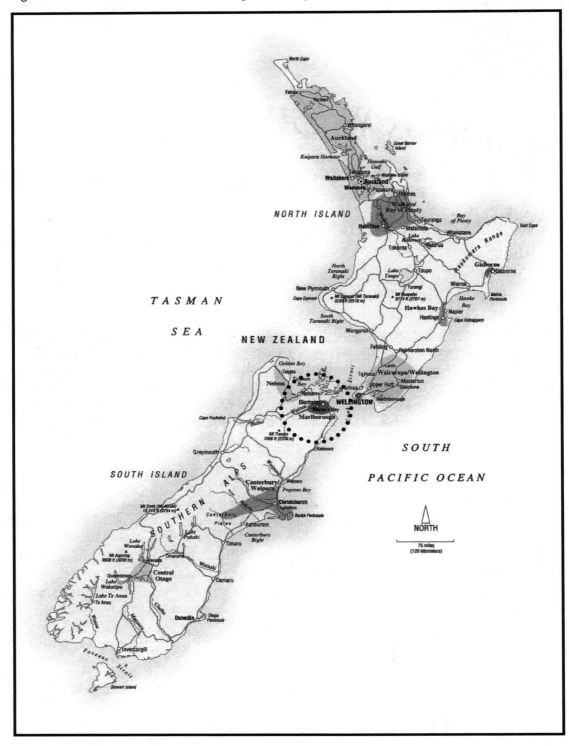

Claire and Mike Allan purchased land in Marlborough in 1990 to found Huia. Their company owns 28 hectares of vineyard area in Marlborough and also sources grapes from four contract growers with properties totaling an additional 26 hectares. In the 2011 vintage, Huia processed 430 tons of grapes and 309,600 liters of wine. The company produces wine varietals such as Sauvignon Blanc, Pinot Noir, Pinot Gris, Gewurztraminer, Riesling, and Chardonnay, as well as rosé and sparkling styles. Huia wines are available in the domestic market, but around 90% of the wine produced by the company is sold in export markets that include the United Kingdom, the United States, Australia, Canada, Germany, Ireland, the Netherlands, Russia, Singapore, and Sweden. Wines sold through the Huia cellar door are priced at NZ $21 to $37 and are available online to US customers at US $18 to $28.

Sustainability has been described as one of the most defining megatrends of commerce in the twenty-first century. Leading global brands have adopted sustainability as a key business orientation. Business executives are recognizing that engagement in sustainability is critical to their ongoing business success. The increasing attention that businesses are paying to sustainability is mirrored within academia, governments around the globe, and nongovernmental organizations. Since the 1990s there has also been a marked increase in the volume of media content that is devoted to the concept of sustainability.

The objective of this case study is to examine Huia Vineyards to see how they have incorporated sustainability within their business strategies, operations, and culture. Huia provides a practical example from which sustainability, across environmental, social, and economic dimensions, can be explored.

THE NEW ZEALAND WINE INDUSTRY

The New Zealand wine industry has expanded rapidly during recent decades but it is a very small producer in global terms. It accounts for about 1% of total global wine production and 1.5% of the global wine trade. Production levels in 2011 are estimated to be around 235 million liters from a harvest of 328,000 tons.

Sauvignon Blanc is the dominant varietal produced in New Zealand. The variety accounted for 69% of the total wine produced in 2011, and eight out of every ten bottles exported are Sauvignon Blanc. The majority of Sauvignon Blanc produced is grown in the Marlborough wine region. Indeed, the harvest from the Marlborough region in 2011 was 245,000 tons and wine production from this single region accounted for over 75% of the national vintage. Other varietals produced in New Zealand include Pinot Noir, Chardonnay, Pinot Gris, Merlot, and Riesling.

The domestic market is still the largest single market for New Zealand wine, and sales grew in this market by 2% in 2011 from the previous year. Per capita wine consumption in the domestic market has now increased to 21.3 liters per annum, but there is clearly the potential for further growth because consumption is much lower than in many Old World wine-producing nations.

The value of wine exported from New Zealand from 2000 to 2011 increased by 294% and now exceeds the NZ $1 billion mark. The top three export markets for New Zealand wine are Australia, the United Kingdom, and the United States. Exports to Australia in 2011 remained level with the previous year, but exports to the United Kingdom grew by 11% and US exports grew by 22%. Bulk wine exports have increased in recent years and now account for around 30% of total exports. This situation has had an impact on the price received for New Zealand wine exports, with the average price of exported wine falling by 3.5% in 2011 from the previous year.

Sustainability

The term "sustainable" is often used rather vaguely to imply everything that is good and desirable; critics argue that the term is used so widely that it has become effectively meaningless. Most definitions of sustainability focus on meeting the needs of the present without compromising the ability of future generations to meet their needs. Definitions typically contain reference to the constrained consumption of resources and to responsibility for effects on the natural world while ensuring ongoing economic viability and healthy stakeholder relationships.

Historically, businesses had a sole focus on profitability. The profit motive was the dominant driver in business thinking for many decades. The introduction of stakeholder theory in the 1980s changed the business paradigm. Stakeholder theory suggests that businesses also need to have a focus on the impact of their decisions on internal and external stakeholders.

The 1990s saw the emergence of the "term triple bottom line," introducing the idea that sustainable businesses should focus on environmental, social, and economic issues and integrate these factors into decision making at all levels within a business. Sustainability combines profit, people, and the planet into a business's culture, strategy, and operations. In other words, business sustainability is seen as addressing the concerns of all stakeholders, the impact on the physical environment, and the ability to remain profitable. Sustainable businesses also consider factors such as job security and the working environment, alongside relationships with the wider community, environmental responsibility, and economic viability.

The establishment of the Dow Jones Sustainability Indexes in 1999 is a further example of the growing focus on sustainability in businesses. In accordance with the triple bottom line concept, the Dow Jones Sustainability Indexes track the performance of companies in terms of economic, environmental, and social criteria. One view of a sustainable business is that it has ongoing financial viability with no detrimental impact on the social or physical environment within which it operates.

Although the term triple bottom line suggests an equal focus on people, planet, and profit, it seems that businesses, consumers, and the media frequently associate the concept of sustainability only with practices that concentrate on environmental protection. There is a high level of knowledge and understanding of environmental issues across businesses and the general public. In many instances, businesses that adopt one or more environmentally-focused practices claim that they are "sustainable." A vast amount of academic research has concentrated primarily on environmental issues (e.g., understanding the drivers for adoption of environmental practices by businesses or identifying consumer attitudes and behaviors toward "green" products). In recent years, the social aspect of sustainability has also had an increased focus, with academic research exploring ideas such as corporate social responsibility or corporate citizenship.

However, there is considerably less research that has truly focused on the triple bottom line nature of sustainability (i.e., people, planet, and profit).

The benefits that businesses can gain through adopting sustainable practices are numerous. These include improved environmental performance, reduced costs, increased efficiencies, market advantages, and improved employee morale and retention. Many claim that sustainability should be added as another dimension of strategic competitive advantage. Sustainability influences the purchase intentions of consumers; however, the direct impact of sustainability claims on purchasing decisions is highly disputed because intentions don't necessarily transcribe into actual behavior. Although consumer awareness of sustainable products has certainly increased, the true importance of the concept and its influence on other product attributes, such as quality, remains largely unknown.

Sustainability is relevant across manufacturing and agricultural industry sectors. It is therefore also applicable to the global wine industry. For the wine industry, sustainability should mean growing grapes and making wine in ways that are sound environmentally, socially equitable, and economically viable. In general, the wine industry has certainly not received as much negative media attention and coverage as other industries. However, environmental issues relating to wine production have gained prominence in recent years. The type of environmental issues associated with wine production include the use of chemical pesticides and herbicides, the loss of natural habitat and species, the depletion of water or of water quality, the emission of greenhouse gases, and the production of organic and packaging wastes. Social issues that exist in the wine industry include employee-related concerns such as workplace opportunity, workplace safety, employee satisfaction, human resource policies, and local hiring, as well as factors such as local purchasing, supporting community events, and ethical business dealings with other companies.

As in other industries, wineries typically think first and foremost about the environmental aspect of sustainability. Not surprisingly, wine producers link sustainability with improved soil and grape quality and enhancement of the character, or terroir, of their vineyards. The implementation of formal environmental management systems (EMSs) by wineries is one area that has received much attention. An EMS is a strategic management approach that defines how a business will address its impact on the environment. Typically an EMS will involve the establishment of an environmental plan, the identification of goals to reduce environmental impacts, the implementation of appropriate actions, and then an assessment of how well the actions have met the goals. Most EMSs are focused solely on improved environmental health, although some also emphasize social responsibility and economic viability.

ISO 14001 is the most widely implemented voluntary EMS program in the world and is one that has been adopted by wineries. However, a number of regional or national wine industry organizations have also developed EMSs that are industry specific. Examples include the California Code of Sustainable Winegrowing Practices, South Africa's Integrated Production of Wine scheme, and New Zealand's Sustainable Winegrowing (SWNZ) program. The number and diversity of certifications and standards adopted in the global wine industry creates confusion for consumers and remains a challenge for the industry to resolve.

There are several drivers that encourage wineries to implement an EMS. Personal values of key stakeholders, corporate culture, industry pressure, industry regulations, employee welfare, cost efficiencies, wine quality, brand equity, product positioning, competitive advantage, and increased sales are all drivers of environmental stewardship in the global wine industry. The key factors that limit the implementation of an EMS include the attendant costs, the time to it takes achieve and then maintain accreditation, the amount of paperwork involved, and the possibility that marketing or cost benefits may not arise.

One difficulty in the global wine industry is that as more and more producers adopt environmentally-focused practices, any possible point of difference or competitive advantage is likely to be negated. Also, consumer confusion over the plethora of environmental claims to which they are exposed (e.g., sustainable, green, organic, carbon neutral, biodynamic, or environmentally friendly) has a negative impact on the realization of any marketing benefits. There is a very real danger that skeptical or confused consumers increasingly view environmental claims as "greenwashing." There is little doubt that some consumers do value environmental claims; however, to a large number of consumers, sustainable claims are likely to be unimportant, misunderstood, mistrusted, or insignificant in comparison to the effect of wine price on their purchase decisions.

Sustainability has had a high profile in the New Zealand wine industry in recent years. The national industry organization, New Zealand Winegrowers, has actively encouraged wineries and grape growers to voluntarily implement a formal EMS. Participation in any of the events New Zealand Winegrowers organize, including wine awards, marketing activities, and the annual industry conference, is open only to wine companies that have implemented an approved EMS. New Zealand Winegrowers are focused on environmental stewardship because of the growing concerns of international consumers, retailers, and regulators. In addition, the positioning and promotion of many New Zealand products, including wine, is often leveraged off the national "clean and green image."

New Zealand wineries have implemented a range of EMSs, including ISO 14001, BioGro, CarboNZero, Demeter, CertNZ, and SWNZ. SWNZ is an EMS that was developed and introduced by New Zealand Winegrowers in the late 1990s. The program has continually evolved over the years and contains sustainable management practices for vineyard and winery operations. SWNZ is based on a scorecard approach that sets targets to improve environmental performance. The program aims to provide quality assurance from vineyard to winery in order to address consumer concerns and to protect New Zealand's global wine markets. Currently 94% of New Zealand's vineyard area is SWNZ-certified and around 90% of total wine produced is from winery operations that are SWNZ-certified.

Huia Vineyards

When Huia owners, Claire and Mike Allan, arrived in the Marlborough region in 1990 they were immediately impressed by its sunshine and wines. The couple purchased land and began to develop their vineyard while gaining winemaking experience at renowned Marlborough wineries such as Cloudy Bay, Vavasour, Corbans, and Lawson's Dry Hills. Both also completed a vintage in Champagne: Mike at Veuve Cliquot and Claire at Taittinger. This experience provided them with skills in making New World wines, giving them an appreciation of the traditions and heritage from the Old World. Further information about Huia can be obtained from their website (www.huia.net.nz). Sustainability is an integral part of the culture and values of Huia; in particular, the owners have a clear philosophy about environmental responsibility. When Claire and Mike Allan founded the company it was with the intention of having "as light a footprint on the land as possible." They believe that the creation of a good wine and a commitment to the environment go hand in hand. The company is focused on the production of elegant, hand-crafted, premium-quality wines that are representative of the unique Marlborough region. The fundamental belief of the owners is that wine is a product that results from completely natural processes—the fermentation of grape juice—and that the purest and highest quality result will thus come from minimizing the introduction of synthetic chemicals into the process. As the Huia owners have increasingly embraced environmental sustainability over time, they have observed that the quality and character of their wines have continually improved and that their vineyards have become clean and healthy places to live and work.

The company was a pioneer in the field of sustainability; with no model to work from, they developed a winery that fulfilled their values by a process of learning as they went along. Huia has taken a number of steps in order to achieve business sustainability. The following sections discuss these steps in detail.

ENVIRONMENTAL SUSTAINABILITY

Huia has been a member of SWNZ for a number of years. It uses a scorecard approach that provides targets or benchmarks to improve its environmental performance in its vineyards and in the winery. Huia maintains its SWNZ membership by meeting the standards required and by undergoing an annual audit process. SWNZ provides wine companies with details of the processes that will enable them to produce high-quality wine through employment of environmentally responsible and economically viable management of their vineyards and wineries. The SWNZ program focuses on sustainability across a number of areas, including site management, soil management, vine nutrition, irrigation management, cover crops, frost protection, crop management, integrated plant protection, and new vineyard establishment.

Resource use and resource generation are central to the concept of environmental sustainability, and reduced resource consumption is a key strategy at Huia. The company has reduced energy consumption, specifically of diesel and electricity, by using a process to evaluate where energy is used, reducing that consumption when possible, and exploring alternative sources of energy. For example, Huia has reduced the use of tractors in its vineyards by avoiding unnecessary trips, and has instigated a policy of turning lights out in the winery in rooms that are not in use. In addition, wastes from the vineyards or winery are almost entirely returned for recycling or reuse.

The ultimate goal at Huia is for the business to operate as a closed system. The company is currently exploring ways to convert vineyard waste into biofuels that could power tractor operations. It is also keen to develop sustainable energy from wind or solar sources, although the establishment costs for these are prohibitive at present.

Huia initially used some chemicals in its operation but over the years it slowly moved toward a fully organic production model. Its own vineyard and those of its contract growers are now all certified as organic under the internationally recognized BioGro Organic accreditation. When Huia began to follow organic principles, the organic movement was still in its infancy, especially in the wine industry. There were few information sources and adoption of an organic approach was thus a risky option for Huia. Over more recent years, a larger number of agricultural producers in the Marlborough region have chosen to farm organically, including several other wine companies. This has allowed Huia to be part of an organic community. The members of this group share similar challenges with each other and work together to identify solutions to some of their key problems. Often the solutions that Huia and others have developed have been very low tech. For example, one of the biggest problems they have faced is the control of weeds; because the conventional herbicide approach was not an option, Huia used sheep to graze the inter-rows.

Huia is also certified, through Demeter, as being a biodynamic producer. Biodynamics is an approach that is more holistic, even spiritual, and that encourages growers to work in harmony with their land. The moon and its rhythms are an important aspect of biodynamics. Tasks such as spraying natural biodynamic preparations onto vines are carried out in accordance with the phases of the moon, which are used to indicate when the vines will best absorb them. Huia has slowly increased the use of biodynamic processes within its business.

In 2006, Huia gained CarboNZero certification. This certification showed that Huia was a carbon-neutral business. To achieve carbon-neutral status, Huia had to measure its carbon footprint in order to obtain a real understanding of its emissions. The winery then had to develop a plan to manage and reduce these emissions when possible and to mitigate any remaining and unavoidable emissions through the purchase of carbon credits. These steps were then externally validated by an outside organization. In Huia's case, unavoidable carbon emissions were mitigated by purchasing carbon credits through regenerating an area of native bush in the Marlborough region. Undertaking the process to become carbon neutral allowed Huia to learn the true cost of its wine production operation. However, more recently Huia made a decision to remove its company from the CarboNZero certification program because of the high financial costs and the time involved with maintaining the CarboNZero certification.

Social Sustainability

Typically wineries will employ contractors, especially for winter pruning and vintage work. Huia made a decision to retain full-time employees whenever possible. One reason for this decision is that following a sustainable model is significantly more labor intensive than conventional wine production. The model also requires specialist techniques and skills, as well as a respect for the land. Although this approach was initially more expensive for Huia, it has found that the benefits outweigh the costs. For example, Huia has greater control of the quality of the outcomes produced by its workforce. In addition, the working environment for staff is more pleasant than in a conventionally operated vineyard that uses chemical sprays.

Huia has made an effort to treat staff as important stakeholders in the business and has involved them in the creation and evolution of the Huia brand and vision. Staff are provided with personal development, training, and assistance with gaining qualifications and skills that will benefit the company. Staff see this as Huia making an investment in them. Huia tries to make the company a fun and enjoyable place to work. They provide staff with good coffee and morning tea each day, which owners and workers share in a collegial and convivial way. They also hold regular social events for staff to attend.

The focus that Huia has on its workforce is repaid not only in the quality of outcomes but also by having a very low staff turnover rate in comparison to other vineyards and wineries. Huia is regarded as being one of the best employers in the region, and this gives it the luxury of being able to choose among the best employees available. Having long-term skilled and experienced employees has created a tone within the company in which staff share knowledge and collaborate to find solutions to problems.

Recently Huia joined with a number of other wine companies in the region who are equally focused on natural wine production methods to establish a formal organization known as Marlborough Natural Winegrowers (MANA). This is a group of seven wineries that work together to promote quality-focused, organic, and biodynamic winegrowing in Marlborough. They learn from each other by sharing experiences and expertise, and they undertake some joint marketing activities and events. Membership of MANA and their previously mentioned membership of an informal organic community are examples of social sustainability in action; Huia is willing to work with others in order to achieve common goals or to gain advantages through numbers.

ECONOMIC SUSTAINABILITY

Although the philosophy at Huia has primarily focused on the effects of the company on the land and people, the fact that the company has been operating since 1990 provides evidence that it is also viable at an economic level. The environmental and social sustainability practices it has implemented have resulted in economic sustainability in a number of ways.

Huia believes that following a sustainable business model requires it to be a much more careful manager of its business. Operating according to organic and biodynamic principles results in viewing the entire business as a network of interactive systems rather than of individual parts. The winery has to be more aware of how a change in one area can have implications in other areas; when taking action the whole system must be considered. This means that the entire business requires constant monitoring of indicators and processes, especially in terms of considering and responding to natural cycles. For Huia, business planning is a continuous process that is integrated into daily business management and that includes detailed observation and awareness of vineyard and winery operations. The quickest and easiest solution to a problem is not always an option to Huia, so it takes a longer-term view of its business; planning is an essential part of this. The fact that the company not only has a 10-year plan but also has a 50-year planning process demonstrates this.

The current global wine glut and economic recession have not affected Huia to the same extent as they have other small wine companies. Huia's long-term planning meant it was better placed to identify the warning signs and to implement strategies to respond to them. The company has reduced some input costs as a result of its desire to be environmentally sustainable. For example, it has no agrichemical costs and has reduced its consumption of diesel and electricity. Huia also has gained a small financial benefit from providing grazing for sheep in its vineyards. It does incur higher wage costs due to the need for a greater level of manual labor and for its preference to hire full-time workers over temporary staff. However, having long-term and loyal staff in the company give Huia a financial benefit in terms of reducing the need for, and costs of, training, and it has found that it is better able to keep skills and knowledge within its company.

Huia's relationships with other organic producers and with MANA members have enabled it to share resources, information, and skills. This collaborative approach to doing business is particularly common among green businesses and provides numerous economic advantages, especially for smaller companies.

The biggest financial advantage that Huia has is with the positioning of its brand. Having a unique selling point in a crowded market allows it to sell high-quality wine at a premium price. Huia's niche is in the production of hand-made, fine wine with a strong sense of terroir and environmental stewardship. The positioning of Huia wines is based on the idea that the quality of wine is attributable to the care with which it is made. Europe is a major market for Huia wines, and consumers in this market in particular are particularly sophisticated, affluent, and looking for products that reflect their own ethical or philosophical values.

The Huia distribution strategy also reflects the positioning of its wines at the premium end of the market; the wines are available in specialist wine shops and premium restaurants but not in large supermarket chains. The owners of premium restaurants, including Gordon Ramsay restaurants in the United Kingdom, are looking for fine wines with a credible story and a point of difference; stocking Huia wines that are not readily available on supermarket shelves provides them with this uniqueness. A large part of Huia's marketing strategy is to tell the story of its company and its philosophies. The owners and even the vineyard manager spend time in overseas markets each year. They travel to shows, attend tastings, and personally visit distributors and selected sellers. The company views relationship marketing as a key factor of its success.

QUESTIONS

1. As a wine marketing consultant and using Huia as an example, identify and discuss the various advantages and disadvantages that a client wine company could expect to attain if it were to adopt a focus on sustainability.

2. Analyze and describe the differences across several wine markets with regards to the importance of sustainability to various stakeholders (e.g., distributors, retailers, and consumers).

AUTHOR'S COMMENTS

The objective of this case study was to examine how Huia Vineyards, a small wine company, has incorporated sustainability within its business strategies, operations, and culture. Huia is a practical example of a company that has embraced sustainability across the triple bottom line dimensions of environmental, social, and economic practices and processes. This case study highlights a number of interesting points to discuss.

First, Huia provides a very good example of a company that has achieved sustainability at environmental, social, and economic levels. Current literature is replete with research examples that have examined only a single aspect of sustainability's triple bottom line. What is lacking is literature that examines sustainability in an integrative way across all three dimensions. Although definitions of sustainability remain contentious, in general they make reference to the constrained consumption of resources, responsibility for impacts on the natural world, ongoing economic viability, and healthy stakeholder relationships. This case study illustrates Huia's commitment to being a sustainable business with an equal focus on planet, people, and profit. These factors have been integrated into the decision-making processes at Huia. Sustainability is a key part of Huia's culture, strategies, and operations.

The Huia case study shows that despite the often unavoidable associated costs, economic sustainability and long-term economic viability can result from the implementation of practices and processes that have an environmental or a social focus. This finding is particularly relevant to the New Zealand wine industry, which is dominated by small- to medium-sized businesses. Most models of sustainability suggest an interrelationship among the three dimensions; this case study provides some evidence that environmental and social sustainability are indeed linked to economic sustainability. In addition, this case study also illustrates that economic sustainability decisions can affect a company's environmental or social practices and policies. Huia's decision to withdraw from the CarboNZero certification was primarily made with the long-term economic viability of the company in mind.

The Huia case study provides an example of how becoming a sustainable business can provide a strategic competitive advantage. The focus on sustainability at Huia begins with the business owners and permeates through the culture, the workforce, implemented strategies, and daily operations. Huia is convinced that it has better business plans because of its implemented sustainable practices, particularly those that focus on environmental stewardship. In addition, Huia has gained marketplace advantage from being a sustainable business with a focus on the natural production of premium-quality, hand-crafted wines.

The Huia case study also illustrates some of the reasons why a small- to medium-sized business may choose to implement sustainable practices and processes. The literature has suggested a number of reasons: the Huia case study illustrates that, in practice, a business can become sustainable for more than a single reason. In Huia's case, the personal values and beliefs of the owners are the primary driver, particularly in terms of environmental sustainability. However, it is apparent that there are other factors that also drive their sustainable behaviors. The company is clearly focused on the production of premium-quality wine. Huia links wine quality with naturalness, which therefore becomes a major driver of its environmental stewardship. This focus on wine quality and Huia's adoption of various EMSs lead to its product positioning and the advantages it gains in the marketplace. There is little doubt that sustainability is a key component of Huia's brand equity. It is also clear that Huia has a focus on employee welfare, morale, and retention. Many of the socially sustainable practices and processes Huia has implemented are driven by a desire to be a respected employer. Huia's focus on its staff gives it greater control of the quality of the outputs from these workers; this focus is actually self-serving because it links to the quality of the final product, which is one of Huia's competitive advantages in an overcrowded wine market.

The Huia story also highlights some of the issues associated with sustainability. In particular, it is clear that the company has felt the need to adopt multiple EMSs. This is an issue that exists not only in the wine industry but also in other industries. Several problems often accompany the implementation of multiple EMSs, including the cost associated with first obtaining the accreditation for each EMS and the time involved with ongoing management and compliance with each EMS. This case study illustrates that, even for a company such as Huia that has a significant focus on environmental stewardship, decisions regarding membership in an EMS are made from economic and environmental viewpoints. This is a good example of the difficulties that wine companies face when they wish to focus on the health of the environment. It is clear that there is not a single EMS that will suffice across all wine producers, whether in New Zealand or globally. At a time when the industry is grappling with issues such as the global wine glut and economic downturn, its members should not be incurring the additional costs and pressures associated with multiple EMSs. This case study highlights the need for the development of a single, all-encompassing EMS for the global wine industry. This would, in turn, reduce consumer confusion over green claims; the wine industry could educate consumers so that they would have greater confidence and trust in the environmental claims being made.

Although the New Zealand wine industry has a clear and significant focus on sustainable production, it should be noted that sustainability is not viewed as important in all wine markets. Sustainability, and especially environmental sustainability, is an important consideration for distributors, retailers, and wine consumers in the northern hemisphere. In many instances, having some form of sustainability credentials is a requirement for obtaining shelf space for wines in some retailers. European countries, the United States, and Canada are major markets for New Zealand wines, and hence the industry body has responded with measures to increase the voluntary adoption of EMSs among its members. Stakeholders in new and emerging wine markets, especially in Asia, have not as yet placed the same degree of importance on sustainability. As large retail companies from the northern hemisphere continue to develop their presence in Asia, it is likely that wine producers will find that sustainability credentials also become increasingly important in these markets.

READINGS

Anders, B., & Gunne, G. (2010). "The effect of environmental information on professional purchasers' preference for food products." *British Food Journal*, 112(3), pp. 251–260.

Darnall, N., Jolley, G. J., & Handfield, R. (2008). "Environmental management systems and green supply chain management: Complements for sustainability?" *Business Strategy and the Environment*, 18, pp. 30–45.

Dyllick, T., & Hockerts, K. (2002). "Beyond the business case for corporate sustainability." *Business Strategy and the Environment*, 11(2), pp. 130–142.

Forbes, S. L., & De Silva, T.A. (2012). "Analysis of environmental management systems in New Zealand wineries." *International Journal of Wine Business Research*, 24(2), pp. 98–114.

Gabzdylova, B., Raffensperger, J. F., & Castka, P. (2009). "Sustainability in the New Zealand wine industry: Drivers, stakeholders and practices." *Journal of Cleaner Production*, 17(11), 992–998.

Hillary, R. (2004). "Environmental management systems and the smaller enterprise." *Journal of Cleaner Production*, 12, pp. 561–569.

Lubin, D., & Esty, D. (2010). "The sustainability imperative." *Harvard Business Review*, 88(5), 42–52.

Marshall, R., Cordano, M., & Silverman, M. (2005). "Exploring individual and institutional drivers of proactive environmentalism in the US wine industry." *Business Strategy and the Environment*, 14, pp. 92–109.

Pugh, M., & Fletcher, R. (2002). "Green international wine marketing." *Australasian Marketing Journal*, 10(3), pp. 76–85.

Renton, T., Manktelow, D., & Kingston, C. (2002). "Sustainable winegrowing: New Zealand's place in the world." *Proceedings of the Romeo Bragato Conference*, September, Christchurch, New Zealand.

Tee, E., Boland, A.M., & Medhurst, A. (2007). "Voluntary adoption of environmental management systems in the Australian wine and grape industry depends on understanding stakeholder objectives and drivers." *Australian Journal of Experimental Agriculture*, 47, pp. 273–283.

Warner, K. D. (2007). "The quality of sustainability: Agroecological partnerships and the geographic branding of California winegrapes." *Journal of Rural Studies*, 23, pp. 142–155.

Zoecklein, B. (2010). "Defining sustainability: What does it really mean for the wine industry?" *Vineyard and Winery Management*, Jan.–Feb., pp. 104–109.

Stella di Campalto Winery

THE BIODYNAMIC PIONEER IN MONTALCINO

Cristina Santini
Università San Raffaele, Roma (Italy)
Armand Gilinsky
Sonoma State University (USA)
Alessio Cavicchi
Università degli Studi di Macerata (Italy)

SUMMARY

Stella di Campalto innovated a niche-within-a-niche sustainability strategy via the creation of an organic and biodynamic winery in the Montalcino region of Tuscany, where the company competed with renowned producers of Brunello DOCG wines. From 2000–2007, Tuscany produced an estimated 10 percent of Italy's premium wines in a diminishing growth, highly fragmented industry. Italian wine exports grew to about 40 percent by value of total country production, increasing slowly as domestic consumption fell. The case describes how Stella avoided the purported "fake Brunello wine" scandal in 2008 by retaining her founding strategy.

INTRODUCTION

Montalcino is a small country village in the heart of Tuscany, in the Siena Province: with its nearly 5,300 habitants, Montalcino is the municipality in the Siena province with the highest aging rate and with a growth in the population trend of 3.2% in the period 2001–2009 (source: ISTAT, 2009). Visiting Montalcino is like having an immersion in a perfect Tuscan postcard: vines, sweet hills, olive trees, country houses, cypresses, tight dusty country roads, plus a wide range of tourism facilities that include restaurants, agritourism, wine bars, hotels, bars and, the most important thing, wineries. In 2004 Montalcino and the nearby Valdorcia were recognized by Unesco as part of the World Heritage.

There is something more than the panoramic view that has been able to make of Montalcino a famous place in the world. This is wine. Montalcino is the Brunello homeland. In 2006 Brunello wine was named as the best wine in the world by *Wine Spectator.*

Among the 250 wine producers in Montalcino, there are a few wineries that are organic and biodynamic. Stella di Campalto ("Stella") was the first wine producer to produce biodynamic wines in the Brunello area; its wines are well known all over the world and its production is synonymous with high quality. Whilst Montalcino emerged largely unscathed despite a dramatic wine scandal, Stella chose to differentiate itself not only from Montalcino big wine producers, but also from other organic and biodynamic wineries.

This case depicts a story of Stella's niche biodynamic winery in Montalcino and provides a perspective on the following questions: how to define the boundaries of a niche in order to ensure a sustainable competitive advantage for the company? What does it mean to be organically certified and biodynamic in an area that is world-renowned for wine production? Does this strategy add value to the product?

THE MONTALCINO WINE SYSTEM
The wine business in brief: production and challenges

Montalcino is a clear example of a wine-driven rural system: visitors can find 36 restaurants, 58 agritourism, 17 wine bars and 10 hotels in an area that covers 243.62 square kilometers, most of which is countryside. In the area there are about 250 wine producers, with 3500 hectares of vineyard (most of them produce Brunello); the average annual production consists mainly of Brunello (6.5 million bottles), and Rosso (4 million bottles), for a total turnover of 104 million Euros per year. The wine is famous all over the world, due to the relevant percentage of product (60%) that is exported.

Besides a few big companies, such as Banfi (the biggest company of Montalcino, owned by the American Mariani family), Biondi Santi, Argiano and Cinelli Colombini, in Montalcino the majority of the companies are very small: 66% of the wineries have vineyards that cover five hectares or less. Tables 1 and 2 summarize the Montalcino wine business.

Table 1. The wine business in Montalcino, companies by type and size (source: our elaboration from CCIAA Siena; Siena Province; Consorzio del Brunello di Montalcino; winenews.it, 2009)

Company info	
Companies (total)	250
Bottling compagnie	200
Merchants	22
Size (% of tot)	
< 1ha	22%
1-3 ha	29%
3-5 ha	15%
5-15 ha	15%
15-100 ha	9%
> 100 ha	1%

Table 2. The wine business in Montalcino, sales and turnover (source: our elaboration from CCIAA Siena; Siena Province; Consorzio del Brunello di Montalcino; winenews.it, 2009)

Sales and Turnover	
Global Turnover (000 €)	130.000,00
Export	60%
USA	25%
Germany	9%
Swiss	7%
Canada	5%
UK	3%
Japan	3%
Domestic Market	40%
Tuscany	7%
Central Italy	5%
Northern Italy	8%
Southern Italy	1%
Montalcino	9%
Montalcino Wineries Direct Sales	8%

Montalcino faced several challenges: on one hand the internal demand for wine was decreasing (Regione Toscana, 2010); on the other the worst scandal in the story of Brunello was just around the corner. In 2008 some wineries were accused of not respecting the productive standards and in particular grapes other than Sangiovese for the Brunello. US temporarily stopped to import Brunello, and some Montalcino companies chose to sell their Brunello under the Rosso label at a lower price. The accidental combination of the scandal with the economic crisis had serious consequences on the local wine business. In an interview, Banfi Wines' General Manager clearly depicted the situation that Montalcino had to face:

> Montalcino leaves the difficult year of 2009 in admirable fashion. The Territory has had to face, for the first time in its young history, an International economic crisis, not with a few hundreds of thousands of bottles to sell, but with a few million. However, despite price pressures, and some problems of overproduction, the International markets have continued to demand Brunello, which seems to have kept its appeal even considering the crises encountered before the economic crisis arrived. (Enrico Viglierchio, General Manager of Castello Banfi, from an interview on winenews.com)

One year later, the scandal seemed far away: after having removed the block for Brunello imports, the US remained the major importer of Brunello wine (25% of total export), and in 2009 Brunello sales reached 7.18 million bottles sold, with a growth of almost 5% compared to 2008. Brunello was still on the top of the mind of consumers that buy wine in specialized shops (AGI, 2011, 2012; Il Sole 24 ore, 2011). Optimistic sales forecasts have subsequently been released by the Consortium (http://www.consorziobrunellodimontalcino.it). Nevertheless, bloggers and other specialized websites still talk about the scandal (Cavicchi et al. 2010; Cavicchi and Santini, 2012).

BRUNELLO, ROSSO AND THE OTHERS

There is no doubt that Brunello is the most popular wine of Montalcino. Brunello is a DOCG wine, where DOCG stands for Denominazione Origine Controllata e Garantita, that is the highest geographical indication. Brunello DOCG is made with 100% Sangiovese grapes and producers must wait five years before releasing the wine on the market after the vintage. All this waiting means a delay in earnings and storage expenses for firms, whilst for consumers purchasing such an old wine means buying a wine for special occasions. Wineries also produce the Rosso di Montalcino DOC wine (DOC stands for Denominazione di Origine Controllata, another geographical indication) that is made with 100% Sangiovese grape, but there is not a minimum aging time prescribed as it is for Brunello, and the maximum wine yield from grapes is higher than for Brunello. As can be guessed, Brunello prices are higher than Rosso ones. Brunello prices usually fluctuate: the quantity of Brunello released every year depends on the quality and volume of the vintage.

Table 3. Montalcino wine production by types @ 2009 (source: our elaboration from CCIAA Siena; Siena Province; Consorzio del Brunello di Montalcino; winenews.it, 2009)

Wine production (Bottles)	
Brunello	7.000.000
Rosso di Montalcino DOC	4.500.000
Moscadello DOC	80.000
San Antimo DOC	500.000
SuperTuscan	500.000
IGT	3.000.000
Grappa made with Brunello	250.000

STELLA DI CAMPALTO WINERY
The origins

Stella di Campalto decided to establish in 1992 the very first biodynamic winery in Montalcino, in a small piece of land owned—and forgotten since the 40s—by her family. After obtaining a degree in viticulture in Bordeaux and having had some experience in the service industry, Stella thought she was ready to move from Milan and start her own business in the Tuscan countryside:

> There were some European funds for enhancing female entrepreneurship in agriculture; I decided to apply for funds for starting the wine production. I do remember myself running with an old Panda car driven by my aunt to deliver my application at the Montalcino office! I could not believe my eyes when I saw that my application was ranked as the first among all the applications in Montalcino.

Montalcino was the ideal place for Stella to grow her family: Steiner's biodynamic principles perfectly suited her philosophy of living in harmony with her surroundings and the best way, in Stella's view, of creating excellent products while respecting nature, by not poisoning the place where she and her family were living.

In the early 1990s Montalcino was growing: large wineries located in the rgion were increasing their production to meet market demand. Stella became a pioneer of biodynamic wine growing. She recalls:

…people thought I was crazy: why produce biodynamic wine? Brunello was having an incredible success all over the world, but I was seeing at what price: natural resources were fully exploited and the land was getting poorer and poorer every day. Some companies have asked their vineyards for too much.

Products and philosophy

The company has been organic certified since 1996 and biodynamic methods were fully implemented by 2002. The winery attempted to respect the main rules of biodynamic wine making: grapes should be manipulated as little as possible, and once crushed, grape juice must get into the tanks by following a gravity system.

Once alcoholic fermentation is complete, the "wine" is taken down to the ageing cellar, where it will mature in small barrels made from thick wood, or in barriques (225-liter casks) or tonneaux (900-liter casks). The ageing cellar is 15 meters deep, allowing the temperature to remain at a constant, natural level. The wine is aged for as long as it takes for it to reach optimum maturity, and each part of the ageing process is carried out in accordance with our quality-control guidelines. (from the company website)

The cellar was built on three levels and hosted some interesting modern art installations, to remind that winemaking is an art; fermentation took place at the lowest level of the building, where temperature could be easily controlled. Processes were organized in order to ensure that every single vineyard vintage be kept separate:

In the cellars, we aim to tap the potential of every single vineyard. The grapes are picked by hand and placed in small trays before being de-stalked, and they are then allowed to fall into 30-quintal wooden vats. (from the company website)

The whole winery was conceived to be part of the landscape: the choice of materials and colors used for the building made the cellar blend in with the surroundings.

Here at the Winery, we work hard to preserve the harmony of the natural environment—we feel fortunate to be guests in a generous land protected by Mount Amiata. We have every intention of continuing to be a small-scale producer with just a few plots—this way we can walk around our vineyards personally and get to know them a little better every day. (from the company website).

Vineyards were managed differently from conventional vineyards: first of all grass was free to grow in the vineyard, because it helped plants to get hydrated and maintain nutrition elements; then the company adhered to Steiner's requirements for composting by implementing the preparation in soil management.[1] Harvest was done by hand. In 2006, the company purchased small bottling machinery, because hand bottling had become extremely time-consuming and labor-intensive.

The estate covered 13.45 hectares, of which 5.5 hectares consisted of six different vineyards, at various altitudes, that produced Brunello, Rosso and Sant'Antimo. As in most Tuscan wineries, besides the vines olive trees were retained: Stella's olive trees had been planted in the 1920s. Each vineyard was conceived and managed as a small cru with distinctive traits: grapes were divided according to the vineyard they belonged to and the wine was aged separately in one or more wooden vats.

> A great deal of time and resources are dedicated to the maintenance of the ecosystem of the area around the vineyards and the company facilities. We endeavour to cultivate grapes that are healthy, powerful, flavoursome and unique to each vintage. In this way, we can produce wines that are pure, unrepeatable expressions of their terroir of origin as it was in the year the grapes were grown.

The company produced internally all the grapes of Sangiovese needed for releasing its Brunello and Rosso. There were five employees in the company and Stella personally followed all the phases of the production, and she was also involved in exhibitions and wine fair organization:

> "I have understood that building stable professional relationships with my employees is fundamental: I have learned that it is easier to work with people who have grown up within the company and know what we are doing and where we are going."

Stella's production choices stressed product quality and wine features, rather than the capacity of a certain product to meet demand: this was the philosophy that inspired Stella not to release Brunello before 2009. Between 2001 and 2003, the market was particularly receptive for Brunello, and the 2003 vintage was ranked as one of the best of all time: although there were favorable market conditions, Stella decided to make Rosso instead of Brunello.

Stella conceived her wine as an agricultural product. In her vision a winery should maintain its original agricultural orientation by focusing on production, rather than struggling to become a symbols or tourist attraction.

This philosophy fully explained the fluctuations in production: Stella's production was, compared with other regional producers, very low, and it changed ever so modestly according to the vintage (*Figure 1*).

Figure 1. Wine production by type and year.

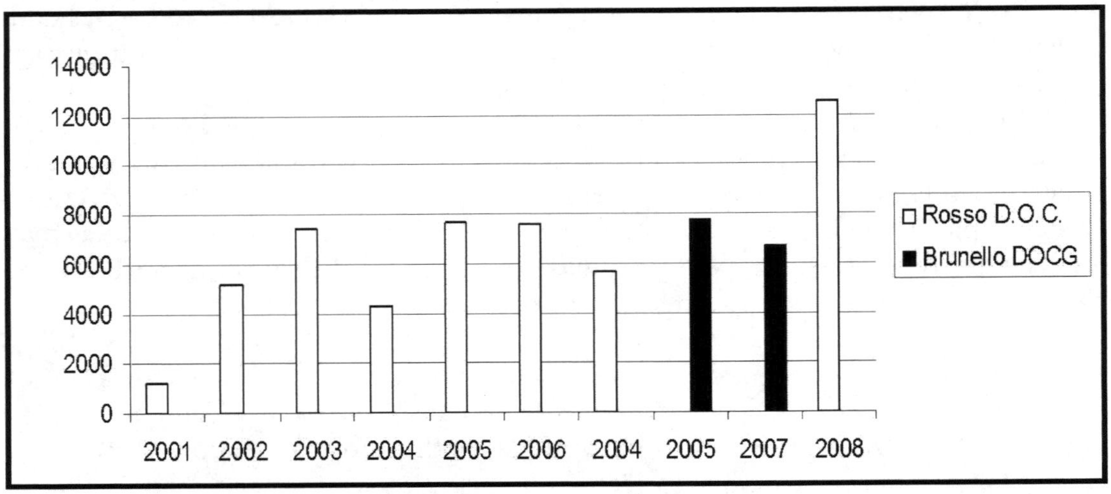

Although production increased, Stella produced 60% less than the maximum productive capacity allowed by local regulations.

MARKET APPROACH

Whilst most of the companies considered Rosso as a second classification wine (lower price, lower expenses, shorter product cycles), Stella regarded her Rosso to be "a great wine," as it was aged at least two years. One wine critic wrote:

> The Rosso di Montalcino 2003 produced by the winery San Giuseppe, run by a young woman with a fascinating name, is already a very good wine and it will surely become a big one as time goes by. It is a wine that is born from a particular philosophy (...) and from the implementation of cellar practices that are as natural as possible." (Franco Ziliani, *Wine Report*)

Stella's Rosso received several awards and in 2010 was ranked as one of the top wines from Tuscany by the Espresso wine guide, one of the leading wine guides in Italy.

Stella's winery competed mainly in the Ultra Premium price segment. Stella's prices for the Rosso were about average, compared with the Rosso released by Biondi Santi, the most prestigious winery in Montalcino, which was the highest priced (Figure 2).[2] Prices for that wine tended to fluctuate, as shown in Figure 3.

Figure 2. Rosso's price comparison

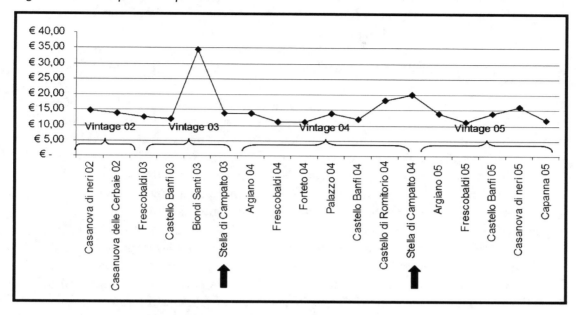

Figure 3, Price history (Euro), Feb 2009 to Aug 2012 (source: wine-searcher.com)

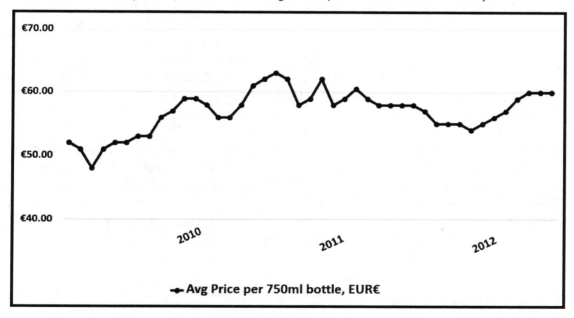

Stella's wines were not designed for a specific category of consumers: she was aware of the importance that Millennials and GenX had for the market, and she also knew that GenX need to be educated about wine in order to become conscious consumers. Still, she was not attempting to target a specific market segment. She explained:

> I am not trying to push my product on the market: my product is available and can be found if there is someone who seeks for a very good wine…I don't want my winery to be open to everyone: we are not plan-

ning to have organized tours 24/7 for improving our cellar door sales. We are not seeking for a notoriety among the mass: we want to warmly welcome those who knock at our door because they really want to taste a good wine, or because they have been told about us, they have read about us, or simply they have been inspired during their journey.

Her basic idea was to build a stable relationship with a few selected people, to communicate with them, provide information and an experience during a brief winery tour: Stella wanted to create an attachment between consumers and her products. Stella decided to add a page to the company website, that is conceived as a journey diary, where she posted comments and shared ideas with visitors to that site.

The company sold its wines mainly to restaurants and specialized wine shops, and those were envisioned to be the main sales channels. Due to small production volumes, the company was not considering selling its wine to retailers, but hoped to enhance direct sales through social media, rather than developing cellar door sales.

Stella was also committed to building export channels: more than 50% of its production was exported to Europe, Britain (where Stella became one of several official suppliers of Italian wine to the English Royal Family), USA, and Japan.

I am currently working on exporting to China and Brazil. Every year I select a couple of new countries and I organize a journey for establishing a sales network there. I need to visit the places, to see how people live there. It can happen to get in contact with some people from foreign countries interested in selling my wine abroad; I start from my contacts and I am happy to say that it frequently happens that the first step is made by other people who seek my product and contact me.

Stella considered her wines as being not competitive in terms of price: other companies, especially the larger ones, had lower prices for Rosso wine. This was because Stella needed to cover the extra cost in producing biodynamic wine and for educating consumers on the sustainable specifications of her wine. Although she believed she was helped by the growing interest in organic and biodynamic, Stella expected to work harder than rivals to justify the premium price she asked for her wines.

THE CHOICE OF BIODYNAMIC

Stella's company was conceived as sustainable-oriented since its beginning: the decision of being sustainable was because sustainability and biodynamic were simply aligned with the owner's vision of the company. Industry and consumer interest in the organic and biodynamic wine market grew over recent years and was thought to address several market segments: consumers strongly motivated by health issues as well as those preoccupied by environmental concerns. A few producers in the global wine industry believed that sustainability might just become a means of product differentiation to justify price premiums, while many others did not.

About being organic or sustainable, Stella laughed:

> Today being "natural" has become a cliché: I am hardly trying to attract consumers because they are interested in the quality of my products. First of all mine should be considered a good wine and, on a second step, it should be considered a biodynamic wine. All the curiosity in consumers for knowing what is behind the wine should arise after the first sip of wine.

Besides biodynamic practices, Stella used solar energy and directed her efforts to reducing wastes and recycling as much as practicable. Her personal values and vision guided her strategic decisions:

> Every company should decide what to do. My choice is the most suitable for me, but I do not judge other's people choices: some other companies have chosen differently and have oriented themselves towards an industrial approach to production. The real point is that every company makes its decisions according to what sounds best for them. Under this perspective every choice must be respected. There is not a best way for doing wine: there are many ways because people are different. I would not say that going green is my strategy, unless you would define strategy as anything else than a coherent behaviour.

In the aftermath of the scandal, a number of local rivals began to recognize the importance of going organic or biodynamic in Montalcino, considering sustainability as a lever for gaining a competitive advantage.

VISION AND FUTURE PERSPECTIVES

Stella says that definitely the crisis had a positive impact on her business:

> The Brunello scandal led the system to a crisis: it is singular that the original meaning of the word crisis—that comes from Greek—is choice, not catastrophe, as many people might think. This crisis forced producers to choose and rethink about how they conceive their products and how they want to produce that. The crisis also shaped consumers' purchasing behaviour: consumers now want to get much more information about the wineries; they want to know how wine is made and the philosophy of the company. Consumers seek something more than just a bottle of Brunello: they seek producers.

Although Montalcino wines lost credibility, the strategy followed by her company has helped her to get more involved with other Montalcino producers, and gave her the strength to make some decisions. Stella released her first Brunello vintage after the market crisis. In 2009, after having abandoned the Consortium of Montalcino, Stella founded an association with three other local producers called "Sangiovese per Amico" (that literally means "Sangiovese," that is the grape variety from which Brunello is made, "as a friend").[3]

> We are three friends, three producers, who live nearby, and we take part in wine fairs together. We are not in competition, because every wine is unique, and all the wineries should perceive it!

With the help of a research institute, they created a system for defining the characteristics of Sangiovese grapes within the vineyard.

> We believe that if our work were conducted only upon commercial and financial criteria, we would deprive ourselves (and others) of the pleasure of experiencing the surprise and thrill and we would probably cause irreparable damage. (from the Sangiovese per Amico website)

The aim of this association, that it is open to anyone who is interested in sharing such a vision, is to promote a specific production philosophy, the Sangiovese grape, and Montalcino:

> Producing wine in an area rich in charm and potential, which has not been fully developed yet, requires a strong commitment. We have taken up the challenge of making, in this territory, from this grape variety, with the utmost respect for production regulations, uncommon wines having a soul and personality. (from the Sangiovese per Amico website)

Future growth must be managed accordingly, as her cellar capacity was limited and could not easily be reorganized because of the installed gravity system. Despite the overall financial conditions that have worsened for the regional wine industry in general, Stella considered the future to be an opportunity for biodynamic wine. The globalization of tastes occurring in the wine industry did not cause Stella concern:

> The iPad has taught people a great lesson: people were afraid that printed books could disappear as iPad has been launched on the market. Bookshops still exist and new small independent publishing companies are editing books that unexpectedly jumped to the top of book charts. There is no logic to it, but things happen, because people are getting back to using inner sensations, feelings and instincts when they make decisions. An iPad can't reproduce the smell of a book, the satisfaction that the buyer has when he gets out of bookshop with a brand new book or the sensation of flipping through a book. The same can happen with wine.

In the future Stella plans to remain a small-scale business: she has gradually increased production, but she doesn't aim to improve consistently the volume of bottles sold. In particular she wants to grow in foreign markets but remain "the same size" in Italy.

QUESTIONS FOR STUDENTS

Case adopters might ask the following questions about the strategy of this wine business:

- After having analyzed the information provided, where is the company now? Where is it going?
- Do you think this company's set of resources could be appropriately exploited for applying and consolidating Stella's strategy?
- What do you think about Stella's niche? Is it too small? What are the differences with other wineries that adopt a niche strategy in Montalcino (i.e., wineries that address their products to the high end of the market)?

AUTHORS' PERSPECTIVES

Adopters who use this case in a wine business course can accomplish the following: (1) illustrate sustainability as a "megatrend" that encompasses building inter-generational equity, corporate social responsibility, and passion; (2) debate the value of "green" or "sustainable" strategies in the wine industry; (3) analyze and compare the "triple bottom line," emphasizing "people, planet and profit," as criteria for measuring success in areas of social, environmental and economic values; and (4) develop and defend recommendations for sustainable practices. Adopters might request student projects to conduct further research into the wine industry, sustainable businesses, or customers who prefer to purchase products and services from sustainable businesses.

Successful enterprises search for a "sweet spot" where harmful environmental and social impacts are minimized, and an adequate rate of return is realized (Nguyen and Slater, 2010). A successful business is conscious of the social and environmental impacts of its supply chain, operations, products and services, and acts responsibly to minimize any negative impacts and remain in business (Phypher and MacLean, 2009). This can involve a range of strategies, such as reducing pollutants and waste, making processes and products more efficient, or even working to ensure the company does not deplete its own supply chain. An example of the latter is found in Chapter 2 of Green to Gold (Esty & Winston, 2006). Unilever changed its fish-buying strategy to ensure it purchases 100% of its supply from sustainable fisheries in order to protect the supply chain and not act to deplete the ocean of fish. A sustainable business must be "born green," streamlined to run lean, profitable and constantly re-defining itself as green innovation continues, but always with a profitable bottom line.

Students should relate sustainability to the wine industry and recognize that for practitioners in the wine industry, priority number one is leaving the land in better shape for the next generation. For instance, most farmers want their children and grandchildren to enjoy the land rather than working the land to get the most amount of money out of it and then discarding it. The latter is definitely not sustainable business. Among the stakeholders in the wine industry are: workers in the vineyards who could be exposed to chemical fertilizers and pesticides over long periods of time, people who live down the street from a winery, or the homes that receive water from the river where a winery releases its used water.

Instructors should remind students that, while sustainability would seem to be a worthy goal for any organization like Stella di Campalto that has a long-term time horizon, there are other Montalcino wineries and indeed, other organizations that do not share that perspective. While regulations to prevent unsustainable actions may be enacted to deter shortsighted behaviors, regulatory controls do not necessarily always result in the desired behaviors from organizations that have no interest in the long term. The Stella case opens a multitude of questions about niche strategy and sustainability of strategy chosen before market segmentation.

According to McGahan (2004:7), growth is a worthwhile objective, but only when its benefits—measured in terms of improved survival or better profitability—outweigh its costs. Too many companies pursue growth for its own sake without considering whether growth will generate a return on investment either in the short or long run. In a broad sense, the appropriateness of a growth objective depends in a sensitive way on both the evolutionary trajectory and the stage of change in the industry of a particular business unit. For example, consider an industry in the shakeout stage of a life cycle: commercial fishing. In this situation, a moderate rate of growth (of the right kind) is essential to both survival and profitability. But once the industry enters the decline stage, additional growth is not likely to generate enough of a return to cover its costs. In other situations, the consequences of an inappropriate commitment to growth can be grave. When the industry is undergoing an "architectural" change (e.g., its core activities are threatened by obsolescence, such as overfishing of shellfish in the Atlantic or tuna in the Pacific), the growth objective may be tantamount to saying that the industry will somehow find a way to support business as usual over the long run. This perspective, if it persists, is almost certain to decrease a firm's potential to generate reasonable returns over the long run, much less survive.

Students should be able to describe and evaluate the competitive positioning of Stella's winery: a SWOT analysis is helpful to allow students to categorize the information contained in the case. Then, Michael E. Porter's 5-forces model can be applied to establish the parameters of any potential future competitive moves within an increasingly unattractive industry context.

SWOT Analysis
Strengths
- Pioneer: Stella was the pioneer of biodynamic in Montalcino, although Stelia doesn't emphasize this aspect in the official company information.
- Soil richness: Production choices have not impoverished the soil.
- Vision: A clear vision inspires company management and is shared among the members of the organization.

- Reputation: The winery has achieved a solid reputation among wine critics.
- Sales Network: Sales network is strongly established and based on Stella's ability to manage relationships.
- Customer orientation: addressing the product to someone strongly motivated would make the loyalty process easier to be effective.
- Uniqueness of product attributes: production characteristics and soil and cellar management provide unique features in every single vintage.
- Sustainability: sustainability plays a leading role in shaping company's vision and mission, and helps the company in achieving differentiation among the other producers.
- Price: price in positioning the company in the upscale market.
- Producer network: being part of a stable network of producers that share a similar business vision enables the company to improve competences and know-how.

Weaknesses

- Production constraints: although the peak of productive capacity has not been reached yet, the company has some structural constraints for future growth. Cellar capacity is limited, vineyards are small-sized and some production choices such as manual harvest or the implementation of the gravity system might limit future development.
- Ownership: even if the size of the winery is very small, an excessive focus on the owner might be risky. Stella covers all the roles in the winery, from winemaking to sales management and customer care.
- Volatility of production: as previously described, wine varies in typology and quantity every year. This would compromise company's capacity to plan in advance any new commercial strategy. If in one vintage the production decreases in typology and quantity there is a risk of not satisfying loyal consumers.
- Limited customer orientation: as described in the case, the company is open to anyone who is curious; Stella decided to invest time and money in others rather than on attracting visitors and customers. People know about Stella because they search for a specific type of wine or because they read wine guides or articles published by some wine bloggers and journalists. It is almost impossible to find Stella accidentally.
- Distribution: although a presence on foreign markets is a plus when domestic market is suffering, Stella's national wine availability is limited and extremely selective. In a period of crisis, where demand for niche wines decreases, a wise recommendation would be to diversify distribution and reinforce, for example, indoor sales, or the domestic market distribution system, in order to be able to diversify the risk.
- Being biodynamic: most consumers don't know much about biodynamic and it might be a deterrent for neophytes. Furthermore, due to the bad reputation

that organic and biodynamic wines have had in the past, some customers may be reluctant to purchase.

- Product Information: the company has the tendency to provide technical information rather than basic information, because it speaks to a selected target customer (see the "product section" in the website); anyway, the presence on some famous wine guides and the location of the company itself would attract many "accidental" customers, who probably don't have a deep knowledge of biodynamic wines and organic cultivation. This could represent a chance not only for increasing brand and company awareness, but also for diffusing information about biodynamic and organic wines.

Opportunities

- Location: Montalcino is famous all over the world and attracts tourists and visitors, although it is not as easily accessible as other locations in Tuscany that are near highways and airports.
- "Tuscany" brand: a wine produced in Tuscany can benefit from a sort of location brand that incentives purchasing.
- New European regulation on organic wines: the new regulation has declared that it is possible to define a wine as organic, rather than "produced with organic grapes."
- Sustainable concerns in consumption: consumers have new inputs in their purchasing behavior that have fostered the search for new "green" products.
- Improved knowledge in wine among consumers: wine consumers are more aware of what they drink and some new categories of consumers, such as gourmet tourists, search for niche products rather than wines that are highly available on the markets.
- Growth in organic and biodynamic wine market.

Threats

- Frauds and scandals: frauds and scandals might affect the credibility of the entire production system, as has previously happened with the Brunellopoli scandal.
- The economic crisis: the global economic crisis is affecting wine consumption and purchasing. This would change consumers' habits.
- Domestic market crisis: the difficult economic situation that Italy is facing has some serious consequences on the dynamics of domestic wine market, with decreased consumption and lower budgets for wine consumers. Market reports say that the percentage of per capita income addressed to luxury and expensive goods is decreased.
- New entrants in the organic wine market: the growing interest shown by consumers for organic wines has stimulated existing companies to become green. Although some companies are not organic-certified they brand their

products as "organic," with the consequence of increasing the population of green wines on the market. The same can be said for biodynamic wines: only a very few companies in Italy and in Tuscany have received biodynamic certification from Demeter (Stella is not Demeter-certified), but their number is growing.

PORTER'S 5 FORCES MODEL

The 5 forces model by Porter can be used for describing Stella's competitive environment.

- Rivalry among existing companies: it is high if considering the whole population of Montalcino wine producers whose production consists of the same type of DOCG, DOC and IGT wines. If considering only the organic and biodynamic wineries, these are fewer. In any case, due to fact that the wine is not sold with the organic or biodynamic certified label, rivalry is high.

- Potential entrants: new entrants in Montalcino are limited, due to the specific regulation that controls new vineyard planting. Existing companies, anyway, can easily convert to organic viticulture, in order to achieve a product differentiation or to implement sustainable principles in their production system. The impact of potential entrants is relatively high.

- Customers: their bargaining power is extremely high. Customers can easily access other wines positioned in the upper market. There is a high availability of good quality Rosso and Brunello wines; this makes easy for those customers who are not loyal to the Stella brand to switch to other wine labels.

- Suppliers: the impact of this force is low. The company is self-sufficient in many aspects (especially for energy concerns) and this reduces the impact that suppliers might have on the firm's competitive advantage.

- Substitute products: there is a high availability of Montalcino wines, as well as organic wines in Italy. Besides wines, consumers who are interested in buying a "green" product can choose among several beers produced locally by microbreweries inspired by environmental concerns.

BENEFITS AND LIMITS OF A NICHE STRATEGY

Adopters of this case should explore Stella's niche strategy—and the pros and cons of that strategy. This winery has adopted a niche strategy by deciding to focus on a specific market segment that includes wine connoisseurs, organic and biodynamic wine consumers and consumers with low budget constraints.

Playing in a niche is a widely diffused strategic behavior among small wineries and in wine it happens under one or a few conditions (Jarvis and Goodman, 2003): because the wine is a very high quality product, because it is addressed to the upper end of the market; because of a product's name; because of how the company is perceived (very exclusive); because of a strong and consistent brand association; because of its packaging or design; or because there is a unique story behind a particular brand.

The biodynamic wine segment in the higher end of the market can be considered as a niche within a niche: Stella's successful choice of not to address her wine exclusively to a biodynamic consumer means remaining open to a wider market segment. Although there's an increasing interest among consumers towards organic and biodynamic products (Hughner et al., 2007), promoting the wine by underlining first its quality and features, and only a second step its production methods, enables the company to avoid several problems: firstly it avoids, as we have already said, the problem of competing in a niche that reveals itself to be too small. Secondly, there is not the problem of sharing a philosophy or a similar set of values between consumers and producers: one of the reasons why consumers buy organic or biodynamic products is because of healthconcerns (Zanoli and Naspetti, 2002), whilst others are inspired by environmental issues (Squires et al., 2001). In some cases consumers seek for a warranty of product quality (Soler et al., 2002), whilst in other cases it is a consumption pattern that is associated witha particular stage in consumers' lives (like the arrival of a baby as observed by Hill and Lynchehaun, 2002), or a set of consumer values (Grunert and Juhl, 1995; Zanoli and Naspetti, 2002).

Stella believed in biodynamic but decided not to brand her products as biodynamic. This is because she is convinced that biodynamic could represent an answer to production needs and it should be evaluated according to its functionality and effectiveness in responding to some specific needs. In Montalcino there has been a growing interest towards what is organic and biodynamic: this is because it is seen as a warranty of quality. Stella is aware of the possibility that a production philosophy could become a cliché and consequently lose its effectiveness as a lever for achieving an effective differentiation. Furthermore, as Grunert has observed (2007), due to fast growth of quality food and beverage production, certifications could lose their effectiveness and could become a surplus in the future. In such a situation, underlining the vision and philosophy that are behind a product is a successful strategy in the long run. In this perspective the work that Stella is currently doing with the Association "Sangiovese per Amico" is extremely important.

Stella felt that a very important part of her job consisted of educating consumers and intermediaries about her wine. However, by not being aggressive in promotion, she was limited to selling her wine only to those clients who were really motivated to purchase an unknown but (for the industry) innovative wine that was recognized some interesting attributes. This strategy might or might not be appropriate for a small- sized company, which surely has difficulties in investing scarce resources to attract consumers. Stella was deeply convinced about the role that inner motivations had in consumers' product perception and evaluation: although market conditions were changing and there is a progressive globalization occurring in the wine industry, Stella might have been persuaded to consider the prominent role that personal motivations, cultural orientation and emotions have for wine consumers—and that those do not necessarily incorporate a bias towards small organic/biodynamic producers. Students might suggest that Stella do more than merely rely on websites to communicate her wines' uniqueness.

That is, what Stella needs to do now, is in consonance with her small association of producers, to attempt to redefine the boundaries of the Montalcino sustainability niche. Adopters might wrap up the discussion by pointing out that growth should be a subsidiary goal to sustainability—i.e., adopted when it is necessary for survival or is tied tightly to realistic objectives for profitability over time. For example, growth is essential to survival when a company must achieve the minimum level of scale or scope necessary to compete effectively as an industry goes through shakeout or changes in leadership—a situation that arises only under specialized circumstances. Growth may be integral to profitability when the company is striving to achieve an advantaged competitive position, or when it is taking advantage of particular changes in industry structure. In each of these cases, the challenge is to link growth to the primary objectives of survival and profitability so that the executive team responsible for implementing the strategy knows how to assess accurately whether growth generates a return over time that exceeds its costs. Another aspect to this discussion involves the differences between private and public companies. Public companies appear to "demand" growth and punish non-growth, while private companies are not necessarily hamstrung by the need for (or absence of) growth.

As Michael E. Porter observed in 1996, niche markets may be rich in opportunity:

> Positioning is not only about carving out a niche. A position emerging from any of the sources can be broad or narrow. A focused competitor, such as Ikea, targets the special needs of a subset of customers and designs its activities accordingly. Focused competitors thrive on groups of customers who are over-served (and hence overpriced) by more broadly targeted competitors, or under-served (and hence underpriced).

The question in 2012 and beyond remains, how long can the Stella sustain her focus and her business? Noy (2010), borrowing from population ecology theory, proposes that for a business seeking a sustainable competitive advantage, a vacant niche strategy is merely a short-range approach, one that ultimately must give way to boundary-spanning (i.e. seeking entry into other market segments) in order to achieve longer-range profitable growth. A firm that remains in an unoccupied niche, once that niche is sufficiently large, is likely to encounter much larger rivals that will alter the competitive structure and profitability of that niche. At that point, a niche player must re-evaluate its strategy—or find a new, unoccupied niche.

REFERENCES AND WEBSITES
Websites

http://archivio-radiocor.ilsole24ore.com/articolo-898511/vino-frescobaldi-2010-fatturato
http://www.agi.it
http://www.consorziobrunellodimontalcino.it
http://www.istat.it
http://www.provincia.siena.it
http://www.regionetoscana.it

http://www.sangioveseperamico.com
http://www.si.camcom.it
http://www.stelladicampalto.com
http://www.unesco.org
http://www.winenews.it
http://www.winereport.com
http://www.winespectator.com

References

AGI (2011), "Vino: Brunello di Montalcino nel 2010 record mondiale di export," available at: http://www.agi.it/food/notizie/201102091316-eco-rt10116-vini_brunello_di_montalci-no_nel_2010_record_mondiale_export (accessed 5 May 2011)

AGI (2012), "Vino: Winenews, nel 2011 superati i 4 mld di export," available at: http://www.agi.it/food/notizie/201201171116-eco-rt10058-vino_winenews_nel_2011_superati_i_4_mld_di_export (accessed 17 January 2012)

Cavicchi, A. and Santini, C. (2012), "Brunellopoli: wine scandal under the Tuscan sun," *Tourism Review International*, Vol. 16, No. 3.

Cavicchi, A., Santini, C. and Beccacece, E. (2010), "Are you ready for the unexpected? The case of the Brunello crisis," in Faraoni, M. and Santini, C. (Eds), *Managing the Wine Business: Research Issues and Cases*, Milan: McGraw-Hill.

Esty, D.C. and Winston, A.S (2006), *Green to Gold.* Hoboken, New Jersey: John Wiley & Sons.

Grunert, K.G. (2007), "How consumers perceive food quality," in Frewer, L. and Van Trijp, H. (Eds), *Understanding Consumers of Food Products*, Cambridge, Woodhead publishing, pp. 181–99

Grunert, S.C. and Juhl, H.J. (1995), "Values, environmental attitudes, and buying of organic foods," *Journal of Economic Psychology*, Vol. 16, No. 1, pp. 39–62.

Hill, H. and Lynchehaun, F. (2002), "Organic milk: attitudes and consumption patterns," *British Food Journal*, Vol.104, No. 7, pp. 526–542.

Hughner, R., McDonagh, P., Prothero, A.. Shultz, C. and Stanton, J. (2007), "Who are organic food consumers? A compilation and review of why people purchase organic food," *Journal of Consumer Behaviour*, Vol. 6, No. 2–3, pp. 94–110

Jarvis, W. and Goodman, S. (2003), "To niche or not to niche?" *The Australian & New Zealand Grapegrower & Winemaker*, October, pp. 108–113.

McGahan, A. M. (2004) *How Industries Evolve*, Boston, MA: Harvard Business School Press.

Nguyen, D.K. and Slater, S.F. (2010), "Hitting the sustainability sweet spot: Having it all," *Journal of Business Strategy*, 32(3), pp. 5–11.

Noy, E. (2010). "Niche Strategy: Merging Economic and Marketing Theories with Population Ecology Arguments," *Journal of Strategic Marketing*, 18:1, February, pp. 77–86.

Phypher, J.D. & MacLean, P., (2009), *Good to Green*, Mississauga, Ontario: John Wiley & Sons Canada, Chapter Five.

Porter, M.E. (1996). "What Is Strategy?" *Harvard Business Review*, November–December, pp. 60–78.

Soler, F., Gil, JM., and Sánchez, M. (2002), "Consumers' acceptability of organic food in Spain: results from an experimental auction market," *British Food Journal*, Vol.104, No.8, pp. 670–687.

Squires, L., Juric, B., and Cornwell, B. (2001), "Level of market development and intensity of organic food consumption: cross-cultural study of Danish and New Zealand consumers", *Journal of Consumer Marketing*, Vol.18, No.5, pp. 392–409

Zanoli, R. and Naspetti, S. (2002), "Consumer motivations in the purchase of organic food: A means-end approach," *British Food Journal*, Vol. 104, No. 8, pp. 643–653

Notes

1. Preparations are identified through a number: there is the 500, the 501 and preparation from 502 to 507. In particular, Horn Manure Preparation (500) increase the microflora and increases the nutrients available in the soil. It is used mainly for developing humus formation and increasing water holding capacity. Preparation 501 is the Horn Silica and helps the plant in assimilating the light and warmth; as a consequence plants provide flavourer fruit with a higher aroma and nutritional quality. the last type of preparation in the Compost Preparations (502 to 507), that are used for improving the dynamic cycles of the macro- and micro-nutrients, via biological processes in the soil and in material breakdown.

2. The prices have been collected in wineries and though some specialised shop's websites.

3. The other producers are: Francesco Leanza, the first to produce organic wine in Montalcino with his company Podere Salicutti and Caroline Pobitzer and Jan Hendrik Erbach, wife and husband, owner of the biodynamic Pian dell'Orino.

Grandes Vinos y Viñedos

WINE COOPERATIVES JOIN FORCES TO REACH INTERNATIONAL MARKETS

Luis Miguel Albisu,
Agro-Food Research Unit, CITA, Zaragoza, Spain

SUMMARY

Traditionally, Spanish wine has been produced through the group efforts of wine cooperatives. In order to address perceived weaknesses in cooperative management and marketing efforts, several cooperatives in the Aragón region in northeastern Spain joined to form the company Grandes Vinos y Viñedos through the help of some government organizations and public interest groups. This company has achieved greater global recognition of its wine brands, though perhaps it is not yet as profitable as it could be.

INTRODUCTION

Wine consumption in Spain has been steadily decreasing in recent decades. Wineries sell their wines in Spain at low prices, especially in years when the supply of wine is abundant due to good weather conditions. Great efforts are devoted to selling wine in foreign countries as well.

Denominations of origin (DOs) have been essential to impel the development of quality wines in the European Union (EU). Currently, EU regulations apply to all member states, although each DO can make specific adaptations to its natural and human environments. The DO Cariñena, located in the Aragón region in northeastern Spain, is one of the oldest Spanish DOs. Cooperative wineries have controlled most of the wine production. They are located in the major villages.

Cariñena wines have been used mainly to blend with wines from other regions because of its high alcohol content and strong taste. There have been notable efforts to transmit other impressions, both at a collective level through the DO Cariñena, where Grandes Vinos y Viñedos is located, and by the company itself. Grandes Vinos y Viñedos has tried to evolve from a previous poor performance and formerly marketing practices, common to most cooperatives, to contend in competitive international markets.

The Framework of the DO Cariñena

Cariñena wines have been recognized even before the DO was formally recognized. In 1932, when Spain first established legislation for wine, the area was mentioned, but the Regulatory Council of the DO was not formalized until 1960. Annual production is around 50 million liters of wine. The Regulatory Council bases its policy on three main lines of action: quality, information, and promotion.

Historically, the geographical area that includes the DO Cariñena has been a land known for its excellent soil and climatic conditions for growing grapes. Ventilated stony soils, as well as a Mediterranean semiarid climate between 400 and 700 meters above sea level, contribute to achieving high-quality wines. The Garnacha variety is considered to originate in this area.

Grandes Vinos y Viñedos has great power in the DO Cariñena, because of its significant size and help received from public authorities, so its development greatly influences the entire collective. However, it is useful to compare some facts and circumstances about what is happening in the DO in order to try to understand the challenges and achievements of the company.

The data presented for the DO are from 1997 and 2011. The comparison of two specific years may not be very accurate due to natural variation between years but, at least, it is indicative of certain trends.

	1997	2011
Wine production (hectoliters)	518,145	545,761
Quality wines recognized by the DO (% of total production)	38	93
Bottling (% of total production)	14	83
Exports in bulk (hectoliters)	6,902	0
Exports in bottles (hectoliters)	28,309	288,977

Grape production, although having a large fluctuation because yields vary from harvest to harvest, has not changed much. The large increase in quality wines has been significant in less than 15 years, and the transition from trading wine in bulk to bottles has been impressive as well as the improvements in capturing foreign markets.

For decades, Cariñena wines have been considered powerful and of high alcohol content. Sales consisted mostly of one-liter bottles and the region was a leader in selling that particular size in the market. The change to three-quarter-liter bottles has been slower than in other DOs because they had a great share of the Spanish market for one liter bottle.

The quality of its wines has changed enormously but the image perceived by Spanish consumers has not kept the same pace. The Regulatory Council of the DO was aware of this problem and created a communications department to better convey the positives of the wines that were launched into the domestic market. The first efforts were started in 1993 and they have continued ever since.

This communications problem has probably been one of the reasons that the DO wants to undertake greater efforts in exports. Consumers in other countries do not have negative images about the DO Cariñena wines and assess their attributes positively, especially the good relationship between quality and price.

A Unique and Complicated Business Establishment: Grandes Vinos y Viñedos

Cooperatives, many of which created in the 1950s, have provided most of the wine supply in the Cariñena area for decades and have sold its wine to strengthen wines of low-alcohol content produced in other geographical areas. However, despite the Regulatory Council's marketing efforts, the amount of bottled wine produced was not as much as desired and the cooperatives were too small to undertake important projects.

The government of the region wanted to move forward and produce a change in its business model and marketing approaches. Small cooperatives were asked to join as larger cooperatives, but it was first necessary to raise capital from public and private financial institutions in the region.

In the early 1990s, the regional government commissioned a study to be undertaken by a consulting firm. The conclusion was that a winery leader should be in each of the DOs of Aragón. As a consequence, the government initiated conversations with the Regulatory Council of the DO Cariñena. The negotiations were arduous because the incorporation of cooperatives was difficult and the most important cooperative resisted at the last moment. It is usual that understanding among cooperatives located close one each other had difficulties to merge because their members do not want to lose their village identities. Grandes Vinos y Viñedos was created in 1997 under the legal rules of a limited company involving four cooperatives from different villages that had a majority of the shareholding. The remaining capital was provided by an institution dependent on the Aragón Government for the development of the region and three private financial institutions. The argument was that common cooperatives were not able to face competitive market challenges. Their management was not appropriately structured to make decisions in short periods of time and their decisions makers were not qualified because poor management education. Joining cooperatives together was a novelty in the Spanish wine sector, which had tried to preserve the cooperative spirit with a different management structure.

There were about 1,000 members in all the cooperatives comprising 5,500 hectares of land. The cooperatives' importance inside the DO Cariñena was clear because it gathering around one-third of the most important production and structural figures. The purpose of the new company was bottling, aging, marketing, and distributing table and bulk wines.

Cooperatives also contributed with their brands and commercial networks, although it must be stressed that one of the cooperatives accounted for 96% of the bottled total production, and they were forced to incorporate all their production into the new company. At the beginning, the bottling and aging of wines were done in the different cooperatives. Then, it was anticipated that the company was planning new investments to provide new facilities to deal with handling, bottling, and aging of wines coming from all cooperatives.

The total quality control was assigned to the coaching staff of the new company and the parameters that had to be analyzed were identified. It was specified to have separate accounts for the bottled wines and the bulk wine. The following premium percentages were established above the average market price for each of the wine varieties: Grenache (18 %), Mazuela or Cariñena (18%), Tempranillo (39%), and Cabernet (71%).

The first two autochthonous varieties of the area received lower price compensations than other varieties, such as Tempranillo, abundant in Spain but not found as much in Cariñena. The foreign variety Cabernet was the most valued. This price policy clearly indicated which varieties were desired for new plantings. Premium prices were allocated to mono varietals. The reason for giving a smaller premium to local varieties was that they represented a high percentage of the total production. Consequently, there was an incentive to produce different wines by introducing new varieties.

The new company brought together vineyards from the different cooperatives, wines were produced in each of them, and then they were jointly marketed in order to achieve greater added value. Higher prices were achieved by selling bottles instead of bulk wine. The claim was to sell all kinds of wines, from common to top line, all of which should bear the label of the DO.

Initially, there were objectives to be accomplished within a five-year period, such as to double the sale of 7.5 million bottles in the first year, that the quality wines increase from 51% bottling production to 80%, and to increase the exports from 25% to 50% of the total wines produced.

Business and Commercial Development

A number of different decisions have been made through the years to enhance business and commercial development. This gives a good indication of how practices have been changing and provides material to evaluate that could enhance crucial adjustments. For example, the first two harvests already showed drastic improvements in increasing the production of bottles and reducing the amount of bulk wine sold.

	1997–1998	1998–1999
Turnover (million euro)	7	14.4
Sales of bottles (million)	6.7	9
Sales on bulk (million liters)	8	5

Since 1997 Grandes Vinos y Viñedos began to promote visits to the winery by creating wine tourism routes together with visits to other places in the area, and participating in a national cycling race in order to reach a greater national audience.

In 2000 Grandes Vinos y Viñedos became shareholders in a company that was devoted to providing image, design, and innovation consultancy services. In this way, they tried not only to improve the production of their wines but also to emphasize other marketing facets. The following year the company went a step further by holding an international competition to design a new bottle that would be used for high-quality wines.

In 2002 the company was operating a new plant with modern facilities, with an investment close to 10 million to cover production tasks in an appropriate manner and comply with the requirements of foreign markets.. New facilities consisted of a building constructed to match the local style and large industrial plants for the entire process of storing, aging, and bottling.

Objectives were fixed for the marketing year 2005–2006 based on new actions related to production and marketing, with the continuing idea to increase the proportion of bottled wines and decrease bulk wine. There was also a clear commitment to achieving a high percentage of total bottles of aged wines. The number of barrels had to be increased dramatically to achieve this objective. Administrative and commercial activities were also improved. Those changes were undertaken to operate in an efficient manner and transmit to the outside an image of a company that was capable of being noticed in the more developed markets and achieving greater added value. A global marketing of 14.5 million bottles and a turnover of 20 million were reached during 2005–2006.

The mission and vision of the company were established. The mission, defined in this new strategic plan, coincided with what was initially expressed at the establishment of the company, but was now described in an explicit manner. Thus, it was stated that Grandes Vinos y Viñedos should be the reference winery in Aragón for its growth and profitability, and recognized in markets for its innovation, quality, competitiveness, and service through the commitment and level of professionalism of its employees.

The company celebrated its 15th anniversary in 2012. Throughout its history, the company has continued its investment in advertising and communication. There has been a transition of efforts from advertising in mass media toward communications aimed more at commercial channels, technical workshops, and tastings. Social networks also receive major attention because they are powerful channels of communication. These efforts are intended to create value in such a way that the number of sold bottles was around 20 million but with better economic results.

Over the years, the company has participated in various exhibitions of wines in Spain as well as in many other countries, such as France, Germany, China, Japan, Sweden, Singapore, and so on. Its presence in the market has been supported, in addition to the quality of its wines, by being able to present certifications ISO 9.001, ISO 14.001, IFS, BRC, and DLG.

RANGE OF PRODUCTS AND BRAND POLICY

From the outset, Grandes Vinos y Viñedos had many brands, but the company has concentrated its business on a smaller number. Monasterio de las Viñas, which was the best-known brand, was focused on the home consumption market and occupied the lowest rung of the price ladder. Corona de Aragón represented wines with a range of higher prices and was aimed to be sold at restaurants. Other brands covered marginal segments of production and were sold at low prices. Currently, the company has a wide range of red, rosé, and white wines. They have also incorporated another brand called Beso de Vino (Kiss of Wine) modern looking and easy to drink. Most commercial and marketing efforts are concentrated on those three brands.

The Monasterio de las Viñas brand has a wide range of wines and a great volume is produced. The white wines come mainly from the Macabeo variety and the rosés are created from the Garnacha variety. But there are many red wines and blends made out of different varieties. In addition, it incorporates the Cabernet Sauvignon variety both as a varietal wine and in blends with other native varieties. It is intended to have a great penetration in self-service establishments.

The Corona de Aragón brand has a lower production because there is higher demand for quality selection. It incorporates two other varieties: Syrah for red wines and Chardonnay for white wines. There are also multiple blends, similar to the Beso de Vino, and whites and rosés are not only varietals but they also have blends. Corona de Aragón brands have a major proportion of Tempranillo compared to other varieties. This brand tries to be in a high-priced segment in the restaurant industry and is marketed with a unique bottle design.

The Anayon brand is part of the Corona de Aragón brand. There is a more stringent selection, which only goes out to markets in particular years. In some of its wines the company uses the term barrel to get some consumer attention from consumers who do not understand other Spanish specifications. Its recognition is based on the variety and the year but has the hallmark of being carefully selected wines of high quality and price. They have, therefore, a less traditional presentation.

There are a number of varietals called Corona de Aragón Disparates, and all varieties have their representation. Their small productions are sold only in certain years. In some cases the wines come from 20– to 40-year-old vineyards. The Corona de Aragón is completed with Muscat, Vermouth, and Garnaccio.

The 2008–2009 season was marked by the launch of the brand Beso de Vino with a new philosophy regarding its presentation, a very casual design, and directed toward young people. This brand, diversified in four varietal wines, has had a large impact on company exports. Despite its recent launch, it is already present in more than 20 countries. It is a break from the image presented by other wines from the company, with a screw cap and a more modern packaging.

In 2011, two new brands were released: Veut with very special characteristics and low alcohol content, made out of Garnacha to reach young audience, and Garnacchio liquor, which is also elaborated with Garnacha. A new society was formed to articulate their participation in another company involving the Cariñena DO—leading companies with the aim of improving the advertising and marketing of the wines of the area. This year reached a record number of bottles sold, with more than 24 million, and a turnover close to 27 million, which means profits that average price per bottle was a little over 1.

Awards and Recognition

From the beginning, one of the policies of the company has been to compete at contests so the resulting awards could give the company the fame it needs to be noticed in the markets where they want to be present.

In 1999, they won the best prize with the wine Corona de Aragón Crianza at the Zarcillo wine contest, which is the most prestigious contest in Spain. The following year they got another important recognition with the Monasterio de las Viñas Crianza at the Golden Baccus contest in Spain.

Through the years, the company has participated in different competitions and has won prestigious awards. It is noteworthy that the company has won the Berliner Wein Trophy for several years, which has had a clear impact in the German market. Grandes Vinos y Viñedos has also garnered awards in contests celebrated in Canada, the United States, France, England, Japan, and so on.

In 2009, the magazine Wine Advocate, led by Robert Parker, included two references of the brand Corona de Aragón and several ones of the brand Beso de Vino. Beso de Vino selection 2009 was the unique Spanish wine under $10 that obtained a 90-point rating. It was a milestone that communicated its achievements to the North American markets but also to the rest of the world, given the projection of its ratings. In 2010 and 2011, there were other recognitions from the same magazine in the 91 score for the Monasterio de las Viñas Gran Reserva. In 2011 the wine brand Veut received recognition at the Wine Innovation Award, an event organized by a leading import group from Holland.

The influence of prescribers is very important in marketing channels, especially magnified by the professional environment around Robert Parker. High ratings from magazines such as Wine Advocate have a positive effect on trade in many countries. However, in other countries, such as England, there are other influences that have more impact such opinion leader Jancis Robinson and many others. Grandes Vinos y Viñedos is aware of these influences but also tries to reach consumers by offering tastings.

Human Resources and Corporate Social Responsibility

Cooperatives are sensitive to local employment and this company has not been an exception. Thus, the constitutional rules of the company provide that it would have special consideration for the recruitment of staff within the cooperative shareholders, although always taking into account the company's needs to comply with business objectives to achieve a sustainable economic viability.

This company has also been able to adapt to new trends by looking for technical personnel who will improve their competitiveness. Hence, in 2001, the winery hired a winemaker from Chile, a very unusual decision in Spain. A wine cooperative in an old world country invited a professional coming from a new world country to design its new wines, thus giving way to a new winemaking philosophy: that preserving the tradition of the wines of the area has to adapt to new trends. It was a step in the right direction, but not easy to carry out in an environment that was not used to changes of that dimension.

The specifications in viticulture and oenology, established by the technical team, tried to upgrade quality wines with an adequate financial compensation for the wine-growers who complied with the requirements. Important investments in oenological technology facilitated that objective. Then, they were adapted to market demands, which means, in some cases, making changes following winery market perceptions and, in other situations, simply producing wines according to customer needs.

Since 2004, the company's export department has been managed by a woman, which is unusual for cooperatives and in the wine sector, because it is usually a highly masculinized industry.

During the season 2005–2006, an agreement was signed with the Down's Foundation, trying to help people with Down's syndrome, to sell a wine emphasizing an image of solidarity. All benefits had to be dedicated to foundation programs and it was the first step in developing a strategy of corporate social responsibility. In 2007–2008, the new wine was launched.

THE EXPORT PATH

In 1998, a few months after the company was started, Grandes Vinos y Viñedos got a contract to export one million bottles to Germany. During the 1998–1999 season, the company started exporting to countries outside the European Union, such as Japan and some South American countries.

During the 2001–2002 season, the company began to think that exports should equal domestic sales by 2005–2006, although progression toward foreign markets was not constant and there were some setbacks. These aims were fulfilled quite soon because the 2004–2005 exports accounted for 40% of the total turnover, and they reached 70% of the total sales figures in 2011, with presence in about 30 countries. The future objectives are to increase the percentage devoted to exports and create more value by going to the best markets.

A program of commercialization has been established countries outside Europe with special attention to Canada, the United States, China, Japan, Brazil, and Russia. That is to say, all countries are raising their imports but altogether there is a mix of developed and emergent markets. Particular efforts have been accomplished in the North American market with the acquisition of a distribution company and the creation of another company for the promotion and export of wines to the Asian markets.

The proximity of the countries of the European Union and the increased wine consumption in many European countries have been two important incentives to direct exports to these destinations. It is logical that the big countries, such as the United Kingdom and Germany, have been the main importers. In 1998–1999, these countries accounted for 68% of the export value of the 18 countries to which the wine was destined,

Germany in the first place (47%), followed by the United Kingdom (21%), Denmark (10%), and the Netherlands and Switzerland (5% each).

In 2011 exports reached 29 countries and the top five markets, regarding total percentages, were the United Kingdom (47%), Canada and Germany (17% each), Russia (5%), and the United States (2%). The high percentage of sales in the United Kingdom is because of penetration on distribution chains. That is, throughout time, destinations have been diversified not only with respect to the number of countries but also of continents. For example, Canada and the United States occupy now the second and fifth place among their exporting countries. Nevertheless, the first five countries reached almost 90%, in both years, showing a great export concentration in a small number of countries.

Profound expansions occurring during the years have been due largely to contracts with retail chains, as happened in Germany, Holland, and England, and to entries in new countries. Exports currently aim to concentrate on the top ten wine-importing countries. The countries of the European Union, jointly with Russia and Switzerland, acquire more than 75% of the exports. However, in the future, it would be desirable that all these countries amount to only about 50% in order to diversify risks and be present in other growing markets.

One of the biggest problems is that the wineries are competing with a large number of brands and references coming from many different countries. The challenge is not only to penetrate markets but also to remain once established. It requires a combination of trying to retain consumers and also attract new customers to the distribution channels. Around 80% of the company's exports are sold under its own brand names. Wine brands produced by this company have high loyalty in England, Germany, Belgium, Switzerland, and Canada.

Wines sold to consumers in the United States at $10 per bottle correspond to a price of $2 at the winery. The majority of the wines sold by this company in the United States are between $7 and $10 a bottle. The range of wines in the Corona de Aragón brand achieved a higher price, surpassing $15 a bottle.

From Brands to Focusing on Variety

The US and Canadian markets are gaining in importance for the company and it is a geographic area where the company wants to promote the presence of its wines. These two markets have been growing with great intensity for the last 5 years and, along with the Chinese market, have evolved more than most other countries.

Both consumers in United States and Canada have high purchasing power. The United States imports about one-third and Canada two-thirds of their consumption, respectively. In both countries, imports are expected to grow because the national supply will not be able to cover expected consumption increases.

Nevertheless, Spanish wines have not gained market share in the last few years. One of the impediments is that consumers are looking for the variety as the main reference to defining wines. In the case of the DO Cariñena wines, similar to other wines that come from the European Union, the DO is the main line of communication. The strategy is to change that approach and the company has chosen wines with the Garnacha variety as the principal support to penetrate the [North American market.

The idea that Aragón is the origin of the Garnacha variety has been supported by many professionals and it is the most planted variety in the region, with more than 30% of the entire production. The varietal composition indicates that almost a third of the production corresponds to foreign varieties that are considered improvers in comparison to traditional varieties. The word tradition has been associated with existing varieties and the word innovation relates to the introduction of foreign varieties and not to innovations introduced in traditional varieties. This varietal composition has a great marketing importance to the identity of the wines from this DO.

The future objective is not only to promote Garnacha varietal wines but also blends with that variety. Wines from this variety have gone from being little known to now being the main avenue to achieving higher market shares in many countries. This change has been the result of improvements in cultivation techniques but mostly of oenological processes as well as of image.

A joint effort of seven DOs from Spain (four from Aragón included the DO Cariñena and three from Catalonia) and three denominations from France, from the Roussillon, has been undertaken to launch an informational and generic promotion campaign of Garnacha wines in the United States and Canada.

The program will be funded mainly by the European Union, but also by Spanish and French institutions as well as wineries. A regional institution in charge of promoting exports, depending on the Aragón Government, has taken the initiative of planning and executing the program. Given the dimension of these markets, actions have been restricted to three states in the United States (New York, Florida, and California) and one region in Canada (Ontario). In both cases these markets have more than 40% of the total imports in each country.

Grandes Vinos y Viñedos is also promoting its wines in the United States and Canada through a program of the European Union linked to the Common Markets Organisation (CMO) of wine. Grandes Vinos y Viñedos tries to combine both activities, with individual and collective actions.

SUMMARY

Cooperatives previously have been blamed for lacking essential internal managerial elements to be competitive in international markets. They assemble a supply of bulk wine but are poor at selling bottles with brands. In this case, a novel approach has been developed by preserving the cooperative spirit under new managerial methods. The idea is how to combine private and public efforts to face new market challenges without losing the rights and philosophy behind cooperatives members.

Spanish wine consumption has been consistently decreasing since the 1980s. Wineries have been forced to emphasize their sales in international markets. Grandes Vinos y Viñedos understood that need and has taken concrete steps to be successful. It remains to be analyzed whether their decisions were the most appropriate to achieving location in the most promising markets with adequate marketing positions.

QUESTIONS

- According to the case but also based on your knowledge, would you say that the shareholders' role has to be specific when managing a cooperative?
- Because there are many actors in the wine world, increasing the added value of a wine is important. How can this be developed?

AUTHOR'S PERSPECTIVE

This unique company raises some questions with respect to the role of shareholders, its development, and its future.

SHAREHOLDERS' ROLE

The initiative to establish the company came from the public sector. It is thought that cooperatives monitored by the public sector usually do not reach optimal performance. In this case, a mixture of public interests, financial corporations, and cooperatives seem to have found a good balance. Public and financial institutions have provided capital and certain guidance.

If the situation continues, it seems that stability is a likely outcome resulting in a good understanding between the cooperatives and other institutions. However, the management of the company probably should be mature enough to continue the development on its own.

THE PATH TOWARD MORE ADDED VALUE

At the beginning, a great part of the production was sold in bulk and there was a great volume of wine. Through the years, bottled wine has increased to the extent that all production now is sold in bottles. The concept is that bottles can reach more value than bulk wine.

However, a simple evaluation of the total turnover shows that at the beginning the price per liter was around 1. At the end, 15 years later, that price was only 1.1. It seems too low and does not represent a great improvement, which means that most of their wines are sold at prices that may be too cheap. Serious questions arise about whether marketing policies have been the most appropriate to get more added value.

SWOT ANALYSIS

With the information offered in this case, readers should undertake a SWOT analysis with respect to Grandes Vinos y Viñedos's commercial strengths and weaknesses as well as to the opportunities and threats occurring in the markets where it wants to place its wines.

This will involve analyzing the commercial development of the company and also collecting some data about international markets. Special attention should be paid to European versus North American markets.

BIBLIOGRAPHY

Albisu, L. M. (2001). Entre lo global y lo local. Viticultura: Enología Profesional, 74, 7–16.

Albisu, L. M. (2004). Spain and Portugal. In K. Anderson (Ed.), The World's Wine Markets: Globalization at Work (pp. 98–109). Cheltenham, UK: Edward Elgar Publishing.

Consejo Regulador DO Cariñena. (2011). El vino de las piedras

Grandes Vinos y Viñedos. (www.grandesvinos.com/english/index.php). Internal documents.

Mainar, J. L. (2012). Creciendo y respirando ilusión. Viñas, Vinos, Vidas, 40, 2.

CASE 4

Winzergenossenschaft Westhofen

A German Wine Cooperative Evaluates Strategic Positioning

Marc Dressler and Anika Kost,
University of Ludwigshafen, Germany

Summary

Winzergenossenschaft Westhofen, a German wine-producing cooperative, evaluates market opportunities and strategic steps for future growth after periods of restructuring and investments. Having created a lean and efficient organization, the CEO intends to exploit direct sales channels as well as to foster exporting its products, specifically to the Americas. The case therefore provides the basis to analyze the industry, competition, and strategic positioning, to create an offer design considering customer expectations in a global context, and to evaluate managerial challenges in the light of specific organizational boundaries, such as cooperative organizations.

Introduction

The Winzergenossenschaft Westhofen (WGW) is a cooperative of about 200 vintners producing and marketing wine from about 340 hectares of vineyards. In Germany, cooperatives deliver one-third of the German wine production. The competitive environment in the German wine industry has resulted in massive restructuring of wine producers in general and cooperative organizations specifically, some of them dissolving and others merging. Despite ongoing concentration, the wine supply side in the German wine industry is still characterized as a fragmented, liberal, and dispersed market. Strategic positioning is therefore of paramount importance to sustainably perform in such a market environment.

WGW sells bulk as well as bottled wine. It is located in Germany's largest wine region, Rheinhessen, and its wine is regarded as quality products constantly awarded and recognized to be of good price value. The distribution portfolio is diverse, covering direct sales to end consumers, sales to retail, and restaurants, as well as exports on a stand-alone basis or via partnerships. WGW is part of an alliance of cooperatives from different regions pursuing jointly national and international marketing and sales for their wines.

In 2009, a new CEO entered the organization. Since then, WGW has extensively restructured with a focus on quality increase as well as productivity gains. A lean organization that creatively exploits market opportunities was realized. Next strategic steps are aiming to further expand direct sales opportunities and access foreign country markets, identified as attractive levers for profitable growth and a sustainable business model for the future.

WG Westhofen Explores Strategic Positioning

Business as usual—a last walk through the facilities to close the doors and turn off the lights—is all standard procedure of a final daily quality check. Dennis Balasus, CEO of Westhofen wine cooperative, extinguishes the lights in the production area, warehouse, and sales and administration facilities, a habit that became routine procedure during the course of realizing massive restructuring and quality increase programs. Having taken the position as CEO in 2009, Dennis reflects on the managerial challenges that he faced in previous years, but also on the ones ahead.

When taking the assignment, Mr. Balasus did not expect such a rich portfolio of managerial tasks to be tackled in such a short period. Intensified market competition, internal incidents at WGW, and difficult weather conditions with lower yields and therefore lower earnings impacted his time at WGW from the beginning. Hence, with some pride at having succeeded despite the challenges, he turned off the computer showing him the latest information on sales and an e-mail stating positive outcome of a foreign country marketing activity.

Indeed, extensive restructuring and process optimization has resulted in a lean organization that is well positioned to compete in a tough German market. An ambitious and challenging change program was created in which all processes and business model components—for example, the payment scheme for the members, new sales approaches and additional channels, strategic partnerships, and the product range—were optimized. In addition to implementing change and restructuring, securing sales was accomplished with a lot of power and creativity: a joint venture for the annual sales of bulk wines, a partnership with other cooperatives for bottled products, and offering slack capacity to outsiders for different steps of the value chain were milestones of fostering sales, efficiency, and profitability. WGW therefore today is totally different than when Dennis entered the organization. A solid organizational and financial basis supported by highly professional processes has been created for a prosperous future in a tough competitive market.

One example is the new grape reception that was finished just the day the harvesting began in 2012. Despite a major investment and a change in one crucial step of the process of delivering and pressing the wine grapes, everything worked at high professional standards and quality levels from the first moment when the press was started. Not surprisingly, most members of the cooperative are now convinced that this change and organizational transformation was needed.

Dennis now shifts focus from efficiency to growth. Sources to increase earnings and profitability that are currently in discussion include intensifying direct sales to end consumers as well as additional export activities. Those two strategic levers seem highly attractive given the German market situation as well as the competencies of WGW. Dennis feels that now is the appropriate time for further concentration on growth ambitions. But are those strategic ambitions in a fierce competitive market realistic? What are the risks of the steps? How should these ambitions be approached? And especially, which markets are best-suited for WGW´s products and organization, and will they increase the profitability of WGW and its members? These questions not only puzzle Dennis when reflecting on the future positioning of the WGW, but also will be raised in the upcoming board and membership meetings. Some members might strive for a rest in the change activities or they might doubt that the steps will result in higher individual income. The story needs a convincing concept to sway the board to accept additional changes.

Context: The Wine Market in Germany

The German wine industry is characterized by changes on the demand as well as on the supply side. Germans drink more than twenty million hectoliters (hl) of wine per year, representing a market value exceeding eight billion euros a year. The average consumption of 25 liters per inhabitant is stable and although it is only about half of France—the benchmark, with highest per capita consumption—Germany is an attractive market for wine. Today, Germany ranks as the number four country in volume consumption in the world, but it is the world champion in sparkling wine drinking and in wine imports. Indeed, with more than 16 million hl of wine imported, more than half of the wine consumed in Germany originates in foreign countries. Furthermore, Germany has developed into a hub for European wine sales, despite its rather small population (DWI, 2012; Rückrich, 2012).

In Germany, wine substitutes for other alcoholic beverages given an overall declining alcohol use but a stable wine consumption. Wine belongs to a modern style of living in developed countries with higher level of wealth, and it is interpreted as more cultural alcohol consumption. German wine consumers are offered a great variety of local, regional, and international wines. Different sales channels compete for the consumers who enjoy wines for a diverse universe of occasions with different preferences and behaviors. They prefer international wines to German products, favor Italian wines, and red to white wines—with a 60:40 split. Italy, France, and Spain jointly deliver more than three-fourths of the imported wines to Germany. (DWI, 2012)

Offer Variety and Channel Diversity

German wine drinkers buy their wine either directly at the vintners' and cooperatives or at different retailers—ranging from local, regional, or national supermarkets to discounters to special wine stores—or they consume in restaurants and on premise. Indirect sales for home consumption dominate the German wine market, with about 70% in volume sold there. These channels, especially supermarkets and discount stores, increase their market share steadily and are seen as a reason for low prices of wines in Germany, given their average sales price of less than 3 euros per liter, alongside imported products that one also characterized by lower average prices. Direct sales of wine growers declined to 15%, a result of channel substitution. As average prices are higher for direct sales, the 15% share in volume constitutes more than 20% in value.

When calculating the wine prices from a consumer perspective, one needs to consider the price premium in restaurants and on-premise resulting in substantially higher prices for the consumer. Hence, with such a perspective the market value of wine in Germany results in annual sales of about 10 billion euros. In such a market view, 40% of the wine market value originates in on-premise sales.

Multichannel view on German market (sales and end customer expenses views)

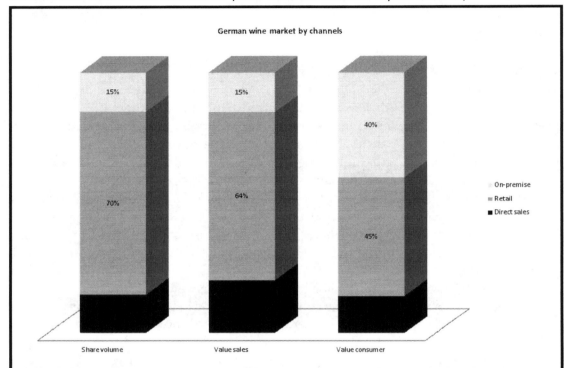

MASSIVE CHANGES ON THE WINE PRODUCTION SIDE

Not only the consumer side but also the production side is characterized by variety and change. Germany produces wine in thirteen regions. The wine regions differ significantly in structural and product matters. Because vineyard surface and location is restricted, constant vineyards of about 100,000 hectares deliver 7 to 11 million hl, depending on the yearly vegetation and natural hazards. Of the production 64% is white and 36% is red wine. Nearly all German wine is rated quality wines. Riesling is grown at about 22% of the vineyards and Pinot Noir at about 12%. Overall, more than 3.8 million hl of wine is exported. Key destinations for the wines are the United States of America, United Kingdom, and the Netherlands. Those three destinations make up for more than 1 million hl of exported wines.

With a loss of about 50% of its producers since the 1980s, the structural changes in the German wine industry on the supply side are massive. Still, almost 50,000 wine growers are active, with about 40% of them declaring wine as their main source of income. Wine in Germany is produced by independent small wineries, cooperatives and their members, and large wineries buying bulk wine from vintners or cooperatives. The market split is about one-third for each producer segment. German producers are generally characterized by extended value chain coverage along with the large wineries concentrating on production, marketing, and sales.

Overview supply side of German wine

	1979	1999	2009
Number of producers	89471	68603	48009
More than 5 hectares	3.349	5.898	5.984
1 to 5 hectares	21.017	13.004	8.914
Less than 1 hectare	65.105	49.701	33.111

The structure of wine production and supply depends on the wine region. Taking the penetration of cooperatives as an example, regions such as Rheingau or Rheinhessen produce less than 10% of the wine through cooperative ventures. Meanwhile, in Baden or Württemberg, almost 80% is produced and marketed cooperatively.

Penetration of cooperatives (in marketed wine per German wine region)

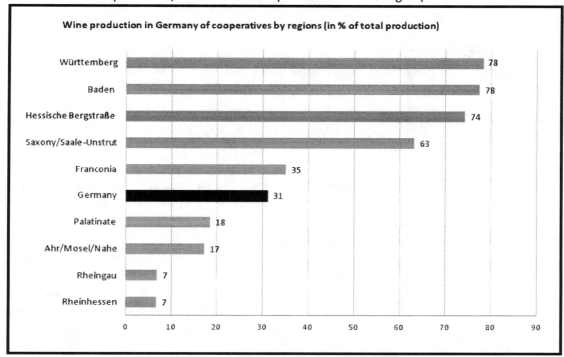

Overall, Germany is a challenging wine market because of the richness of products, low margins, and its complexity, which is also due to regulatory requirements, framing production decisions as well as marketing ideas from a federal but also a European perspective with the intention of securing transparency, quality, and honesty in the interest of the consumers. To just mention a few examples, labeling is strictly defined as is treatment with sulfur, or methods how to treat wine in case of acidity reduction or increase. But since the market is liberal and consumers are curious in regards to offers, products, and channels, there are entrepreneurial opportunities for success. Despite a low average of profitability in the market, new players enter and the recognition for good products as well as entrepreneurs in wine business is high in German society, and therefore compensates for eventual financial restraints.

COOPERATIVES AS IMPORTANT PLAYERS IN THE GERMAN WINE INDUSTRY

The idea of cooperatives in the form of mutual arrangement with integrated value chains and joint ownership dates back to the mid-nineteenth century. During that time the rural population in Germany had to deal with profitability challenges given low prices for their products but high costs, for example, rising interest rates. To counter the resulting poverty, local and regional communities of interests were formed in solidarity to share costs and jointly build market power. First, cooperative banks and agricultural cooperatives were founded. Wilhelm Raiffeisen and Hermann Schulze Delitzsch are seen as the godfathers of the German cooperative movement. Cooperative principals are (Grosskopf, et al. 2009):

- Voluntary and open membership
- Democratic member control
- Economic participation by members
- Autonomy and independence
- Joint education and training on the basis of information exchange

The first viticultural cooperatives in Germany date back to 1852, and the oldest still-existing wine cooperative, Mayschoß-Altenahr, was founded in 1868. It claims to be the oldest wine cooperative in the world.

A wine cooperative is therefore an organization in which regionally tied viticulturists join their forces and create a joint entity to market the products. While the owning, planting, growing, and harvesting are mostly pursued by individuals on an entrepreneurial basis and membership in the cooperative, the wine production as well as sales and distribution are pursued in joint interest by the cooperative body. Cooperatives therefore exploit economies of scale for their owners and create market power, advantageous in the wine business with high fragmentation on the producer side and a concentrated distribution as an intermediary to the final customers. Furthermore, given the seasonality of the activities and the impact on investment needs and financing, such an organizational approach can enhance savings.

Today, about 200 cooperatives exist in Germany. Given the average joint output of about 3 billion liters of wine, cooperatives in sum produce about one-third of the German wine. The output consists of 87% bottled and 17% bulk wine. Bulk wine is sold to wineries for wine production or bottling to serve to national as well as international markets via distributors.

The landscape of wine cooperatives has changed massively. With a peak at around 1960 with more than 500 cooperatives and about 68,000 members, the 1980s saw the population begin to decrease to a current level of about 200 cooperatives with 49,000 members today. Because the planting surface remains rather stable with more than 30,000 hectares, the reduction in members has led to an increased portion of business for the remaining members. (DRV, 2012)

Overview on cooperative landscape in Germany

	1900	1938	1980	2011
Number of cooperatives	113	493	342	188
Members in cooperatives	1,000	29,000	67,000	49,000
Hectares covered	Not stated	Not stated	34,935	32,002

STRATEGIC POSITIONING OF COOPERATIVES

Wine cooperatives in Germany tend to position themselves as generalists serving local, regional, and, depending on the size of the cooperative, also national or international markets. They are often positioned at the lower to mid end of the market and therefore target more basic or mass market segments. Given the size and distribution power of the cooperatives compared to smaller individual vintners, they can serve retail channels with their requests for constant quality and a certain yearly quantity.

A strategic profiling can be derived by looking at size and therefore quantity of the cooperative versus extent of direct sales to consumers. The larger the cooperative, the more the retail channels dominate the client portfolio. Shelf place in retail is needed for sales of larger volumes of bottled wines, but considering volatile yearly yields and the international competition it is also a challenge to fulfill the agreements every year.

COOPERATIVE-SPECIFIC CHALLENGES

Cooperatives face several specific challenges besides the market challenges which are induced by cooperative ownership. Individual members might feel restricted in their entrepreneurial ideas. Brand development is not easy because German consumers might connote a lower quality with cooperatives. Strategic positioning and decision making are more difficult because of the diverse portfolio of interests, ambitions, and perspectives of the members, as is alignment of the members. Indeed, the decision making in cooperation might be more complex than in single-ownership entities. Often, local or regional interests of the communities are considered in addition to all other aspects.

Overall, cooperatives often have to fight a rather negative quality image. This might be the result of years of focus on quantity of production instead of quality. The profitability of members of cooperatives on average is lower than for independent vintners (Oberhofer, 2012).

TRANSFORMATION OF WINZERGENOSSENSCHAFT WESTHOFEN

In the following, the cooperative WGW will be presented by looking at its historic development, describing its actual situation—especially the massive managerial transformation that was initiated after a change in the management of the cooperative—and by providing insights into current strategic decisions in regards to the future development to exploit market opportunities for growth and to increase attractiveness for customers, and also for members of the alliance.

HISTORY OF WGW

The cooperative "Winzergenossenschaft Westhofen eG" was established in 1920. Twenty-nine members agreed to found a joint entity and to deliver all their grapes to the newly created cooperative. At the time of creation the cooperative was located in two facilities in Westhofen, one for production and one for storage. In 1976, WGW bought a former furniture factory, today's facility for receiving and pressing the grapes. A bottle storage location (1978) and an office building (1987) followed. The original warehouse was used until 1993.

Three phases of historic company development followed the starting phase. Decades of growth in members resulted in 139 members in 1955 and 290 members in 1996, respectively. In the 1980s, a phase of investment into facilities and equipment laid the foundation for more professional wine production. The third phase started with the new millennium with a focus on customers as well as new sales approaches for further company development.

WGW is located in Rheinhessen, a region that has greatly increased its quality performance and perception by customers in the German wine market. Rheinhessen benefits from production cost advantages because the area lacks the difficult-to-harvest steep hills of other wine-producing areas, and the size of the plots allows exploitation of economies of scale.

WGW milestones of investments

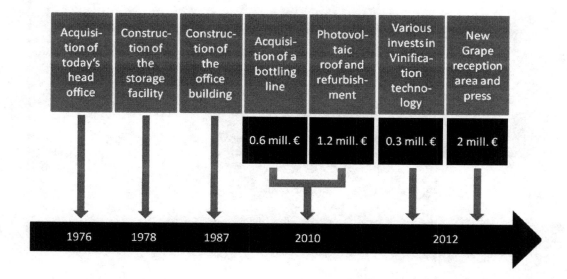

Investment milestones of WGW

CURRENT SIZE AND OUTPUT OF THE COOPERATIVE

WGW counts about 200 members with, 50% of them actively delivering their harvest. Only 5% of the delivering members market their own wines individually instead of only through the cooperative, although members are free to decide on capacity delivered. Having reduced their active members but still keeping an overall constant surface for production, the average size of the active members has increased over the years. The membership portfolio is heterogeneous, with the larger ones cultivating more than 40 hectares, far more than the German or Rheinhessen average. One-third of the members deliver two-thirds of the vine. Membership within the cooperative can be cancelled any time with a two-year notice. WGW is convinced that the only way to sustain itself in the future is to be attractive to members and not by establishing lock-in strategies.

On 350 hectares the cooperative produces on average 3.7 million liters of wine. Of this, about 65% is marketed as bulk wine disposed completely by the partner "Erzeugergemeinschaft Goldenes Rheinhessen" and 35% is sold as bottled wine. WGW covers direct and indirect sales of the bottled wine, including to restaurants. It is also active in foreign countries, though to a smaller extent. The retail market is its dominating sales channel, selling more than 60% of its bottled products.

Sales channels of WGW for bottled products

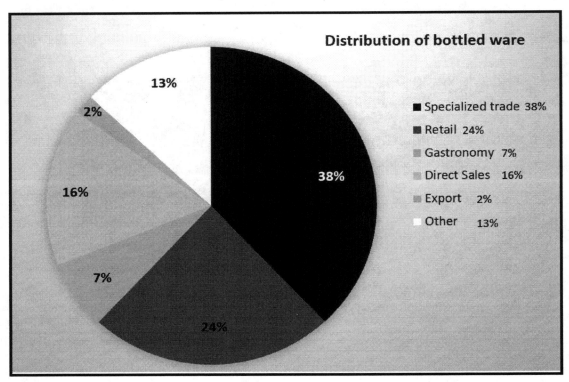

The capacity of WGW is not at its limit with its 8 million liter storage capacity of wine in tanks. Indeed, the strategic aim is also to increase wine production from its current level of about 4.4 million liters and of 400 hectares processed to 500 hectares in the future.

Change and Optimization—Transformation of WGW

WGW has restructured with a strong focus on quality increase as well as productivity gains, for example, staff reductions, ISO certification, forming an international cooperative distribution alliance, offering logistic services to optimize warehouse capacity, and so on.

Top Management Change as Starting Point

Before entering WGW Dennis Balasus gained entrepreneurial experience in watering systems and long-standing sales experience for a US company in the steel business. Covering the world for the sales job, Dennis traveled extensively through Eastern European and Asian countries. Indeed, his experience before joining the wine world left its marks with professional ideas on export activities and production processes know-how. As well, working for a US company resulted in a constant search for optimization opportunities.

Family relations built the basis for Dennis's affinity for the wine industry and to WGW. In his wife´s family there are a number of long-standing members of WGW delivering their grapes to the cooperative. The offer to become part of the management board in WGW therefore provided the opportunity to transform the cooperative by exploiting his experience outside of the wine industry to the advantage of the members, and therefore also to the profit of his own family's wine activities. Dennis also perceived that the job allow a change in his lifestyle to be closer to his family and friends, paired with apparently sufficient challenges for his managerial ambitions.

Shortly after he took over the assignment, a fraud case in the accounting and sales department was discovered by prosecutors. In the course of the investigations the former CEO, in that position for decades, had to resign, and Dennis Balasus moved from the side chair to become the main driver of the cooperative. Being an experienced practitioner with a lot of business sense, Dennis quickly seized the need to massively reduce costs, invest in new technologies, exploit the just-started sales alliance, and change the payment procedures and member relations. He therefore initiated a vast portfolio of change activities.

POSITIONING AND PRIORITIZATION

The strategic orientation of WGW is to produce good wine quality based on reliable processes to ensure constant quality delivery. The bread and butter business is to provide quality wine for the mass market. Producing premium wine is the free exercise. Therefore, costs need to be controlled with quality processes in place, and flexibility is of paramount importance to win retail clients against strong competition of larger providers, not fancy offers.

Dennis decided that the cooperative needed to reduce the number of employees to increase the productivity of the remaining personnel, and use external HR in peak times to become much more cost-efficient and diminish waste and slack in the processes. Hence the staff was reduced to a minimum team and flexibility was increased. Delivery, for example, was to be done by external providers. Staff reductions in accounting, warehouse, order management, and other functions was also carried out. Events and catering are now provided by external service providers. In the course of the HR portfolio changes, the average age of the team was significantly reduced.

Dennis introduced a new payment system for the members. Not only did the basis of payments change but also the pay-out system. WGW switched from a complicated to a transparent system, because nowadays the bulk wine prices lay the foundation for payments to the members. Liquidity is provided by installments within one year and members can decide whether to leave their share in individual accounts with paid interest. As a result, members receive payments earlier with more transparency. By paying the price of bulk wine on the open market they reflect volume and quality effects for that specific year, and therefore the risk for the cooperative is reduced.

The warehouse capacity was increased by more efficient sales processes and logistics optimization. Freed-up capacity is now rented, for example, to a joint venture called "Weinallianz, csz" increasing the income of WGW. Of the 2,000 square meters, currently one-quarter is rented out. Wine production is also opened to individual vintners on an as-needed basis. Interested wineries can use the capacity for needed wine production and logistics processes. Because of the low costs after all the optimizations and ISO certification processes, this offer represents an attractive opportunity for the vintners as they can profit from scale effects. Not surprisingly, WGW´s wine laboratory, which performs at very high standards, is used 80% by external customers.

The roof of the warehouse was replaced and covered with solar energy panels. Besides the needed roof refurbishment for the wine processing, this investment of about 1.2 million euros generates constant additional income by selling electricity into the public net and increases the sustainability of WGW.

CREATIVE PRODUCTION OPTIMIZATION AND BULK SALES SECURIZATION

A partnership with the "Erzeugergemeinschaft (EG) Rheinhessen" was another milestone in the managerial transformation. Since 2010, bulk wine sales are carried out entirely by the EG, an alliance of 240 vintners with more than 2,000 hectares, and therefore one of the most important bulk wine producers in the region. WGW benefits from reduced costs and synergies because EG Rheinhessen offers a market power for lucrative price negotiations and vast experience. In addition, a fixed demand is ensured so that sales are guaranteed for WGW. The cooperative venture, settled formally in 2011, intensifies the collaboration on grape processing, must, and wine, and also in sales. A first step was the agreement that the vintners located in the south of Rheinhessen could deliver their grapes to WGW—located closer to their vineyards—instead of delivering to the more distant EG. Quick processing of the grapes increases the quality. The process is supported by modern technology to guarantee efficient processes: microchip-based identification is used when delivering the grapes at whatever location.

LEVERAGE ON MARKETING AND SALES—THE MODEL OF WEINALLIANZ

In addition to a secured marketing of the bulk wine, the other focal point of managerial change on the sales side was the active push of the "Weinallianz," a joint venture of selected cooperatives used as a powerful vehicle to serve customers with a broader product range. It therefore increases buying efficiency for the channel partners because the offered portfolio exceeds one brand or one supplier. Today, eleven cooperatives form the alliance, jointly marketing their bottled products via their own sales organization.

Overview of the joint venture "Weinallianz"

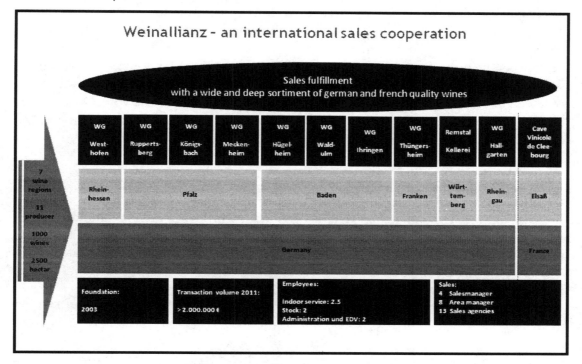

The members profit from better usage of the sales forces capacity as well as better service to their customers. Export activities of individual members can be utilized by the partners, and the experienced sales team offers a broader product range with an extended geographical scope—national and international. Furthermore, the alliance develops brand recognition and quality efforts of the individual members and also the joint Weinallianz brand. With the addition of the "French Cave Vinicole de Cleerbourg," the alliance is now international, increasing the attractiveness of the portfolio and earmarking a milestone in international cooperation.

ENTREPRENEURIAL EXCELLENCE—USING EXISTING PLATFORMS AND ORGANIZATIONAL ENTITIES

Dennis inherited further residuals and platforms that he used to increase professional activities. The "Weinkontor" initially served as joint sales organization with another cooperative, and when the partner merged into a larger entity, the platform was left inactive. This platform was reactivated. Activities that exceed the core business of WGW of transforming incoming grapes into wine and selling them on the market are now pursued via that entity. As a result, the business income on solar energy, laboratory services, bottling for externals, and other activities are realized from Weinkontor platform. It increases transparency and flexibility, and allows for adequate cost allocation. It is also an attractive vehicle given taxation complexity in the German wine business.

It has to be considered that management in cooperatives is regulated to reflect the interest of the members. The executive board of WGW comprises four part-time members, and Dennis Balasus, as a full-time member, represents the cooperative externally and is responsible for management decisions. The supervisory board is composed of four different members elected by the general assembly who control the executive board and report to the assembly. This committee is the highest decision-making body of the cooperative. Each vintner who is a member of WGW has one vote. During their annual meeting they approve, for example, the annual financial statements and the allocation decisions.

PRODUCT OVERVIEW

Looking at the grape varietals, WGW is oriented toward Germany's plantation mix of 64% white and 36% red, and Rheinhessen's split of 69% to 31%, because the members grow 61% white and 39% red vines.

Grape varietals in Rheinhessen

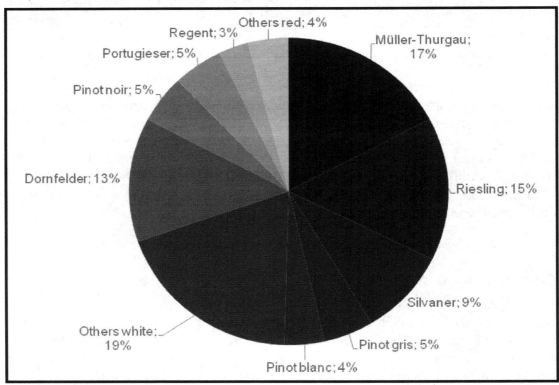

Müller-Thurgau and Dornfelder are Rheinhessen's as well as WGW's common grape varieties, followed by Riesling and Silvaner for white and Spätburgunder and Portugieser for red wines. Furthermore, the cooperative matures rare grapes such as Faberrebe or Blauer Lemberger. The average price range for the bottled products is about 3 euros for white and 3.50 euros for the red wines.

Grape varietals at WGW

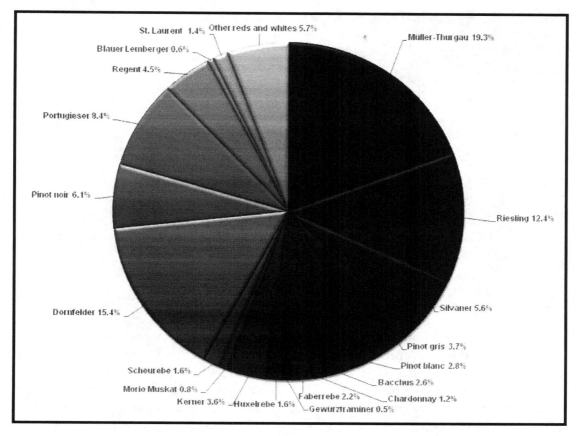

The assortment is divided in two main product lines: Wonnegau wines and Premium—"Aureus"—wines. The price list of the Wonnegau wines entails 70 wine products, 20 types of sparkling wines, seven liqueurs and spirits, and three grape juices. Ten white wines are offered in liter bottles with a price range of 2.90 euros to 4.15 euros, and 25 white wines are offered in 0.75 liter bottles going up to 4.60 euros (14 quality, 2 Kabinett, and 9 Spätlese wines). Fans of rosé wines can choose among nine products, ranging from 3 euros to 4 euros. Six red wines in a liter bottle and ten red wine products filled in a 0.75 liter bottle constitute the red choices, beginning at 3.60 euros for a cuvee in a liter bottle and ending at 7.90 euros for a merlot. Thirteen noble sweet wines build the top of the quality pyramid in price from 5 euros up to almost 30 euros a bottle.

The wide product range is continued in multifaceted product designs—starting with transparent bottles, emblems, and screw caps, ending with dark bottle colors, birds on the label, and traditional cork. The portfolio evolved from customers' decisions on their preferred vineyards, grape varieties, and flavor, but also considered packaging on the basis of habitual preferences and customers' individual historic buying behavior.

Screen shot of the regular web page/wine shop of WGW

In contrast, the premium-line Aureus delivers a quite homogenous picture. Five white wines, three red wines, and two cuvees in an elegant décor constitute the offering. An antique gold coin is used on the label as eye-catcher to represent quality and significance. A rating program in the vineyard with additional payment for the vintners guarantees extraordinary grape quality. Handpicking, a gentle maturization, and permanent quality controls result in high end products.

Screen shot of the Aureus web page

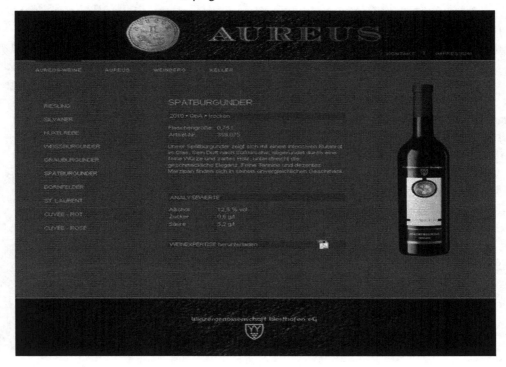

For the enthusiasts of premium wines Aureus has its own web page. In Germany, the product line is offered from 5.60 to 8.40 euros. Aureus wines are expected to build the basis for future export: internationally comprehensible, attractive figurehead, and a price level that allows satisfying margins and still ends up in a reasonable range of customer pricing.

Export Activities

WGW accesses foreign markets either directly or via the cooperative venture Weinallianz. In its direct export activities WGW covers Japan, Belgium, the Netherlands, and Poland. Poland serves as an example that some activities are a result of serendipity rather than of strategic programs. Based on a request from a Polish entrepreneur to actively sell WGW products on the Polish market, WGW delivers and states active sales for that destination.

China as well as other interesting markets are generally served by the Weinallianz and its sales staff. This approach secures a larger product portfolio and is therefore interesting for importers. An efficient logistic system enables sending products from all members of the alliance with shipping centralized out of the warehouse in Westhofen.

Currently, of the whole production capacity of WGW only a minor output is sold as bottled products to foreign countries. Benchmarks in the German cooperative landscape show a significant gap of export activities.

Overall Transformation and Rejuvenation—Providing Perspectives

The business transformation has resulted in significant business improvements. The managerial drive to consequently exploit all opportunities for efficiency and profitability increase by investing in technology and processes resulted in benchmark production costs. Furthermore, attractive payments to the members are possible because of low costs as well as a stabilized income situation. Given the difficult market environment, with other cooperatives merging or failing, a solid foundation for success in the future seems to be provided.

The changes in staff with a reduction of a third of the workforce led to the creation of a young and ambitious team of twelve employees. An entrepreneurial paradigm characterizes Dennis Balasus, his business approach, and his leadership for the team. One pillar of the team is Tobias Wagner, the production manager. He started in 2010 directly from university and was quickly given responsibility for the production process, despite that Tobias's background was not from grape but from cherry wine. Another example of entrepreneurship is that the team members are provided a playground for creativity and managerial autonomy but maintain a strong backing and support from Dennis when needed.

How to Compete Successfully on a Sustainable Basis in the Future

The next step of optimization is to more strongly exploit direct market sales and export opportunities. Dennis Balasus is evaluating strategic steps to make use of market opportunities abroad. He wants to commit personally to this goal because of his experiences in exports. The premium quality product line Aureus is regarded as attractive for foreign destinations. In addition to the marketing activities with the joint venture, first steps for new markets will be tried out on a stand-alone basis in Westhofen. In case of success, the Weinallianz will follow, which will then provide opportunities for all members.

Indeed, on the basis of insights garnered from international wine fairs and also from exchanging thoughts and ideas with other professionals in the wine business, Dennis Balasus identified two potential target markets for short-term market entry: Brazil and Mexico.

Brazil as a Possible Target

Brazil represents the largest economy in Latin America, with a population of more than 190 million inhabitants. Brazil's wine market accounts for about 3.7 billion USD and 350 million liters volume. The market is growing at a rate of 4% by value and slightly less in volume. Still wine accounts for about two-thirds of the market. Fortified wines and sparkling wines, including Champagne, make up a high proportion of the market. The distribution systems for wine are well developed. Most of the wine is sold via specialist retail (37%) and on trade (31%). Supermarkets sell only one-fifth of the wine. (MarketLine, 2012a)

Brazil has a significant wine production of its own that is under international competitive pressure. For this reason, the country's government is considering raising import tariffs. The bureaucratic hurdles to ship wine to Brazil are rather high. Nevertheless, German wines are already established in the market and there is a certain interest in light dry white wines, which Germany certainly can deliver nicely.

Mexico as a Possible Target

people. Mexico's wine market is about 600 million USD and 60 million liters. The market is growing at a double-digit level value and volumewise, with high potential for further growth. Still wine accounts for almost 90% of the market. Wine is mostly distributed via supermarkets (38%) at comparatively low prices. Specialist retail (25%) and on trade (25%) sell about one-half of the volume. (MarketLine, 2012b)

The Mexican consumer has a preference for full-bodied, tannic red wines. Still, wine is in tough competition with beer and liquors (i.e., tequila). The country attracts many international tourists, which could be an interesting way to market German premium wines.

Indeed, both markets with their projected volume growth seem to be interesting for WGW:

Wine markets of Brazil and Mexico (MarketLine, 2012 a/b)

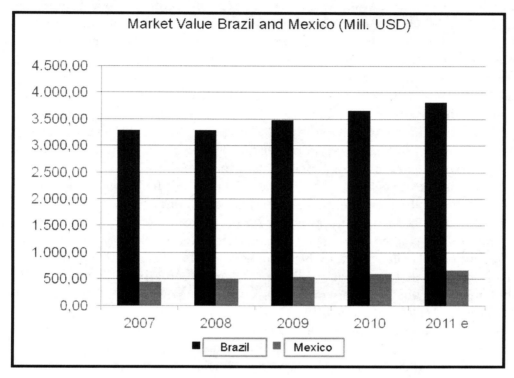

INCREASING DIRECT SALES

Direct sales to end consumers are highly attractive for wine producers. Direct customers pay higher prices and their negotiation power is limited; therefore almost no rebates or discounts are to be deducted from the price list. Aditionally, it is a cost-efficient sales channel. German consumers enjoy direct buying as part of their wine experience. About 15% of the wine in Germany is bought directly from the producers. Because of higher prices the value share is about 20%. Looking at German products, about 40% of volume and half of the value of the German wine is sold directly.

Although an attractive strategic option, increasing direct sales is not an easy road. Competitors also aim for direct access to the customers by building fancy new sales rooms, offering packages, creating attractive events, and increasing their CRM activities (Dressler, 2012). The success of Rheinhessen is also due to young and dynamic, well-educated winemakers creatively exploiting market opportunities, especially in direct sales. WGW's sales room and tasting facility were built in the 1980s. Westhofen is not a destination for wine tourism, and the building of the cooperative is not located conveniently. WGW offers open house days two times a year, attracting a remarkable number of clients. In order to increase penetration and to win new customers, leapfrog approaches and creativity are vital.

REFLECTION, STATE OF MIND, AND OUTLOOK

Indeed, walking through the facility at the end of the day, Dennis looks back with some pride on the achievements of the transformation in a competitive market. He knows that he has accomplished some major strategic switches and operational success. He is happy that this year´s harvest was processed without problems despite new technology implemented just days before the first grape delivery. The open day for the public and clients resulted in very positive feedback, underlining the impression that Dennis has made gains in interacting with his members, friends, and colleagues.

Overall, Dennis does not regret his decision to take this job opportunity although it turned out to be much more "sailing rough seas" than expected. His young and loyal team as well as the professionalized processes in the cooperative are a great foundation for next adventures. He feels that the cooperative is on the right track and the next transformation phase can be started. In his words, "The real work starts right now!" Financially solid with attractiveness for customers and members, WGW can approach new dimensions and perspectives in the business. Dennis also feels ready for personal involvement in the next adventure. He has a preference for one of the considered markets and will soon contact promising partners for his preferred option.

Two interrelated challenges—a solid strategic storyline for the growth ambitions and winning his board colleagues and the members—lie ahead of him. Therefore, three questions need to be answered: What are the challenges and a possible roadway for stakeholder management in the case of WGW—considering ownership issues, organizational design, and strategic analysis tools? Which market is best suited for the export ambitions—analyze consumer preferences, sales channels, access to the market, market risks, fit of WGW products or German wines, and strategy for implementation? What could the strategy to enhance direct sales look like—on the basis of competitor analysis, changing customer needs and behavior, investment restrictions, strategic positioning, and strategic evolution? Creative ideas need to be developed and challenged.

FINANCIAL STATEMENTS

AKTIVA	01.09.10 until 31.08.11	01.09.09 until 31.08.10	01.09.08 until 31.08.09	01.09.07 until 31.08.08	01.09.06 until 31.08.07
	Euro	Euro	Euro	Euro	Euro
A. Anlagevermögen	3,064,697.73	2,742,726.00	2,259,368.00	2,356,344.25	2,414,537.80
I. Immaterielle Vermögensgegenstände	8,993.00	11,512.00	2,453.00	3,485.00	7,285.00
II. Sachanlagen	3,030,504.73	2,706,014.00	2,231,715.00	2,327.659,25	2,382,052.80
III. Finanzanlagen	25,200.00	25,200.00	25,200.00	25,200.00	25,200.00
B. Umlaufvermögen	3,667,543.35	10,173,684.15	4,986,848.59	5,257,417.40	5,484,676.01
I. Vorräte	984,117.57	1,389,705.71	1,267,041.83	1,040,219.21	1,185,465.19
II. Forderungen und sonstige Vermögensgegenstände	1,116,504.95	1,056,227.63	947,340.81	1,133,942.61	687,144.33
III. Kassenbestand, Bundesbankguthaben, Guthaben bei Kreditinstituten und Schecks	1,566,920.83	7,727,750.81	2,772,465.95	3,083,255.58	3,612,066.49
C. Rechnungsabgrenzungsposten	0	0	1,331.97	7,886.31	0
Summe der Aktivseite	6,732,241.08	6,916,410.15	7,247,548.56	7,621,647.96	7,899,213.81

PASSIVA	01.09.10 until 31.08.11	01.09.09 until 31.08.10	01.09.08 until 31.08.09	01.09.07 until 31.08.08	01.09.06 until 31.08.07
	Euro	Euro	Euro	Euro	Euro
A. Eigenkapital	1,741,327.22	1,740,028.43	1,755,006.53	1,906,467.02	1,995,719.12
I. Geschäftsguthaben	927,915.38	929,021.98	945,413.74	918,047.94	907,497.42
II. Kapitalrücklage	2,736.54	2,736.54	2,736.54	2,736.54	2,736.54
III. Ergebnisrücklagen	809,472.60	807,563.09	1,085,485.16	1,085,485.16	1,019,396.63
IV. Bilanzgewinn/Bilanzverlust	1202.7	706.82	0	0	0
B. Sonderposten mit Rücklageanteil	209,776.55	0	1,345,560.71	0	0
C. Rückstellungen	816,886.68	976,715.86	4,146,981.32	1,499,664.30	1,388,130.90
D. Verbindlichkeiten	3,964,250.63	4,199,665.86	4,146,981.32	4,215,516.64	4,515,363.79
Summe der Passivseite	6,732,241.08	6,916,410.15	7,247,548.56	7,621,647.96	7,899,213.81

AUTHOR'S PERSPECTIVE

The case study provides material for students to analyze strategic options for a German wine producer in the light of competition, changing market environment, organizational boundaries, and a history of strategic evolution. Therefore, a basic strategic review with industry assessment and SWOT analysis could be the starting point using the case study in the course of strategic management courses. Furthermore, managerial challenges in the field of strategic marketing, international marketing and sales, organizational change, sales and distribution, and customer management can be explored on the basis of the case. Asking the students to sell their results to the other board members, the members of the cooperative, the region, or other stakeholders serves to illustrate a valuable stakeholder and appropriate management approach.

Indeed, the provided information on the realized transformation offers the potential to use the case to discuss organizational change, implementation of strategic programs, leadership, or managerial challenges in an organizational context such as cooperatives or joint venture management. Additionally, with the raised interest of WGW in expanding the export business as well as fostering direct sales, students can assess international marketing and sales activities as well as customer relationship measures. Hence, they explore marketing strategies, strategic positioning, and management of export strategies. Indeed, a task for students could be to create market-entry strategies by analyzing the two raised markets of interest—Brazil or Mexico—or other markets such as China or European markets. However, market exploitation strategies for direct sales can be analyzed, considering changes in consumer behavior, especially changes in channel usage and multichannel buying behavior, but also developing strategies on the basis of changing social interaction and new media and technology.

The strategic development of wine cooperatives in Germany is of great interest given their market importance and their specific organizational and strategic challenges. Cooperative management and the positioning of cooperatives in the competitive German wine market need to be considered. Indeed, the challenging wine market in Germany is characterized by massive structural changes, with suppliers and producers exiting the market and some question marks with regards to successful strategic positioning in general, and especially for the future of cooperatives in that market.

INDUSTRY ANALYSIS

An industry analysis of the German wine business should reveal the extensive structural changes on the demand and supply sides and the need to adapt and change to cope with the changing environment. Wine in Germany enjoys an overall stable demand, and given the reduced overall alcohol consumption, wine substitutes for other alcoholic beverages, such as beer. But despite an apparent volume equilibrium the market is in constant change: German consumers increasing their demand for international wines, a far-reaching switch to red wines, a different portfolio of varietals as of today, a multichannel as well as a diverse universe buying behavior, and reduced loyalty are just a few examples serving to illustrate the massive change. Competition is fierce, with suppliers exiting the market but still high fragmentation. Overall wine quality has increased, and offering very good quality has become a necessity, not a comprehensive solution for market success. The need for strategic positioning and offering additional value is vital.

Overall, customer-centric offers as well as innovative access to clients are pursued by a lot of players in the market, all trying to escape the market challenges of a strong market power of the indirect sales channels, low price levels, to deliver on offer attractiveness and convenience demanded by direct customers despite decreasing loyalty, to react to changing customer preferences and to better manage the inherent risks of a naturally influenced production. Cooperative organizations are especially squeezed in their market positioning, serving attractive products and exploiting new market segments to secure future sales. The aim to conquer new markets abroad or to win new direct customers and penetrate existing ones due to higher prices and lower channel costs is therefore not a unique solution but rather common sense. A strategic roadmap with realistic operationalization and a solid financial background is needed.

SWOT ANALYSIS

A SWOT analysis will certainly discover that Dennis Balasus has created a very lean organization with massively reduced risks. But the changes and especially the staff reduction might raise the notion that the resulting centricity of the organization around the CEO constitutes a bottleneck when pursuing new entrepreneurial ventures. Are there enough resources with adequate experience to successfully conquer new and far markets or steer the organization toward new strategic positioning?

Possible results of a SWOT analysis

Strengths	Weaknesses
Solid quality of the wine	Location
Awards and recognition of wines in Germany	Investment needs to create attractive sales facilties
Partnerships	Image of a cooperative
Broad sales approach	Broad sales approach
Lean organization	Portfolio of grape varieties
Low headcount	Resources for risky export ventures
IFS 5 certification	Experienced resources besides CEO
Size with 340 ha	Down to earth image/appearance
Experience in export (Weinallianz)	
Entrepreneurial flexibility	

With regard to accessing new markets with premium products and also fostering direct sales, a SWOT analysis might reveal the need to change the image and also to define creative access to consumers. Neither are the current sales facilities modern, nor is Westhofen located conveniently or in an attractive site for tourists. Reaching and accessing new clients therefore might need very creative approaches on the basis of new media and technology. All activities require adequate marketing and investments in marketing activities, channel access, fancy facilities, or convenience offers. Creating a creative business model for WGW to reach new clients is therefore a challenging but rewarding exercise for the students.

STRATEGIC POSITIONING

The discussion could start on the basis of generic strategies—cost leadership, differentiation, and niche strategies—by providing representative examples of the wine industry as well as inherent challenges for the German wine market for each strategic positioning. The previous years with lower yields for German producers show that operating in mass market segments is challenging because distribution agreements with indirect sales gained in tough competition need to be fulfilled even in years with lower production. Buying needed stock on the spot might destroy already small margins and therefore jeopardize profitability. It also risks the quality of the production. Playing in the premium segments needs adequate investments into products, offers, and marketing. This strategic route is quite challenging for cooperatives because their image is generally more tied to mass rather than premium markets.

Indeed, Dennis Balasus has created a lean organization embedded in multiple partnerships to increase all possible cost-reduction opportunities of economies of scale in and within organizations and to cushion the organization from market risks. Hence, cost leadership has determined strategic measures so far. The managerial changes resulted in a cost position that enables WGW to successfully market mainly in the mass market segment in Germany with a very attractive price-value relationship.

The next strategic ambitions might require a strategic shift toward more premium positioning. Students could be asked to explore the challenges of such a strategic shift, the suitability for WGW, and the attractiveness, taking into consideration a different business model needed to sustainably play in the premium segment. Considering market risks and investment needs and taking the perspective of the individual winegrowers as owners of the cooperative will provide a rich portfolio of arguments supporting but also rejecting risky strategic shifts, especially because a lot of other players in the market are already pursuing, or aiming to pursue, related measures in order to increase their price levels and to grow into other market segments and customers.

Organizational Perspective

Cooperative entities with their democratic decision making, multiple owners with individual ambitions and intentions, and a historically affected image should be discussed by assessing the advantages and also the disadvantages of such joint ventures. Strategic repositioning of cooperative entities might be more difficult because decision making in cooperatives is more complex than for independent vintners; individual versus collective perspectives need to be integrated; and strategic focus might not be possible for all cooperatives (e.g., size versus quality). Hence, the students can discuss not only strategic options but also the development of organizations and therefore the structural changes of the wine industry when repositioning in the market.

We propose to use the cooperative with its steering mechanisms as a possible setting for results delivery. The exercise could be framed asking students to present at the annual membership convention. In preparation for that meeting, not only the strategic analysis and the resulting business case are important, but also stakeholder management should be carefully planned: winning members, how to prepare, how to deal with opposing members, how to win the region, and so on.

EXPORT STRATEGY—ACCESSING INTERNATIONAL MARKETS

Furthermore, with a focus on export markets the case study delivers a very actual playground that producers currently try to exploit. The success of this strategy is surely not yet to be taken for granted: export market opportunities are often interpreted as an easy way out of the local competition for German wine producers, especially because of market growth rates in foreign countries and price levels in export markets, but the managerial challenges and costs to conquer the market are often underestimated.

Export strategies require an assessment of the targeted markets as well as a suitable and profitable market-entry strategy. Indeed, assessing target countries for wine export should include the following aspects:

- GDP and growth of the country
- Size and volume (population, alcohol consumption, wine substitution, society and alcohol, etc.)
- Wine production
- Wine imports
- Wine market segments (e.g., mass versus premium products)
- Price levels (wine, other alcoholic beverages)
- Consumer perspective: wine consumption, channels, clusters, and so on
- Channels
- Access and restrictions for exporting countries (systems, tariffs, taxes, customs, etc.)

Once the attractiveness of the foreign market with its peculiarities is worked out, an interesting exercise could be to assess the fit of German wine products in foreign markets. Students might be asked to conduct interviews to evaluate perceptions of German wine in the targeted countries, or might even integrate some wine tastings.

Possible evaluation result Mexico versus Brazil

Mexico	Brazil
➢ Massive growth potential for wine	➢ Dynamic market
➢ High tourism	➢ Big sport events
➢ Stable import requirements	➢ German companies sponsoring the sport events (creative approach for quick start)
➢ Predictability (e.g. NAFTA)	➢ More fairs
	➢ Apparently developed channel structures
	➢ More developed wine market

Brazil and Mexico seem attractive after looking at the growing populations, their economic profiles, and their developing wine markets. In the meantime Mexico seems more predictable and reliable, also supported by its integration into NAFTA. Brazil seems attractive because it hosts large international events—for example, the world soccer championship—at which wine might be placed nicely to get a foothold in the market.

BIBLIOGRAPHY

Dressler, M. (2012). Innovative Weinwelt: Der "aktive Kunde." Der Deutsche Weinbau, 6, 16–18.

DRV (2012). Weinwirtschaftsjahr—Auszüge. Retrieved from www.deutsche-winzergenossenschaften.de

DWI (2012). Deutscher Wein Statistik 2012/2013. Mainz.

Grosskopf, Werner, Münkner, Hans, H., & Ringle, Günther. (2009). Unsere Genossenschaften-Idee, Auftrag, Leistungen. Wiesbaden: Deutscher Genossenschaftsverlag.

MarketLine (2012a). Wines in Brazil. MarketLine industry profile.

MarketLine (2012b). Wines in Mexico. MarketLine industry profile.

Oberhofer, J. (2012). Faßweinbetriebe sind 2011/12 die Gewinner. Der Deutsche Weinbau, 20, 22–25.

Rückrich, K. (2012). Entwicklung der Stillweinimporte. Der Deutsche Weinbau, 22, 9.

CASE
5

Recovering from Bankruptcy:

TOWARDS A NEW MARKETING STRATEGY FOR MONT TAUCH COOPERATIVE

Hervé Remaud, KEDGE Business School, France
Philippe Dunoguier, Vidi Vini Vidum Consulting

SUMMARY

Being one of France's largest cooperatives did not prevent Mont Tauch Cooperative from being put into receivership in April 2013. With its 250 members, Mont Tauch produces about 10 million bottles of wine. The receiver, who was nominated to assist the board of the cooperative, knows that many decisions of directors urgently need to be made to find new (export) markets for the wines produced by the cooperative. In the meantime, a new marketing strategy has to be proposed to ensure sustainable development for the company.

INTRODUCTION

On the 2nd of April, 2013, the Mont Tauch Cooperative was put into receivership. This very unusual decision was made by the board of directors of the cooperative and accepted by the Court of Narbonne. After five years of financial difficulties, the cooperative had an agreement in 2011 to postpone the reimbursement of its debts in exchange of austerity measures. This was not enough, and so the decision was made to go under administration. This gives the cooperative from six to eighteen months to find solutions.

By extension to the cooperative difficulties, 20% of these growers are facing tremendous economic difficulties: their revenues have been reduced to one-third while in the meantime they have to pay back loans contracted in their respective wineries. The cooperative buys grapes both from its shareholders, the growers (mainly located in the AOC Fitou zone), and also buys wine outside their areas of production. Not only has the cooperative had difficulties selling wines produced by its shareholders; the company has also been losing a lot of money on wines bought outside their areas of production and sold below cost.

In 2005, the company invested around 20 million euros of its own resources (without any bank loan) on new vats and cellars which were obviously too large for the cooperative's own production. In order to maximize the production capacity and cover the fixed costs, the cooperative bought a huge volume of wines from outside the local area of production and pushed the salespeople to take market share with very aggressive prices (selling sometimes below cost).

By contagion, wines produced from the local growers were also sold below cost. As in the meantime some foreign markets went down, Mont Tauch cooperative plunged into the red year after year, to end up in 2011 with 7 million euros in losses. It has been established that most of the losses came from the export markets, where the cooperative sells its wines at below cost.

The receiver, who was nominated to assist the board of directors, knows that many decisions need to be made, and you have been recruited to assist that person in his duty to return to profitability next year.

HISTORY OF THE FITOU AOC

Wine produced under the *Fitou Appellation d'Origine Contrôlée* (noted AOC) can only be produced with grapes from the following communal areas: Fitou, Caves, Treilles, Leucate, La Lalme (with these five zones located beside the sea, between Narbonne and Perpignan), and Cascastel, Paziols, Tuchan, Villeneuve (all located in the *Corbières* countryside). See map in Appendix 1.

Documents going back as far as Philip Augustus, Louis XIII and Louis XIV bear witness to the long-standing reputation of Fitou wines. Rabelais particularly appreciated the "vin de Palme" which now is sold under the Fitou AOC name.

The vineyards are set out on chalky and argil calcareous soils with exceptional exposure to the sun. The countryside, whose relief consists of hills, slopes and plateaus, has the advantage of a particularly dry climate that is often swept by a high wind, named the "Cers."

The Carignan grape is at its very best in this countryside: here it ripens to perfection to give strong, full-bodied wines with real substance and a rich, deep color. The Grenache grape is the ideal complement to the Carignan, bringing its fine, smooth, mellow qualities. A small percentage of Syrah and Mourvèdre also bring its richness in flavor and a delicious aftertaste worthy of the greatest of wines. From the marriage of these varieties of vines is born the harmony which characterizes the Fitou wines.

From these grape varieties, the wines produced by the cooperative include young, full-bodied wines with the fragrance of flowers and fruit, rich in noble tannins. Then, beyond two years of age, we encounter wines with a real structure, having a dark, deep color and a nose with a hint of violet, liquorice, thyme, rosemary and the flowers of the Provencal moorland. These wines are always elegant and deliciously mellow. In most cases, the wines are only made available for consumption after a period of twelve to eighteen months of maturation. A singular characteristic of an *AOC Fitou* is its capacity to mature and improve with age. Thus, extremely good bottles of *Fitou* are four or five years old and sometimes much older still.

"Omnia fecit deus, Fitou homines": without a doubt, one of the symbols of the majesty and munificence of Fitou wines is the *Mesnie des Chevaliers*, created in 1987, which celebrates both the Bacchus land of Fitounia and its finest wines, having contributed to their renown ever since its creation. Thus, constituting a hundred or so chapters, under the direction of its Grand Master, over 600 celebrities have been initiated into the brotherhood. Every year, in its name, a jury of connoisseurs awards a coat of arms to Fitou wines of the highest quality. The coat of arms, appropriately, depicts the four villages of High Fitou (red) and the five villages of Coastal Fitou (blue), Aguilar castle and a cluster of Carignan grapes. Its motto: "Omnia fecit Deus, Fitou homines," "God made all, men made Fitou," full of southern humor, is a nod in the direction of the "divine origins" of the Fitou A.O.C, the first red wine of Languedoc.

Mont Tauch Winery and Wines
Vineyard

Set in the Languedoc's dramatic landscape of picturesque hills and Cathar castles, Mont Tauch is one of France's largest cooperatives, based in the heart of the Fitou appellation in southern France. With its 250 members, Mont Tauch produces just over three-quarters of a million cases (10 million bottles) of Fitou, Corbières, Vin de pays du Torgan, Vin de Pays de la Vallée du Paradis, Vin de pays d'Oc, Muscat de Rivesaltes and Rivesaltes.

Mont Tauch covers 1,913 hectares made up of 3,800 small vineyards dotted around the villages of Tuchan, Paziols, Villeneuve and Durban. Each village is recognized for its specific terroirs and for the character of its wines. Mont Tauch is surrounded by wild *garrigue* (or bush) - the Mediterranean terrain rich with the scent of thyme, rosemary, lavender and juniper.

Mont Tauch's wines are a genuine expression of these terroirs, which have been shared for centuries by the vignerons and the many wild boars that roam the hills of Fitou, gorging themselves on the grapes and gnawing at the vine shoots. Indeed, the wild boar is used as the Mont Tauch logo. It is not surprising that boar hunting, along with rugby, is one of the region's most passionately pursued sports; and nothing washes down a wild boar casserole or saucisson better than a satisfying glass of Mont Tauch Fitou.

Mont Tauch's vineyards are owned by its members (the growers), giving the co-operative full control of vineyard management. Mont Tauch vines are planted in some of the most diverse soils of the entire vineyard land in France. To help to classify these terroirs, Mont Tauch has identified over twenty specific types of soil, of which there are six major ones: Schistes, Calco schistes, Poudingues, Red Mediterranean soils, Colluvions, Calcaires and Marnes du Trias. Thanks to the soil classification, Mont Tauch has carried out separate vinifications from specific vineyards. Such concern for detail is exceptional for a cooperative the size of Mont Tauch.

Conscious of a long tradition of wine production, Mont Tauch has retained the best Carignan and Grenache vines, which grow on the surrounding steep slopes or coteaux. The average age of these vines is fifty years old. They are naturally low-yielding, and this factor, along with the region s low rainfall and poor soils, contributes to the quality of the wines. There is also a smaller proportion of the old "cépages nobles"

Grenache Blanc, Gris, Maccabeu and Muscat (petit grain and d Alexandrie), as well as some Cinsault.

The vineyard structure has been gradually reorganized, and individual growers are encouraged to restructure their plantations by regrouping plots through exchanges and replanting vines with more adapted grape varieties. This has led to increased plantings of Syrah, first set here in 1982 to bring added finesse to Fitou, and now accounting for 20% of Mont Tauch's vineyards. Merlot and the newest grape variety, Marselan (a cross between Cabernet Sauvignon and Grenache), have been introduced in richer soils to enhance the Vins de Pays portfolio.

History of cooperation in the South of France

The first cooperatives were created by grouping together a multitude of small independent producers. This was an attempt to survive in an unstable market, which culminated in the wine sales crisis of 1907. The *Cave Cooperative de Mont Tauch* was established in 1913 in the village of Tuchan and is one of the oldest cooperatives in the Languedoc. In 1936, along with eight other villages of the Corbières, Tuchan was awarded the appellation Cotes d Agly for its Vins Doux Naturels, which became Rivesaltes in 1943. This recognized the quality of its wine.

In 1948, Fitou became the first red wine to achieve AOC status in the Languedoc. Corbières has also been recognized here since 1951 (Corbières Supérieures VDQS) before it became an AOC in 1985. Although the blend of Carignan, Grenache and Syrah is essentially the same for Corbières and Fitou, Fitou are selected vineyard sites within the larger Corbières Appellation.

In 1993, the Mont Tauch cooperative merged with the neighboring coop in Paziols, thus doubling the Cooperative's production capacity. On the 1st of July, 1999, the Villeneuve and Durban cooperatives also merged to form the new Mont Tauch entity.

The winery

Over the last decade, Mont Tauch has invested over 22 million Euros in renovating vineyards and winery facilities. The new facilities include a gleaming, modern, state of the art vinification plant called *Chais Egrappé* with near 150 stainless steel vats with capacities of 50hl to 500hl. Finished in 2001, the Chais Terroir has 52 stainless steel vats of 100hl to 230hl capacity, which allow the flexibility to make wine in small batches from individual and fragmented terroirs.

Furthermore, the old cave has been renovated and specially equipped as a carbonic maceration center with 40 concrete vats of 400hl each. The winery has a total vat capacity of 180,000hl, representing double the Cooperative's annual production.

The varied-sized vats enable Mont Tauch to store small amounts of selected grapes in their own vats, allowing greater control and increased scope for blending. Individual growers have the chance to taste their own wines for the first time and thus the vignerons become wine producers rather than just grape growers.

Various styles of wine are produced, embodying both the charm of the region with its eclectic mix of soils, microclimates and herbs, and the determination of individual coop members to demonstrate the maximum character from their own terroir.

Mont Tauch has its own bottling line along with a stock of over 2,000 barrels, and the Mont Tauch bottling plant has recently acquired a screw cap machine.

A three million bottle storage and oak aging cellar, and a new wine shop and visitor center at the winery have been built. To manage the entire entity, Mont Tauch Cooperative has recruited sixty people.

The growers

Mont Tauch Cooperative has always considered the involvement of its members to be of vital importance in the management of the company and one of the key factors in the quality and character of its wines. Mont Tauch Coop thrives on each grower's desire to do well. Focusing on quality means that income is dependent on the value given to each grower's efforts, whereas historically, coop members were paid on volume and potential alcohol.

In 1998, a vineyard selection scheme was set up to encourage the growers to produce a better quality of grape (and wine). Under this scheme, each grower registers his best vineyards according to soil type, yield and general viticultural practice according to detailed guidelines.

A tasting panel then determines the reward the grower will get: from 25% to 100% extra payment for the best wines. The selection scheme has different levels of contracts from simple «selection» to top «selection grand vin,» and therefore payment varies depending on the type of contract. This gives the growers responsibility for the wine's quality from start to finish.

Sustainable agriculture and cooperative management

In 2000, Mont Tauch Coop initiated *Lutte Raisonnée*, a form of sustainable agriculture. Today, about 80% of its growers adhere to the scheme. *Lutte Raisonnée* scheme guarantees effective traceability and restricts use of chemical treatments. For example, one time-sensitive method growers now use to prevent insect damage is targeted treatment during the mating season, causing sexual confusion (amongst the insects) and making them unable to reproduce.

The innovative nature of this sustainable development involvement of the growers is due to the integration of environmental and social problems in the management of the company. Supported by the Cooperative Wine Institute, this approach minimizes ecological impacts and brings quality of life to those involved (winegrowers and employees) in order to bring eco-citizen products to the market. Human welfare is at the forefront of the cooperative's concerns. Through the way it is managed, it aims to unite through a shared and sustainable project. The cooperative cellar relies on its land and brings it to life. The cooperative is therefore fully signed up to the values of fair trade.

The Winegrowers for Sustainable Development scheme includes 37 specific objectives (see appendix 2).

Brands portfolio

The range of Mont Tauch wines is quite large. It covers all consumers' segments, from "basic" cheap wines to rather expensive icon wines.

Brand range

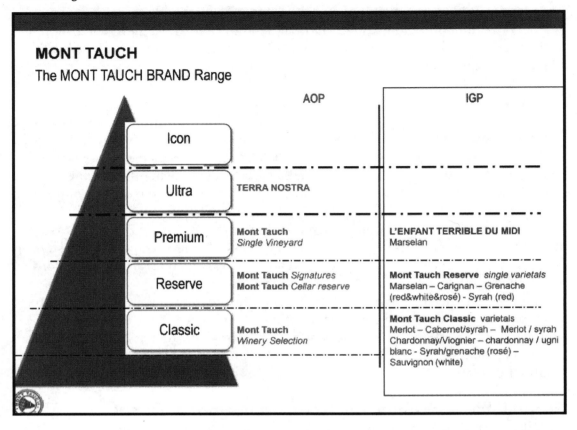

More details about Mont Tauch range of wines and brands can be found on the cooperative website: http://www.mont-tauch.com/.

Sales

Volumes of wine bought / produced vs. sales

(unit = hl)	2007	2008	2009	2010
Wine produced (from the growers' grapes)	59000	72000	55000	55000
Wine produced sales	28000	30000	41000	32000
Wine bought (outside of the local area)	59000	55000	67000	70000
Wine bought sales	58000	54000	70500	68000

Average sales prices vs. average cost prices (wine bought not included)

(unit = €)	2007	2008	2009	2010
Average production cost price	1,75	1,75	1,55	1,6
Average sale price	1,85	1,75	1,75	1,4
Profit vs. loss per unit sold	*0,1*	*0*	*0,2*	*-0,2*

Sales by country in 2010 and 2011

(unit = %)	2010	2011
France (off trade)	41	43
France (on trade)	5	5
UK	22	12
Germany	11	13
Belgium	7	9
Netherlands	4	6
Scandinavia	2	2
Other countries	8	10

Export markets facts

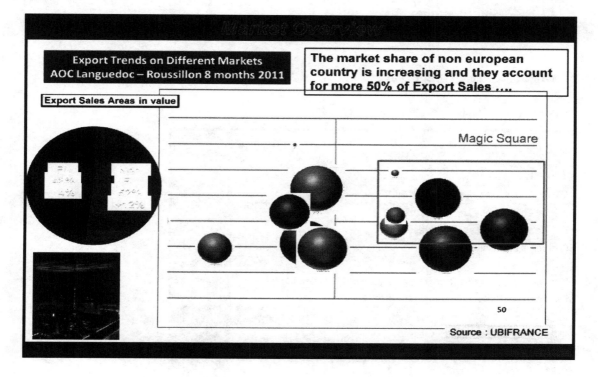

EXPORT (K€)	2007	2008	2009	2010	Rank	Market Share
Germany	19 505	19 757	20 239	18 837	1	15%
Canada	15 488	15 920	14 341	15 926	2	13%
Belgium	17 184	17 300	16 588	14 664	3	12%
UK	24 164	18 809	16 177	13 403	4	11%
Holland	13 050	14 255	13 490	11 707	5	9%
Switzerland	8 785	10 480	10 993	10 601	6	8%
China		2 467	6 487	10 377	7	8%
USA	8 736	7 718	7 857	9 516	8	8%
Japan	6 127	6 818	4 492	5 042	9	4%
Denmark	4 984	3 557	2 946	2 067	10	2%
Sweden	1 934	1 112	1 134	745	11	1%
Others	12 218	8 926	9 057	12 150	12	10%
TOTAL	132 175	127 119	124 783	125 035		100%

Professional price chart

Some Prices Ex Cellars to Professionals

Products	Export
WHITE	**€/excellar**
IGP Oc Chardonnay Mont Tauch Classic	1,90
IGP Oc Chardonnay Le Village du Sud	2,25
IGP Oc Chardonnay Les Garrigues	2,05
IGP Oc Sauvignon Les Garrigues	2,20
Corbières Blanc Ancien Comté	2,15
ROSE	
IGP Torgan ou Paradis Grenache Gris Les Garrigues Grande Réserve	2,35
IGP Torgan Grenache Gris Farmer Bernard	2,50
RED	
IGP Oc Merlot Mont Tauch Classic	1,85
IGP Oc Cabernet Sauvignon Les Garrigues	1,85
IGP Oc Merlot Les Garrigues	2,05
IGP Torgan ou Paradis Grenache Noir Les Garrigues Grande Réserve	2,35
Corbières rouge Château La Condamine	1,60
Fitou Domaine St Roch	2,05
Fitou Mont Tauch Cellar Reserve	2,60
Fitou Mont Tauch *Single Vineyard* MONTLUZIS	3,25
Fitou Château de Ségure (Caisse Bois)	4,30
Fitou Château de Ségure Olivier de Termes 75 cl	6,00
VINS DOUX NATURELS	
Muscat de Rivesaltes Cuvée prestige 75 cl	3,00
Rivesaltes Villa Passant	3,35
Muscat de Rivesaltes Amphora Ruscinosis	4,30

Financial facts

Simplified Income Statement 2005–2010

(K€)	2005	2006	2007	2008	2009	2010
Total Income (K€)	24119	23082	26271	25381	26247	20951
Total consumption of goods and raw materials	11964	13568	17004	16609	17279	13850
Gross Margin	12155	9514	9274	8772	8968	7101
Operating Costs	8716	10249	11556	12854	12476	13996
Subventions					-1658	
Operating Result	3440	-735	-2282	-4082	-1850	-6895
Financial Result	355	395	101	-561	-172	-406
Exceptional Result	-1709	326	-892	-60	14	-272
Pre tax Result	2070	-14	-3073	-4703	-2008	-7573

Urgent decisions to be made...

As mentioned at the beginning of the story, the nominated receiver and the cooperative board know that many decisions need to be made urgently, and you have been recruited to assist him in his duty to return to profitability next year. First he asks you to:

1. Complete an internal and external environment analysis related to the Mont Tauch situation.
2. Summarize the situation to make it clear and easily comprehensible for him.
3. Present a plan detailing:
   - The two most important (export) markets on which the company should focus on (including sales targets);
   - The brands portfolio that would fit best with these two selected markets;
   - In each of these two selected markets, channel(s) of distribution that should be selected;
   - The pricing strategy in relation to these markets.

APPENDIX 1: MAP OF THE MONT TAUCH AREA

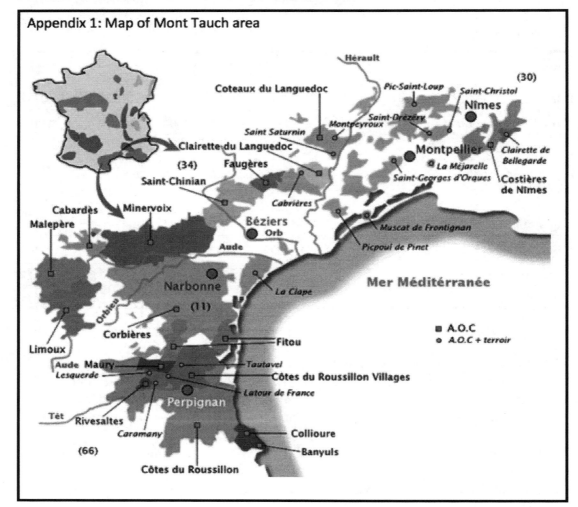

Appendix 1: Map of Mont Tauch area

APPENDIX 2: THE WINEGROWERS FOR SUSTAINABLE DEVELOPMENT SCHEME

Winegrowers for Sustainable Development guarantees that economic development will go hand in hand with respect for the environment as well as respect for social and community impacts. From planting the vine to serving the wine at your table, we guarantee the quality of our product while ensuring respect for our employees, partners and other stakeholders as well as the environment.

> "Sustainable development is part of the innovative strategy of our companies, by transforming constraints and restrictions into development opportunities."

The following 37 objectives have been defined in order to meet the requirements of this approach

Governance and managerial practices

1. **Management commitment:** The commitment of the management covers the three pillars of Sustainable Development (economy, social and environment) from planting the vines to selling the products.

2. **Strategy, policy and objectives:** The strategy, policy and objectives draw on the three pillars of Sustainable Development.

3. **Management System:** The performance of the company is measured through a management system including the social and environmental dimensions.

4. **Organization and responsibilities:** The role and responsibilities of each employee in terms of Sustainable Development are defined.

5. **Staff participation, involvement and motivation:** Staffs are consulted; employee motivation is an important issue for managers.

6. **Internal communication:** Our internal communication is transversal, organized and regular.

7. **External communication:** The company initiates communication with interested parties; the Sustainable Development report is issued each year.

8. **Monitoring of regulation:** Monitoring of regulation is organized.

9. **Consideration of universal principles:** The main principles are applied as initiatives (use of environmentally friendly products, strict compliance with the guidelines issued by the International Labor Organization, etc.).

10. **Consideration of interested parties:** Interested parties are identified; their expectations are prioritized and translated into challenges for the company.

11. **Eco-design:** Environmental parameters are included in the design of company processes and/or products.

12. **Purchasing Policy:** Wine, products and services are mainly acquired from suppliers that are part of the Sustainable Development movement and that have terms and conditions that include Sustainable Development requirements. We listen to suppliers and take their interests into consideration.

13. **Wine producing Policy:** The Sustainable Development requirements are applied to the wine-growing operations that represent at least 50% of the harvest

14. **Risks linked to wine producing:** A risk prevention plan (awareness, evacuation exercises, etc.) is put in place, the site is made secure.

15. **Storage:** Best practices for storage are applied: first in, first out, good storage conditions, removal of dead stock.

16. **Employee transport:** Employees are encouraged to use methods of transport other than driving alone (walking, cycling, car-sharing, etc.).

Economic performance

17. **Client relationships:** The clientele is expanded; ways of handling customer relationships are drawn up and applied.

18. **Productivity:** Improvement in productivity is done in conjunction with an improvement in working conditions.

19. **Investment:** The company has a balanced debt-equity ratio.

20. **Profitability and sharing of the added value:** When the company makes a profit, this profit is shared with employees.

21. **Performance measurement:** The performance indicators distributed within the company include economic, environmental, and social data.

Social responsibility

22. **General working conditions:** Employees are involved in the improvement of working conditions (work stations, meeting places, staff events, etc).

23. **Equality:** The principles on non-discriminatory employment, inclusion of disabled individuals and transparency of our remuneration terms and conditions shall be met.

24. **Jobs, skills, training:** An annual training plan is drawn up; an annual interview shall determine employee needs; and HR indicators (level of training, skill level, etc) are included in the company performance indicators.

25. **Hygiene, health and safety:** Training on hygiene, health and safety rules is given to all employees. A management system on health and safety at work is in place.

26. **In the Community:** The company initiates and gets involved in collaborative action aimed at improving the quality of life with in the community and participating in the development of the community. Employees and producers are encouraged to take part in community life (festivals, culture, sports).

27. **Product responsibilities:** A management system is in place to anticipate and prevent risks related to product use (regular audits of the food health and safety system, IFS/BRC/ISO22000 certifications), effects of over-consumption of the product are displayed on the products, and communication complies with the regulation.

Environmental responsibility

28. **Water consumption management:** Water consumption is monitored; a system is in place to limit the consumption of water at the posts where consumption levels are highest.

29. **Water pollution:** Handling waste is carried out in compliance with regulation. We are constantly researching new and clean technology.

30. **Energy consumption:** Posts that consume the most energy shall be subject to plans aimed at reducing these consumption levels.

31. **Air pollution and greenhouse gases:** The carbon footprint is drawn up; a plan to reduce usage levels is drafted for posts with the highest usage levels.

32. **Waste:** Waste is processed and this procedure is included in the terms and conditions of all companies involved in waste processing.

33. **Soil management and pollution:** The quality of the soil at the company's site is identified, the effluents are channeled away and the soil is stabilized.

34. **Biodiversity in the community:** A local analysis and diagnostic is carried out.

35. **Impact on the Landscape:** Action aimed at preventing and improving the quality of the landscape is put in place; particular care is given to the area around the company and all industrial buildings.

36. **Noise and smell:** Measures to limit and handle noise and smell are in place to limit the impact on the neighborhood.

37. **Transport and logistics:** An action plan shall be drawn up for logistics and reducing traveling distances.

Mont Tauch Authors' Perspective

On one hand, this case study focuses on international marketing strategy and, on the other hand, on brand portfolio development.

In the French wine industry, many wine producers would claim that they can't be market-oriented: what they produce has to be sold! *Fitou* wines may be classified in that category to a great extent. In the meantime, many wine companies around the world have been able to develop a range of wines and brands that match far better consumers' expectations and preferences for wines.

The objective of the case and the objective for Mont Tauch is to find a market for its (produced) wines and for produced wines (the ones that are bought outside the area) that can be marketed. Therefore, the first key job that can be asked to the students doing this case is to assess the internal and external environment as two dependent aspects. In other words, what market has the greatest chances to absorb wines produced by the shareholders of the cooperative (the growers), and what wines can be produced (wines that are sourced outside the area) to serve and deliver value to consumers in the export markets?

As a given, the cooperative has too much capacity and therefore should find a way to use it. Finding the wines to be made to deliver value in specific markets is critical, but other ways to use the production facility can also be investigated in order to use the production facility as much as they can. Students are invited to think of other ways for the cooperative to use its facility: renting the facility for producers or other wineries wanting to develop their own brands; creating small "cuvees" with higher margin, etc.

Another critical aspect of any winery activity is selling the wines that have been made. On the export markets, it has been decided in 2011 that all wines will be distributed by Grand Chai de France. If there is no intention for the cooperative to stop this agreement, there is a need for the cooperative to know where their wines can be valued, for Grand Chai de France to distribute them. In other words, Mont Tauch cooperative can't just assume that Grand Chai de France will sell all wines that are produced. This is where the students can add value by reviewing a few markets and focusing on a couple with realistic recommendations.

Assessing the internal and external environment

As mentioned above, the internal environment assessment should be conducted with a distinction between local appellation brand (mainly related to Fitou and Corbieres AOP that are produced by the cooperative) and brands produced with wines sourced outside the region. The key issue for the local appellation brand is to review the worldwide market keeping in mind the key characteristics of Fitou and Corbières wines, and to find out the most promising markets to focus on/target. On the other hand for the wines and brands produced with wines sourced outside the region, the key issue is to produce wine that can match wine consumption markets with the highest (potential) sales growth.

Any market report is useful here to use in order to review the consumption markets' characteristics. Students are invited to get their school databases, and any other websites that provide market insights. A nice and easy tool to be used is the one that is developed by Hollensen (2008), where the market selection process is conducted using two concepts or proxy variables:

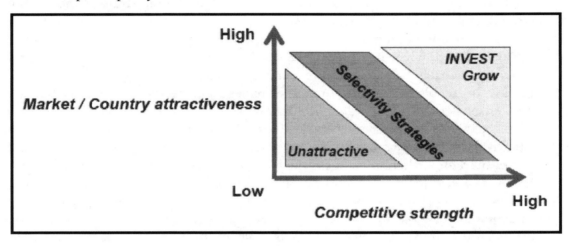

On the market / country attractiveness axis, the idea is to compare several markets or countries using specific variables, usually split into two categories: the macro-environment (country risk, tariff barriers, import duties, infrastructure, currency change risk), the industry environment (competitive intensity, average price of imported wine, wine consumption per capita, size of the wine market, ease of wine distribution).

Example:

UK	Very Poor (1)	Poor (2)	Medium (3)	Good (4)	Very Good (5)	Weight factor	Result (rank*Weight)
wine consumption per capita				4		20	80
size of the wine market					5	25	125
etc							...
Total							

Belgium	Very Poor (1)	Poor (2)	Medium (3)	Good (4)	Very Good (5)	Weight factor	Result (rank*Weight)
wine consumption per capita				4		20	80
size of the wine market			3			25	75
etc							...
Total							

On the competitive strength axis, the idea is also to compare several markets or countries using the strongest competitors as a point of comparison, from a price point perspective. Other characteristics that could differentiate Mont Tauch wines against its main competitors are used, for example: product fit to market demand, quality, aroma, etc.

By adding the points for each of these two axes, one can spot on the figure what market(s) seem to be more attractive to focus on first for Mont Tauch cooperative. Again, we encourage students to distinguish the two wine categories that are produced by Mont Tauch: the one produced by the growers' grapes and the wines bought outside the local area.

Once a market or a few markets have been selected, a typical international marketing plan can be developed, with the following aspects to be covered:

- Marketing objectives per market (mainly volume to be sold in these markets).
- Brands positioning in each of these markets.

  In the French market and in most of the export markets where the range of wines is broad enough, it can be suggested to the students to consider the creation of an umbrella brand, such as "Mont Tauch Wine Growers" for the wines produced with grapes harvested in the area, and "Mont Tauch Wine Makers" for the wines produced with grapes harvested outside of the area.

  The idea here is to facilitate wine purchase by consumers with a brand big enough for them to remember. Students could look at "Castel Family" umbrella brand to think about an idea.

  The creation of such a brand should be done in line with a specified positioning for Mont Tauch wines: good value for money in each of their categories, including the entry level. Students are invited to work on the brand equity of "Mont Tauch Wines," focusing mainly on regular wine consumers, and reminding the consumers of the sense of place of the Fitou area.

- Product adaptation (labels, support services).

  In most of the export markets, there will be aspects of the label to adapt, as well as dedicated support services.

  It can be suggested to the students to consider tender made by major monopoly in the wine markets: Canada, Sweden, etc. Because Mont Tauch Wine Makers can select the grapes and the wines to be made, this would be an aspect for the students to consider to better value these wines.

- Distribution channels to select and use (including market entry strategy).

  In order to grow their market share, the key aspect for the students to have in mind is that Mont Tauch should maximize the penetration rate of its brands (See Sharp B., 2010). Therefore, multiple distribution channels should be found to reach the maximum number of wine buyers. In France and in the major markets, large retailers should be part of Mont Tauch marketing strategy. This is where an umbrella brand can be used with different wine labels to satisfy retailers' exclusivity.

  On the export markets, including the US, it can be suggested to the students to consider a national sales company which would facilitate trade in multiple states and minimize the risk for Mont Tauch.

  In early 2013, Mont Tauch signed an agreement with Les Grands Chais de France, a major French wine distributor. All export markets would be directly traded by that Group. Mont Tauch would continue to manage the overall production process and the French wine domestic market. It would be interesting to have the students to assess this option (as opposed to a deal with foreign distributors) on different aspects: management, marketing and trade and if it is salient for the long term future of the cooperative.

- Promotion and marketing support.

  It should be advised that Mont Tauch not break the price reference line with too many price promotions in retail outlets. A key aspect to consider is trade shows, such as ProWein in Germany, Vinisud and eventually Vinexpo in Bordeaux.

  In the countries where a distributor is used, materials should be created to facilitate the job of the partners.

- Pricing determination (including price escalation issue).

  Pricing is a difficult component of the mix to work on, due to the many intermediaries and cost, when exporting. In most countries, there will be costs associated excise duty and import taxes. In the US, the price of a bottle of wine will be multiplied by two with an importer, and again doubled with a distributor. This means that the wine will be almost three times more expensive.

A specific attention should be given to the following points:

- Mont Tauch cooperative and its growers are engaged in a sustainable development initiative. This initiative increases slightly the cost of production of a bottle of wine, but could also be valued by consumers in some markets. So students are invited to include this aspect as part of the environment analysis and as part of the international marketing plan (in the product characteristics as well as the promotional aspects of the wines).

- Because Mont Tauch has based its strategy in the past on large volume at low price, price increases should be considered with caution. In other words, the biggest current clients of Mont Tauch may not accept a price increase if there is no added-value to the wines offered. This can be overcome with a new branding strategy and/or sustainable initiative.

- In brief, the best way to increase price of Mont Tauch wines may be to develop a new brand in a (new) market where French wines are valued and well perceived. Opportunities exist in the US market, to play around the brand FITs TOO (Fitou) to make it fun and affordable for US consumers.

- Another aspect that the students could look at is the creation "micro cuvee," single vineyard wine, single block, with the name of the grower, so a story can be created around it.

Marketing Chilean Wine Domestically

COMPARING WINE SALES AT SUPERMARKETS AND SPECIALTY WINE SHOPS

Marcos Mora
Rodrigo Escobedo
Cristian Adasme
Universidad de Chile, Chile

SUMMARY

The Chilean wine consumer has evolved because of Chile's great expansion in wine production since the 1980s. This case considers three factors that consumers use to evaluate their wine purchasing experience at supermarkets and specialty stores: the level of wine quality differentiation, the availability of oenological advice, and the availability of parking at their respective facilities. Although the amount of wine purchased in Chile has lessened in recent years, consumers are now buying higher-quality wines.

SOME BASIC INFORMATION ABOUT THE CHILEAN WINE INDUSTRY

Since the mid-1980s, Chile has become one of the major wine-producing countries of the new world. It has achieved this status through a trading strategy based on the positioning of trademarks, highlighting productive vineyards that are focused on improving the expression of their varieties and mixtures, refining oenological practices, practicing a market orientation throughout the value chain, and incorporating various business practices, among other tactics. This accomplishment is remarkable because of its productive and commercial dynamism, which is expressed in the generation of wines designed for clients in increasingly distant new markets (Figure 1). This achievement has been possible because of the unique climate and soil conditions that are present in the wine valleys of Chile, the proper selection and location of vineyards, the existence of producers who create wine grape varietal expressions desired by the end customer, the level of investments wineries and vineyards have made over the years, and obviously, the work of specialist winemakers, most of whom have managed to create what the market demands. Finally, from the 1990s to the present, there has been a steady growth in export volume, and from 2006 onward exports have exceeded 7 million hectoliters, even in 2010, when there was a loss of about 1 million hectoliters due to the earthquake.

Figure 1. Evolution of Chilean wine exports by volume (hectoliters).Source: PROCHILE.

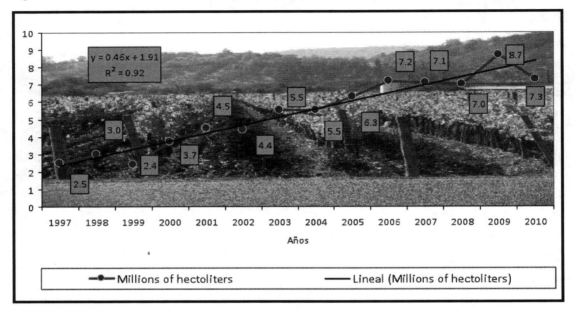

The value of the sector is reflected in Table 1, which shows that the amount of wine exports in 2011 reached a total value of US$1.702 billion, mostly from bottled wines (Vinos de Chile, 2012). It is also interesting to note the unit values of sparkling wines and wines with fruit pulp. As noted, the wine industry in Chile aims itself principally at the export market because it is the most profitable. Exports during 2011 were distributed 40.6% to Europe, 24.9% to North America, 21.2% to Asia, 10.2% stayed in South America, 2.3% to Central America, and 0.6% to Africa. By country, the largest volume markets are the United Kingdom, the United States, Holland, Brazil, Japan, Canada, and China (Fitch Rating, 2012).

PER CAPITA WINE CONSUMPTION IN THE CHILEAN DOMESTIC MARKET—A STRUCTURAL CHANGE TOWARD QUALITY

Wine consumption per capita in Chile has presented a relatively steady decline over time, similar to other countries with a viniferous tradition; although wine consumption generally decreases, the consumption of quality wines increases (Stasi et al., 2011). In the 1960s, the consumption of wine per capita stood at 68 liters per year and was primarily generated in the domestic market. Currently, per capita consumption is estimated at 13 liters and competes with beer, which has a per capita consumption of about 39 liters (SAG, 2012). For domestic consumption, the main vineyard producers are Concha y Toro, San Pedro Tarapacá, Cono Sur, Santa Rita, and Santa Carolina, which together account for 85% of the domestic market and represent 32% of the export market in 2011. The rest of the available supply of wines is generated by approximately 400 wineries,

Table 1. Structure of Chilean wine exports, amount, value, and unit value

Product	2011
	Volume in millions of liters
Bottled wine	396.6
Bulk wine	210.2
Must bulk	6.0
Other wine packaged	49.5
Sparkling wines	3.8
Wines with fruit pulp	1.7
Total wine exports	**667.7**
	Value in US$ million
Bottled wine	1,321.5
Bulk wine	245.2
Must bulk	14.6
Other wine packaged	98.7
Sparkling wines	14.7
Wines with fruit pulp	7.5
Total wine exports	**1,702.2**
	Unit value in US$/liter
Bottled wine	3.33
Bulk wine	1.17
Must bulk	2.43
Other wine packaged	1.99
Sparkling wines	3.86
Wines with fruit pulp	4.47
Total wine exports	**2.55**

Source: ODEPA (2013), SAG (2012), and INE (2011).

which are strongly concentrated in the Maule, O'Higgins, and Valparaiso regions, in that order. Also, many of these wineries sell their wines locally; however, others orient themselves mainly to the export market.

One of the marketing strategies that has developed most in recent times is a distribution channel that strongly emphasizes selling in large area supermarkets and increasing the number of different wines at convenience and exclusive shops, the latter having a wide range of international and Chilean wines. In Chile, the supermarket has increased its shareholding and positioned itself as the leading wine marketing space in terms of volume of sales. Moreover, since about 2000, supermarkets as retailers have attracted public recognition (Mora, 2012) as suppliers of a high level of differentiation, although in terms of market share they do not exceed 15%. Zeithaml (1988) defines quality as a "consumer´s opinion about the superiority or excellence of a service or product." This opinion is formed by three factors: (1) the intrinsic attributes of the product, for example, in the case of wine, the color, aroma, astringency, and so on;(2) extrinsic attributes such as brand, packaging and label design, advertising, and so on; and (3) the price, an extrinsic attribute that must be considered separately because of its special influence on the perceived quality. In particular, the distribution channel has been considered an explanatory variable in the quality that a customer perceives within the group of extrinsic attributes, and has been linked positively to the availability of different wines in retail establishments (Mora, 2010), the availability of parking, and the assistance of a seller during the purchasing process (Lockshin & Kahrimanis, 1998; Taylor &Barber, 2012).

In Chile, there is a strong concentration of commercial distribution. A few actors are responsible for a large percentage of total sales, such as supermarkets and hyper-markets, department stores, home and construction facilities, and pharmacy chains (Lucchini, 2010). In this regard, four companies account for 88% of retail market sales, which together sell about US$10 billion per year. Specifically, the largest market share is held by the D&S (now Walmart) chain (Líder Supermarkets), followed by Cencosud (Jumbo Supermarkets and Santa Isabel), SMU (Unimark Supermarket), and Supermerca-dos del Sur (Bigger) (Arias, 2011). Regarding the wine distribution channels, the majors are supermarkets (Líder and Jumbo), wine shops (The World of Wine and The Wine House), liquor stores, hotels, restaurants, and online stores. Here we review three cases: a high-differentiation supermarket, a generic supermarket, and a specialized wine shop. According to Stern et al. (1999), there are two major trends that cause specialized retail outlets to increase polarization. The first is the proliferation of retailers who carefully manage their product lines and are extremely specialized. They offer wide assortments responding to the personal needs of their customers and a high-quality retail experience (high touch, which in this case corresponds to the experience of purchasing in stores). The second trend is the proliferation of large stores, which has developed because of the powerful technology applied to the inventory and their ability to move huge amounts of product (high turnover) with very low margins. There are specialty retailers of high technology (hightech, which could be similar to supermarkets).

In Chile, wine shops first appeared in 1997, when the Wine Lovers Club (also known as the CAV) decided to open a store dedicated exclusively to selling wines. With time they added other products such as imported wines, distilled spirits, and wine ac-cessories. To date, the CAV has three stores located in the eastern sector of Santiago. In 1998, they opened a second store specializing in wines from Chile, called The World of Wine. This shop is characterized by a wide range of domestic and imported wines, and additionally, a large collection of imported and domestic distilled spirits. Currently it has five stores (three in Las Condes, one in Providence, and one in Talca). The third competitor in this area is Vinoteca. This company began operations in 1997 as a dis-tributor of wines to restaurants and supermarkets, and in 2003 decided to set up a wine shop promoting wines. To date it is housed in a single store in the Providencia district.

REPRESENTATIVE SALES OF CHILEAN WINE: THE WORLD OF WINE, JUMBO SUPERMARKET, AND LÍDER SUPERMARKET
The World of Wine: A specialized wine shop

The World of Wine is located in Las Condes, the eastern part of Santiago, which repre-sents the commercial hub, financial and tourist capital, and has a concentrated area of high-income people (Adimark, 2010). This population purchases and consumes wine frequently, especially premium wines on the weekends (Camussi, et al., 2006). The World of Wine has five branches: four in Santiago and one in the city of Talca. This distribution channel is known for its wide variety of foreign wines along with having trained sales personnel to guide the purchase, home delivery services, and the packaging of wines and wine tastings; exclusive accessories (cups, decanters, screws, books, gourmet products); and other liquors, though it does not have parking space. The wine is found on shelves, arranged by varieties, valleys, international wines, and promotions. This tactic supports the findings of Lockshin and Kahrimanis (1998), who argue that the key attributes that a wine consumer is looking for in a store are visibility of prices, ease of finding the wine, decor, the feeling of the purchase experience inside the store, and delivery and proximity factors to home or work. The buying public for this segment is a relatively cosmopolitan Brazilian, Asian, American, British, and Chilean shopper. The store offers 1,200 bottles of 23 wine grape varieties representing six countries (Argentina, France, Italy, New Zealand, Australia, and Chile). They eventually plan to offer Spanish and American wines. The minimum and maximum price range per variety is the most noted among the three analyzed distribution channels (see Table 2).

Table 2. Price of wines sold at The World of Wine (in Chilean pesos)

Average			Price minimum	Price maximum
$31,448			$5,280	$57,615

High differentiation: Jumbo Supermarket

Jumbo Supermarket of the Cencosud chain is considered a high-differentiation distribution channel, but Líder Supermarket of the D&S chain is considered a generic or low-differentiation distribution channel. Both supermarkets are located in Maipú, the western part of Santiago. According to 2012 census projections, Maipú is the most densely populated district in the country (734,494 inhabitants). It is one of the most representative areas in terms of socioeconomic status to Santiago because it has a similar socioeconomic distribution to the metropolitan region as a whole. Demographically, the district is largely inhabited by middle-class families and lower-middle-class people, leading to a great influx of people who like this store for its economic benefits (Reardon & Berdegué, 2002). At Jumbo Supermarket, there are approximately 800 different wines on 11 shelves, one of which is intended for a "tetra" format (cask wine), another with magnum bottles (1.5 liters), one with premium wine, and the other eight for red and white wine bottles (750 cc). Also, the wines are displayed by wine type (red or white), grape variety, reserve or varietal wines. The market offers a traditional wine setting, trained personnel to assist the buyer, and parking availability. The wines mainly come from Chile and Argentina. At the Jumbo Supermarkets that are located in higher-income areas, there is a greater supply of imported wines, including French and Italian. The wines are arranged in four shelves of white and red wines and are displayed by brand or vineyard. The minimum and maximum prices are shown in Table 3.

Table 3. Price of wines sold at Jumbo Supermarket (in Chilean pesos)

Average			Price minimum	Price maximum
12,384			$1,918	$22,850

Low differentiation: Líder Supermarket

Líder is a generic or low-differentiation supermarket located in Maipú, in the west of Santiago. It sells spirits, but there is a section exclusively for wine that has six shelves, one for tetra wines and 1.5 liter magnum bottles, one for white wines, and four for red wines of 750 cc (0.75 liter). The wines are arranged by brand or vineyard, with two levels of varietal wines and two levels of reserve wines. Inside personnel are not available to advise the sale but the property has parking spaces. Table 4 shows the prices from the five total shelves of red and white wines of 750 cc size.

Table 4. Price of wines sold at Líder Supermarket (in Chilean pesos)

Average			Price minimum	Price maximum
$5,333			$1,904	$8,762

Each of these venues offers a distinct strategy. The World of Wine has a marketing strategy that aims to provide more than 5,000 wines at a minimum price of 5,280 Chilean pesos (about US$12 dollars a bottle). It offers a great range of wines, as reflected in the number of varieties of wine grapes (23) and the six countries of wine origin. Jumbo Supermarket offers some variety of wines but with less differentiation than The World of Wine. It has high and low average prices of greater magnitude than Líder but less than The World of Wine. Likewise, Jumbo presents an intermediate number of wine grape varieties (18) and countries of wine origin (only two). Líder offers a positioning strategy that highlights convenience and low prices, with low product differentiation. These trading strategies generally are maintained throughout all stores in Chile, but there are nuances. The World of Wine analyzed is located in one of the highest-income communities in Chile, whereas Jumbo and Líder are located in middle-income communities. In this sense, the greatest difference between the maximum and minimum price is evident in The World of Wine. Jumbo and Líder Supermarkets also have retail locations in high-income areas. In this case the range of wines is more diversified in terms of products and prices.

Wine trade at the level of retail sales agents: objective, method

In order to deepen the described information, we have constructed a case study whose main objective is to characterize the consumers' attitudes and preferences concerning the three retail distribution agents of bottled wine according to their level of differentiation. To do this, we designed a questionnaire that was administered between October and December 2012 to a sample of 300 people who shop regularly or occasionally at these commercial agents. These surveys were conducted outside of supermarkets and wine shops by stopping women and men over 18 years of age who were considered habitual consumers of wine. According to Durán (2010) the supermarket owns 76% of the bottled wine market. Specialized wine stores comprise 10% of the market and therefore of the total surveys. Thus, we worked with a sample that was proportional to its representation in the market (Table 5).

Table 5. Sample characteristics of surveyed consumers

Businesses	Market share (%)	Number of questionnaires
Supermarket (Jumbo and Líder)	76	264
The World of Wine	10	36
Total	86	300

The survey was the main source of information for our case and included the following aspects:

- Descriptive characterization of wine consumption
- Preference for place of wine purchase: wine shop or supermarket
- Socio-demographic data

The statistical treatment of the data was performed by a univariate analysis (mean, mode, variance, and dispersion measures) and a multivariate analysis technique called conjoint analysis, which helps explain how respondents develop preferences for a product or service on the grounds that consumers evaluate a product, service, or idea according to the utility that is assigned to the product's attributes (Hair et al., 1999). The attributes to be considered in this analysis are the willingness to pay more at a particular business establishment (10% more, 0%, 10% less), distribution channel (The World of Wine, Jumbo or Líder), advice on purchase site (yes or no), and parking availability (yes or no).

Authors' Perspective

According to the characterization of the wine shelves at The World of Wine, Jumbo, and Líder, The World of Wine corresponds to a highly differentiated distribution channel in terms of wines. It has the largest range of minimum and maximum prices, along with having the largest amount of wine varieties and number of international wines; it also has trained personnel to guide the purchase, gourmet products and accessories, but it does not have parking space.

Jumbo Supermarket can be considered from the observed data as a high-end supermarket that has a level of intermediate differentiation of wines concerning price range, minimum and maximum number of wines, international wines, number of varieties, and shelves, exceeding the data for Líder. It must be emphasized that Jumbo has trained staff to guide the purchase, offers a wine-oriented atmosphere, and has parking space. Líder can be considered a generic or low-differentiation distribution channel because it offers no assistance from sales staff and no wine atmosphere, but it does have parking.

PURCHASED WINES FROM EACH CHANNEL

In order to examine the results, it is evident that as one moves from less-differentiated to more-differentiated brokers, there is a shift toward buying more expensive wines. The percentage of wines from $5,000 to $10,000 Chilean pesos increased from Líder Supermarket to The World of Wine (Table 6).

Table 6. Price levels in different actors involved in the marketing of wines in the Chilean market.

Broker	Price (Chilean pesos)	Frequency	Percentage
Líder	From $2,000	30	21.7
	$2,000 to $3,000	44	31.9
	$3,000 to $5,000	49	35.5
	$5,000 to $10,000	15	10.9
	Total	138	100
Jumbo	From $2,000	20	15.9
	$2,000 to $3.000	46	36.5
	$3,000 to $5,000	43	34.1
	$5,000 to $10,000	16	12.7
	More than $10,000	1	0.8
	Total	126	100
The World of Wine	$2,000 to $3,000	7	19.4
	$3,000 to $5,000	6	16.7
	$5,000 to $10,000	16	44.4
	More than $10,000	7	19.4
Total		36	100

CONSUMER PREFERENCES TOWARD THE ATTRIBUTES OF THE THREE WINE SELLERS

From the conjoint analysis performed, we can identify preferences for attributes of commercial agents. In this sense, the segment was directly shaped into three parts by gathering the survey data from consumers who were buying in certain commercial premises. The first group of people was called The World of Wine segment, which was characterized by a more positive assessment than the other commercial agents analyzed (.325). Data reflected some extended loyalty to this place, which was reinforced by the relatively minor WTP (willingness to pay) variable, that is, the price was a secondary end point in terms of relative importance. The most valued attribute to this segment was the advice at the time of purchase. However, parking availability had a neutral rating for Jumbo and a negative one for Líder. The Jumbo Supermarket segment received positive comments (.263), The World of Wine neutral comments (.022), and Líder Supermarket negative comments (−.285). Consumers appreciate the advice at the time of purchase and the availability of parking. Finally, consumers' willingness to pay at this location is at the minimum payout level (−10%) because it provides lower profits (−.150).The Líder Supermarket segment reflects a relatively neutral preference to Líder Supermarket and The World of Wine and a positive preference toward Jumbo (.156), which may be related to the aspirational aspect of Chilean society: Jumbo is a supermarket oriented to segments that have a higher willingness to pay. Parking, advice, and willingness to pay are at a minimum when buying at Líder Supermarket. However, the beta (linear relationship between preference and price) of lesser magnitude is presented by The World of Wine (.150). These results are relatively similar to those reported by Lockshin and Kahrimanis (1998) (Table 7).]

Table 7. Preferences for attributes of wine-marketing agents in Santiago de Chile

Variable and level		The World of Wine		Jumbo Supermarket		Líder Supermarket	
		IR	Utility	IR	Utility	IR	Utility
Broker	Jumbo	28.851	.075	27.793	.263	28.042	.156
	Líder		-.400		-.285		-.078
	TheWorld of Wine		.325		.022		-.078
Advice	Without	29.531	-.553	26.676	-.378	27.849	-.407
	With		.553		.378		.407
Parking	Without ESIONAMIENTO	23.741	-.406	22.868	-.239	23.992	-.345
	With ESTACIONAMIENTO		.406		.239		.345
DPA	Less than 10%	17.877	-.150	22.663	-.245	20.117	-.203
	0%		-.300		-.489		-.406
	More than 10%		-.450		-.734		-.609
Constant			3.141		3.308		3.203
DPA(beta)			-.150		-.245		-.203
	Value		Sig.	Value	Sig.	Value	Sig.
Pearson's R	.843		.002	.745	.011	.71	.007
Kendall's Tau	.722		.003	.444	.048	.535	.023

PROBLEM FOR STUDENTS
What distribution channel choice for a wine on the market?

At the consumer level, if you are looking for a special occasion wine, a wider range of wines is found in stores like World of Wine and Jumbo supermarkets. In contrast, low differentiation supermarkets, like Líder offers less diversity of wines. It is noteworthy that a supermarket's physical location affects the diversity of products offered. A supermarket like Líder, usually offers increased product range if it is located in a high-income area. Moreover, specialty shops generally have a expert advisors to guide the customer's purchase. Expert assistance in supermarkets is less frequent.

Besides the aggressive advertising campaigns and semi-annual promotions, large chain supermarkets like Jumbo-CENCOSUD and Líder-Walmart, have demonstrated escalating consumer consumption of more valuable wines. These activities offer communication rebates of up to 50%. Also, many wineries offer their own mega-promotion conducted every year in different locations to increase awareness of wine from Chile. This has contributed to the increase in consumption of higher quality wines. Specialty stores are also showing this same trend, but with a smaller market share. Specialty sales volume is very likely to increase, since in this type of transaction the customer is buying for special occasions, and therefore seeks different wines. In contrast, supermarket wine sales with high and moderate differentiation require convenience, price, fee payment incorporation, and large volume, particularly in the case of wine segments that are less than $ 5/bottle. In general, these wines are marketed by large companies (Concha y Toro, Santa Rita, San Pedro Tarapaca and Conosur). In specialty shops there is room for different wines from smaller wineries that do offer large volumes, but do offer consumers a wide range of wines. The Maule region has many small vineyards.

CONCLUDING REMARKS

Since the 1980s Chile has evolved into a major wine producer. There has been an increase in production and exports every year. Moreover, there has been a change in domestic consumption toward higher-quality wines, which has led to the development of an increasingly sophisticated market that now distributes to specialized shops and some supermarkets. It is easy to distinguish a highly differentiated wine supermarket from other wine-oriented supermarkets that have a low differentiation but offer a very attractive value for the money. On those grounds, consumers who wanted differentiation preferred The World of Wine compared to Jumbo Supermarkets. Furthermore, the study demonstrates a willingness to pay a little more (negative coefficient but of lesser magnitude) in specialized stores compared to other markets. The study distinguishes the analyzed agents in terms of the advice at purchase. Oenological developments are creating more complex products, so consumers look for staff to help them in their purchases. The study assesses the availability of parking, which is associated with the demands of an urban lifestyle, and requires safe facilities. In the future, with an increasingly competitive economic scenario, we will have to find new economies and new ways to operate in Chile's wine distribution channel, such as online sales, which currently has a usage rate of around 1.5 to 2.0%.

READINGS

Adimark (2010), "Mapa socioeconómico de Chile," available at http://www.adimark.cl/medios/estudios/mapa_socioeconomico_de_chile.pdf.

Arias, A. (2011), "Nota informativa sobre los canales de distribución en Chile," *Oficina Económica y Comercial de España en Santiago de Chile. Embajada de España,* available at www.oficinascomerciales.es/icex.

Camussi, G. Padrón, D., & Sarazola, C., (2006), "Caracterización de los canales de distribución de vino fino en Uruguay," *Panorama Socioeconómico,* 24(32), pp. 8–16.

Durán, K. (2010), "Análisis del comportamiento y actitudes de consumidores chilenos frente a vinos tintos varietales embotellados con D.O. Memoria de Titulo Ingeniero Agrónomo Universidad de Chile," *Facultad Ciencias Agrarias,* Santiago de Chile.

Fitch Rating (2012), "Sector Vitivinícola," available at http://www.fitchratings.cl/Upload/Presentaci%C3%B3n%20Vitivinicola_Abril%202010.pdf.

Hair, J.; Anderson, R.; Tathan, R.; Black, W. (1999). *Análisis multivariante (5th ed.),* Madrid, España, Prentice Hall.

INE (Instituto Nacional de Estadísticas) (2011), "Estudio de la situación de bodegas de vinos," available at http://www.ine.cl/canales/menu/archivos/Bodegasdevino2011_29062012.pdf.

Lockshin, L.; Kahrimanis, P. (1998), "Consumer evaluation of retail wine in store," *Journal of Wine Research,* 9(3), pp. 173–184.

Lucchini, F. (2010) Desarrollo de una metodología para el análisis del comportamiento de la industria del retail en Chile. Memoria Ingeniero Civil Industrial Universidad de Chile Facultad Ciencias Físicas y Matemáticas, Santiago de Chile.

Mora, M. (2004), "Estudio de las actitudes y percepciones de los consumidores hacia los vinos de las Denominaciones de Origen de la Comunidad Valenciana," doctoral thesis, Departamento de Estudios Económicos y Financieros, Universidad Miguel Hernández de Elche, Campus Orihuela, Alicante, España.

Mora, M.; Magner, N.; Marchant, R. (2010), "Segmentación de mercado de acuerdo a estilos de vida de consumidores de vino orgánico de la Región Metropolitana de Chile," *Idesia*, vol 28(3), pp. 25–33.

Mora, M. (2012), "Conociendo al consumidor chileno de viños para construir una relación comercial de mayor plazo relativo. Encuentro Nacional de Facultades de Administración y Economía de Chile—ENEFA 2012," Universidad de TalcaTalca, Región del Maule, Chile.

ODEPA (2013), "Boletín de vinos y pisco: Producción, precios y comercio exterior," available at http://www.odepa.cl//odepaweb/serviciosinformacion/Boletines/BVinos_0113.pdf;jsessionid=2897E1365B5229E075872459B8EAC976.

Reardon, T., & Berdegué, J. (2002), "The rapid rise of supermarkets in Latin America: Challenges and opportunities for development," *Development Policy Review*, 20(4), pp. 371–388.

SAG (Servicio Agrícola y Ganadero). (2012), "Informe ejecutivoproducción de vinos 2012: Elaborado por el Subdepartamento de Viñas y Vinos," available at http://www.sag.cl/sites/default/files/informe_ejecutivo_produccion_vinos_2012.pdf.

Stasi, A.; G. Nardone, R.; Viscecchia and A. Seccia (2011), "Italian wine demand and differentiation effect of geographical indications," *International Journal of Wine Business Research*, Vol. 23, (1). pp. 49–61.

Stern, L., El-Ansary, A., Coughlan, A.,&Cruz, I. (1999) *Canales de comercialización (5th ed.)*, Madrid: Prentice Hall.

Taylor, C., and Barber,N. (2012), "Measuring the influence of persuasion marketing on young wine consumers,"*Journal of Food Products Marketing*, 18(1), pp. 19–33.

Vinos de Chile.(2012) "Resumen de exportaciones," available at http://www.vinasdechile.com/contenidos/informacion/estadisticas-anuales/.

Zeithaml, V. (1988) "Consumer perceptions of price, quality and value: A means-end model and synthesis of evidence," *Journal of Marketing*, 52(3), pp. 2–22.

Brunello di Montalcino Wine Farms

REMAINING COMPETITIVE THROUGH FULL-COST ACCOUNTING

V. Alampi Sottini, GESAAF: Department of Agricultural, Food and Forest Systems Management, University of Florence

M. Bertocci, UniCeSV: Centre for the Strategic Development of the Wine Sector, University of Florence

N. Marinelli, GESAAF: Department of Agricultural, Food and Forest Systems Management, University of Florence

E. Marone, UniCeSV: Centre for the Strategic Development of the Wine Sector, University of Florence

S. Menghini, GESAAF: Department of Agricultural, Food and Forest Systems Management, University of Florence, Centre for the Strategic Development of the Wine Sector, University of Florence

SUMMARY

Wineries need to adjust how they assess their cost structures, particularly when expanding their markets from local to global. This case study explores how an Italian wine farm producing Brunello di Montalcino uses full-cost pricing analysis to improve its understanding of the costs that go into each bottle it yields. Such analysis enables the winery to make more effective decisions along the entire winemaking process to enhance profitability.

THE PROBLEM: PRODUCTION EXCELLENCE IS NOT ENOUGH
IN A GLOBALIZED SCENARIO

In several Tuscan and Italian wine farms, the introduction of cost-accounting tools confronts a culture that remains strongly product-oriented and subject to organizational and managerial choices only marginally related to the market, rather than to economies of scale. These farms found that competing only with one another in local markets, with exclusively local consumers and producers, a product-oriented approach was adequate. However, when competition moved to global markets, the success of those farms was no longer solely related to the quality of the wines they were able to produce, but also to the efficiency of their relationships with external markets.

The widening of market borders in which wine farms operate causes producers to face increasingly complex challenges in which they are forced to compete with a greater number of competitors and satisfy a growing range of capricious and selective consumers. Thus, it becomes increasingly important for wine producers, given the structural rigidities that do not allow for easy adaptation and adjustment of the supply in the short term, to be fully conscious of the environment in which they operate and the characteristics of their farms (see figure 1). It becomes fundamental for the farm to be fully aware of the production costs for each bottle because that information is necessary for any pricing decision and, more generally, for product positioning.

Figure 1: The Macro Environment for a Winery

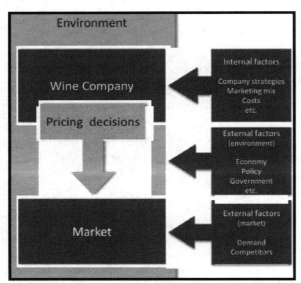

COST ACCOUNTING IN ITALIAN WINE FARMS: TOWARD FULL-COST PRICING

Over time, Italian wine farms began to understand the importance of developing pricing strategies through an increasing analytical knowledge of production costs. Initially, Italian farms, including market-oriented ones, exclusively focused their attentions on explicit costs because they were highlighted by ordinary accounting. This is because the farm's primary requirement was to ensure that sales were sufficient to cover real monetary expenses; very little attention was paid to the analyticity with which the costs were divided among the individual product lines and phases, and none was paid to the implicit costs, directly linked with the inputs provided by the farmer. The price at which the farm was willing to sell its product x was set by applying a mark-up m^x only on the explicit direct costs that the farm incurred to produce product line x:

$$p^x = \frac{dc_e^x}{1-m^x} \quad (1)$$

This was the payment for the inputs directly provided by the farmer and, in best cases, it also covered the expenses associated with the depreciation of the farm's capital be- cause share of the depreciations were included in the value of dc_e^x.

In the typical conditions of the Italian wine market up to the 1970s, this approach was linked to farms that were completely product-oriented when the farmer had a completely passive role in the setting of the prices for their products on the local mar- ket[1]. Thus, the mark-up at that time was not a value fixed by the farm but a variable dependent on the price and explicit costs set by the markets:

$$m^x = \frac{P^x - dc_e^x}{pi} (2)$$

Farmers measured their efficiency by ensuring that the selling price was higher than the direct explicit costs and verifying, only at the farm level, that the mark-up was at least sufficient to cover the indirect explicit and implicit costs (direct and indirect), also allowing the latter to include underpayments.[2]

Soon, increasing competition demanded greater analyticity and the farms began to quantify their mark-ups by considering all of the direct costs for their single x product, Dc^x, thus calculating not only the explicit costs, dc_e^x, but also estimating the implicit ones dc_i^x:

$$m^x = \frac{P^x - Dc^x}{pi} \quad (3)$$

$$\text{with } Dc^x = dc^x + dc^x$$

A further step toward a more analytical approach was also taken by paying increasing attention to the indirect costs ascribable to each product. This led to the definition of a selling price in which the mark-up was established by accounting for all of the direct costs by including the farm's indirect explicit costs, ic_e, measured as a share α attribut- able to the specific x product:

$$P^x = (Dc^x + ic_e^x) * (1 + m^x) \quad (4)$$

$$\text{with } ic_e^x + \alpha\, ic_e$$

By doing so, the mark-up identifies a sum that covers implicit indirect costs and, even- tually, some profits.

At present, it is possible to state that the more analytical approaches for price defi- nition aim to precisely quantify the full indirect cost, Ic^x, considering not only indirect explicit costs but also indirect implicit costs ic_i^x, thus obtaining a full-cost quantification for the x product Fc^x:

$$P^x = (Dc^x + Ic^x) * (1 + m^x \quad (5)$$

Furthermore, if all implicit costs (direct and indirect) are quantified at market prices, the fixed mark-up reveals the profit that farmers are willing to receive, considering the selling price they intend to set.

Thus, from formula (5), the minimum price at which the product x is to be sold, setting a profit equal to zero, will be equal to the full cost of production Fc of the single product x:

$$P^x = Fc^x \quad (6)$$
$$t\,T = 0$$
$$\text{with } Fc^x = Dc^x + Ic^x = dc_e^x + dc_i^x + ic_e^x + ic_i^x$$

At present, the most advanced methodologies for cost accounting applied to the pricing strategies, in conjunction with this full-cost quantification logic, cause farmers to face difficulties related to the following:

- The quantification of implicit costs
- The distribution and allocation of indirect costs
- The temporal distribution of the costs related to fixed assets that allow their productive utility to extend over more years

These issues require the collection and, partially, the estimation of additional accounting data that can be conducted with different levels of accuracy, implying expenses for the farms that may be relevant: an analytical model applied to the farm has to evaluate these expenses, considering the economic size of the business to be examined and the usefulness that such details may convey, that is, irrelevant costs.

However, all of these different approaches are still adopted by Italian wine farms according to their specific needs and specific management sensitivities and skills.

CASE STUDY

The Montalcino area is located in the province of Siena, Tuscany. With a surface area of 3,821 square kilometers, Siena is the second largest Tuscan province in terms of territorial extent. The agricultural sector comprises 8,449 farms, 20% of the total number of companies in the region]ISTAT, 2010), covering 275,239.5 hectares of Tuscany's total agricultural area; thus, the rural component plays a very important role. Within this context, the wine sector is of primary importance, emblematic of the entire territory and contributing to the local economy as a component of the agrifood sector and as a draw for tourists. The Province of Siena has consistently been the largest Tuscan vine cultivation area (with 18,330.39 hectares of vineyards, 31% of the regional total) and also very important on a national scale, guaranteeing the wide supply of its products as evidenced by the many geographical indications (GIs) that cover the wine-growing areas of the province. There are 880,000 hectoliters of wine produced in the province, 31% of the regional total.

Within the province, the Montalcino area represents one of the best examples of excellence in Italian wine production. The cultivation of wine in this area dates back to the Etruscan period, and since that time, the economy of the area has been substantially based on the production of wine and olive oil. There are a total of 332 wine farms comprising 3,925 hectares of vines (with an average farm size of 11.8 hectares). Most of the production (more than 116,000 hectoliters) is represented by DOC and DOCG wines, the most important and renowned of which is Brunello di Montalcino. The Brunello DOCG covers 2,020 hectares of vines belonging to 311 farms, for a total production of approximately 80,000 hectoliters per year, and is the only DOCG in the area. Three DOCs (Rosso di Montalcino, Moscadello di Montalcino, and Sant'Antimo) are produced in the Montalcino municipality along with the Tuscan IGT.[3]

More than 70% of the bottles of Brunello di Montalcino are exported, the United States being its most important market (approximately 25% of total production). On the Italian national market, Brunello is primarily sold in restaurants and wine shops and little is distributed via major retail chains.

The choice of a Montalcino wine farm as a case study, and in particular the choice of the production cost of Brunello di Montalcino wine, is due to the relevance of this product in the context of Tuscan and Italian viticulture and its role on the international market. Furthermore, analyzing a farm in such a territory allows for an exemplification of how traditional, local, high-quality producers that operate with high-quality products need to update their management skills by introducing new, more refined, and more appropriate tools to react to changing market scenarios. The case study is particularly appropriate because most Montalcino wine farms represent complex farm typologies that are responsible for all phases of production, from field activities to processing, aging, and bottling.

Company background

The analyzed estate was started in 1970 and is located on the slope of Montalcino Hill, on its northeast side. The total estate comprises 60 hectares: 20 are cultivated with cereal crops, 20 are covered by olive trees and woods, and the final 20 are given over to the vineyards. Of these last 20 hectares, a large part is registered to the Brunello di Montalcino DOCG appellation and the rest to the Rosso di Montalcino DOC.

The vineyards, all planted with the Sangiovese varietal, are divided into seven separate plots of equal quality, but the individual characteristics of the vineyards differ. The 20 hectares of vines are planted at altitudes between 330 and 150 meters above sea level. The total wine production is approximately 60,000 bottles per year, divided into two product lines: Brunello di Montalcino DOCG and Rosso di Montalcino DOC.

The Brunello di Montalcino DOCG produced by the analyzed farm is an excellent example of the Sangiovese variety, beginning with the meticulous selection of the best bunches in the vineyard: each lot is then harvested, vinified, and aged separately. The final assemblage (blending) of the different lots to produce the Brunello di Montalcino is decided 13 months after the harvest. The Brunello is then sent on to complete its 24 months of barrel aging in French barriques. Eighteen months of bottle-fining follow. The annual production of Brunello is approximately 30,000 bottles.

The farm's Rosso di Montalcino DOC represents the estate's second product line. The owner has awarded this wine equal attention to that paid to the Brunello. Moreover, the grapes used for the Rosso come from the same vineyards as those used for the Brunello. The choice of the wine to use for the Rosso is made only when vinification is complete and after several tastings have been performed.

From an analysis of the farm's sales, it is possible to note that, for this case study and the entire Province of Siena, the main market is the foreign one: over 70% of total revenues come from exports and the remaining 30% come from the regional and national markets and, to a limited extent, the local one. The main foreign customer is the United States, which accounts for approximately 50% of the market, followed by Belgium, the Netherlands, Luxemburg, and Switzerland. Other minor European customers are the United Kingdom, Denmark, France, Austria, and Germany. In recent years, the farm's Brunello di Montalcino reached Canada, Australia, Russia, Japan, and Southeast Asia (Hong Kong, Singapore, and South Korea).

With respect to placement, the estate does not engage in direct selling: in the local market, the product is sold directly by the estate to several restaurants and wine shops. At the regional level, the estate collaborates with an agency that collects orders from customers, which are primarily restaurants, wine shops, and quality food shops. Abroad, the estate sells its product through an importer and distributors who, collaborating with them, promote the wine and periodically organize exhibitions and tastings for final customers. The farm's wines are not sold at the major Italian retailers.

CASE PROBLEM: DESCRIPTION OF THE METHODOLOGY

The management of wine farms is becoming increasingly complex, not only in terms of technical-productive aspects but also economic and financial ones. The internationalization of the markets and the consequent increase in competition force the farms, including those with the highest-quality products, to implement innovative solutions capable of supporting more efficient and efficacious management.

How is it possible to reconcile the need for managerial control with the limited economic resources typical of the average farm? Is it possible to conceive of managerial control irrespective of cost accounting, which by definition represents one of its unavoidable instruments? The answer is likely no. However, it is possible to wonder if, for the average wine farm, it is sufficient to have a limited amount of information and thereby hypothesize a simplified theoretical, practical, and applicable model. Cost management represents one of the main tools for managerial control. Moreover, cost management is one of the indispensable elements for the definition of product prices, and a useful instrument for determining the efficiency of different phases of the production process. Thus, cost management provides elements of essential knowledge for efficient farm management, although not enough for the implementation of a true management control system.

Nevertheless, nearly all wine estates are multi-product farms, thus facing objective difficulties in ascribing the indirect or joint costs. Joint costs are generated by productive inputs used in more than one productive sector and, within the same productive sector, for more than one product. Thus, cost management is typically performed by combining the joint costs in a cost center, but an activity-based cost method, which attributes those costs to management activities that generated them, is also employed. In the first case, the smaller cost center has to be determined (productive, auxiliary, and functional) with respect to which costs, indirect for the single product, become direct for the cost center. Accounting for an individual activity, conversely, makes it possible to identify the causes that generate each cost, with positive implications for the formulation of future management programs for the farm.

The use of mixed systems could make it possible to limit data gathering to the essential information needed to determine the few cost centers that each farm is usually able to detect and apply (for instance, plants, workforce, raw materials, etc.) sufficiently to provide the necessary data to determine the cost of a specific activity (for instance, the cost of the agronomic phase of grape production). Once the cost-per-activity is calculated, if this cost significantly differs across the different vineyards (and thus for the different wines contributing to the final products), it can be distributed with respect to the parameters (soil conditions, vine specificities, etc.) that are determined to be the causes of these differences.

The case study discussed here concerns the Brunello di Montalcino DOCG produced by the analyzed farm. For this case study, the necessary data for the implementation of the management control model established by our research team were detected with the aim of calculating the production cost of a single bottle of wine.

The proposed model

To ensure that the cost-accounting model is adaptable to the different situations that exist in the sector, the control model, aimed at the development of full-cost accounting, has been applied in a manner that separated the grape production phase from the processing one. By doing so, the model is applicable to any farm, irrespective of the degree of integration in the production process, according to the different technical and economic characteristics of the filière (production chain). For this reason, the model identifies four phases, each of which is characterized by phase inputs and different half-processed products that are technically and economically transferable (figure 2):

- Phase 0: Production (from the vineyard to the grape)
- Phase 1: Processing I (from the grape to the fermented wine)
- Phase 2: Processing II (from the fermented wine to the aged wine)
  - Sub-phase: aging wine in wood
  - Bottling
  - Sub-phase: aging wine in bottle
- Phase 3: Marketing (selling activities)

In addition, being a production process structured over several years with a minimum length of six years from harvest to selling the bottles, the model has a multi-period development. Therefore, in case a phase is longer than the accounting period, the model tracks the value and the relative costs of the product in the maturation phase for each year.

Figure 2: The Wine Production Process

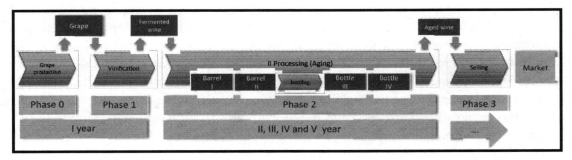

The wine farm conducts production phases that are highly differentiated, and in each of them it is possible to have the product of the previous phase and one acquired externally as inputs. Moreover, in each phase it is possible to either transfer the product to the subsequent phase or sell it on the market. For instance, in phase 0, the model accounts for the units of planted vines and the respective grape varietals and all of the inputs linked with agricultural activity. It considers the grapes as outputs. For phase 1, the system identifies the grape varieties and associates them with the corresponding processed wines. For phase 2, the model identifies the aged wines produced, correlating them with the respective processed wines from which they originated, and, in phase 3, the link between the final product and the source mix is defined. Therefore, the system allows the product to be traceable because the model is able to go back, for each label, to the original grapes and vineyards.

Beginning with the vineyard and concluding with the bottle, the proposed model elaborates, for subsequent phases, the costs of the grapes, vinified wine, aged wine, and the bottle for each label, thus providing a budget plan and a final economic balance able to support the business's strategic decisions. Through the use of a value chain, it is possible to analyze the individual activities of the wine farm, determining the relative costs and revenues. The proposed model follows a similar approach and, by including information on costs and revenues in each phase, it calculates the value generated by each activity.

The described model was input into software that begins with a classic input area (IA) and ends with an output area (OA). The input area is organized into a farm info system (FIS) and a drivers set (DS), which then transfer the collected data into an analysis area (AA), which is divided in two linked databases, AA1 and AA2. AA1 includes the input data from the productive process, divided into phases, and the relative costs that allow for the calculation of the production cost of the phase and the single product. The output of the AA1 database is then used and elaborated on by AA2 by applying the drivers set to the indirect costs (figure 3).

Figure 3: Scheme of the Cost-Accounting Process

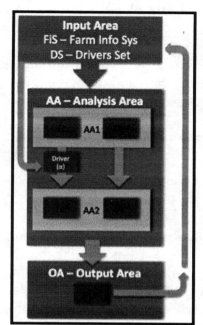

Clearly, to obtain such a result, the farm should use a cost-accounting system capable of providing the information necessary for determining the values of the individual products that will be marketed, in this case identified as the labels. The proposed model can also be employed if a rigorous cost-accounting system is not present by suggesting reclassification schemes for the general accounting data available. The initial results of the model, if current analytical data are lacking, will obviously be only approximations of the real production cost of the nth label, but thanks to the segmentation of the productive process into phases and analyses of the cost structures for each phase, they will allow the farm to understand which sectors of the productive process are most relevant and which require a system for the analytical detection of their costs. In substance, over time the model will more accurately identify production costs, thus allowing the investments related to the implementation of the cost-accounting system to be repaid through reduced expenses and higher revenues achieved through the improvement of the farm's management.

Analysis Area AA1

Database AA1 provides the organization for each year of the information on the production process for each of the four identified phases and separates any information that is not immediately ascribable to the final product (explicit and implicit indirect costs) from the explicit and implicit direct costs. Regarding the indirect costs, the model creates the introduction of information regarding the use of productive inputs ascribable to the following categories: machines, labor, tanks, and general costs. The cost per unit is given for each factor and will be divided among the different phases and products in a subsequent phase. When the data from AA1 is transferred to AA2 it employs a set of drivers (DS) that will be described in the following paragraphs.

Based on how direct costs are treated in database AA1, it is possible to highlight that they are managed through two informational levels:

- In the first, the productive inputs used for each productive phase are listed.
- In the second, for each of the previous inputs, quantities and values are determined, derived from the market price (if the inputs concerned were purchased outside the farm) or by considering the production cost if those inputs are half-processed products obtained within the farm.

All of these directions are repeated any time a process differs in any of these phases. For instance, if the productive techniques in the vineyards differ, the model considers the specific production process applicable to each vineyard. The same process occurs if differences in the vinification, aging, or marketing phases take place.

If a component of production costs has a significant effect on the total cost, it could aid the farm in deciding to apply specific cost-detection activities that could make it possible to understand the specific product and input linked to a given cost. In so doing, the farm would be able to link agronomic activity in the vineyard and the consequent effects on the characteristics of the final product, with the cost it requires and the possible increase in the value of the product.

All inputs considered in the first database, according to the production process(es) characterizing the phase, are elaborated to detect the production cost for each of the products identified for that phase.

Analysis Area AA2

AA2 is also organized in phases. This enables the elaboration of the costs for all four phases of the wine production process and provides profit-and-loss accounts.

This database, using the data derived from database AA1 as inputs, divides the indirect costs according to the drivers (algorithms for the repartition of the indirect costs) for each phase and each product. The model makes it possible to define the drivers on the basis of simple repartition indexes, such as surface areas, production, sales, and so on, or inserting the results of any additional extra-accounting data detected. The choice of the type of driver employed can be made not only within each single phase but also for each of the costs characterizing the phase, choosing more or less accurate drivers on the basis of the importance of the costs considered. After the drivers are identified, the software visualizes the direct and indirect costs and calculates the total costs and the unit cost associated with the final product of each phase, ultimately determining the production cost of the individual label.

The total production cost for the final product and the different half-processed products is divided into direct and indirect costs and explicit and implicit costs. If the length of a phase spans several years, as is the case in phase 2 (the current regulation for the DOCG states that the wine has to be aged for two years in wood and two in a bottle), the model maintains detailed costs for each year, not only allowing for a full-cost analysis for each of the three phases but also a full-cost analysis for all four years of the aging process. As a result, the farm, after the aging requirements imposed by the DOCG are fulfilled, can evaluate the value of extending the aging duration because it is able to compare the marginal cost of each additional year of aging in the bottle with the marginal increase in the consumers' willingness to pay for the same product aged an additional year.

RESULTS

The application of the described model to the examined estate makes it possible to conduct an analysis of the structure of the farm's total production cost for a single product, eventually highlighting the difficulties in the organization and management of the production process.

The farm selected for this case study, although exhibiting a marked sensitivity toward the analysis of the production costs, did not employ a system of cost accounting and, thus, lacked any systematic method for the detection of useful additional accounting data. This required the nearly exclusive use of the repartition drivers to determine the indirect costs according to the previously given terms.

To simplify the description of the results for the case study, the analysis of a single farm product was conducted, namely, the production cost of a specific label produced by the farm in a specific vintage year i.

As previously discussed, the model first analyzes all the required inputs, separating them into fixed and variable costs and considering whether they are direct or indirect costs for the specific label of wine examined:

- Fixed costs:
- Labor: family and nonfamily labor
- Depreciation expenses: depreciation shares for property assets, machinery, equipment, tanks (cement and stainless steel), wooden barrels (large and small), and vine planting
- Other fixed costs: energy, insurance, consulting, education and professional training, financial costs, long-term and ordinary maintenance and renting liabilities, interest on land assets, and planting rights
- Variable costs:

  nonfamily labor, nondurable products and services (i.e., pest management, fertilization and materials for the vineyard, fuels and lubricants, materials for the winemaking process, subcontracts and outsourcing, marketing costs, packaging, and DOCG certification)

The other information that the system is able to provide, which is however strictly linked with the farmer's entrepreneurship and the characteristics of the specific farm, is a further classification of the previous costs with respect to their explicit or implicit nature according to the following scheme:

- Explicit costs: nonfamily labor, other fixed costs (net of the interest on land assets and planting rights), and variable costs
- Implicit costs: family labor, depreciation charges, and interest on land assets and planting rights.

  The aggregated results of the cost analysis by cost typology (table 1) make it possible to observe their relative weights and the relevance of the implicit costs in the total costs. In our case study, the total production cost per bottle is €12.94

Table 1. Composition of the Production Costs for Label Wine per Cost Typology

Cost	€/bottle	%
Nonfamily labor	2.83	21.87
Other fixed costs	1.48	11.43
Variable costs	3.61	27.87
Total explicit costs	**7.92**	**61.17**
Family labor	0.35	2.74
Depreciation charges	3.99	30.84
Interests on land assets and on planting rights	0.68	5.24
Total implicit costs	**5.02**	**38.82**
Total	**12.94**	**100**

This result can also be achieved if a cost-accounting system is not implemented: clearly such information provides specific suggestions regarding product pricing but no indications regarding the improvement of the firm's internal organization or that among the different phases.

The most important result of this analysis is the detailed description of the total production costs per phase through the adoption of specific drivers that can be identified either through objective tests or eventually estimated.

In detail, the case study reveals that the agronomic phase (grape production) is the most important contributor to the overall process (42%), followed by the aging and bottling and marketing phases. This cost distribution appears even more interesting if the explicit costs are distinguished from implicit ones.

Table 2. Composition of the Production Cost for the Label Wine per Production Phase

Production phase (value)	Explicit Costs (€/bottle)	Implicit Costs (€/bottle)	Total (€/bottle)
Grape production	2.90	2.54	5.44
Vinification and processing	0.62	0.50	1.13
Aging	3.00	1.94	4.95
Marketing and selling	1.38	0.04	1.42
Total	**7.92**	**5.02**	**12.94**
Production phase (%)			
Grape production	36.61	50.59	42.04
Vinification and processing	7.82	9.96	8.73
Aging	37.92	38.70	38.23
Marketing and selling	17.50	0.73	10.99
Total	**100**	**100**	**100**

The cost-accounting system can now verify the relative weights of the different cost components for each phase of production. In the case study, grape production is characterized, as we could expect, by the significant influence of labour costs and depreciation charges. These costs were ascribed to this phase using the drivers estimated from the property. However, is important to note that for some of the costs of the processes in this phase, the estimation should be free of attribution errors (considering the harvest and the types of machines employed), but for some other costs more analytic surveys should be conducted (considering the different agronomic techniques that can be employed in a vineyard and the implications that these techniques may have on the use of labor, machines, and raw materials).

The same process can be performed for the other phases of the production process, as shown in table 3 and figure 4. From the analysis in this case study, it appears clear that the general costs were equally distributed across the production phases because a cost-accounting system is absent.

Table 3. Composition of the Production Costs for the Label Wine from Each Production Phase

Cost entry	Grape Production		Vinification		Aging		Marketing and Selling		Total	
	€/bottle	%	€/bottle	%	€/bottle	%	€/bottle	%	€/bottle	%
Labor	1.82	33.52	0.34	30.09	0.94	19.00	0.08	5.58	3.18	24.57
family labor	0.13	2.39	0.09	7.96	0.06	1.21	0.08	5.58	0.36	2.78
nonfamily labor	1.69	31.12	0.25	22.12	0.88	17.79	0.00	0.00	2.82	21.79
Capitals: depreciation charges and interests	2.40	44.20	0.41	36.28	1.83	36.91	0.02	1.67	4.66	36.01
Other costs	1.21	22.28	0.38	33.63	2.18	44.09	1.33	92.74	5.10	39.41
other fixed costs	0.50	9.21	0.33	29.20	0.53	10.73	0.13	9.00	1.49	11.51
other variable costs	0.71	13.08	0.05	4.42	1.65	33.35	1.20	83.74	3.61	27.90
Total costs	**5.43**	**100.00**	**1.13**	**100.00**	**4.95**	**100.00**	**1.43**	**100.00**	**12.94**	**100.00**

Figure 4. Composition of the Production Costs for the Label Wine per Cost Typology and Production Phase

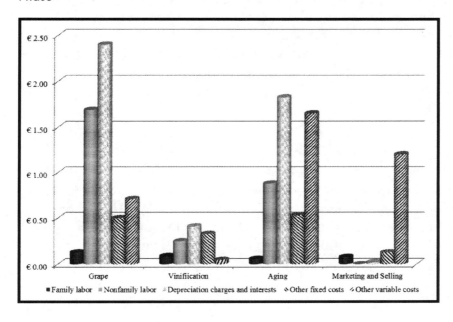

Finally, knowledge of the costs per production phase, and thus of the half-processed product, allows this cost to be compared with the relevant market values. It also provides the farm with the opportunity to evaluate the benefits of purchasing the inputs for the entire production process on the market or selling its half-processed products on the market.

Conclusions: The New Challenge for the Future

The case study aims to describe a significant example of a larger Italian wine-production system. Even very small farms understood the importance of being competitive on the global market, investing not only in technological innovations to improve product quality but also organizational and managerial tools, and investing in human and tangible resources. In this scenario, cost accounting represents one such innovation that, together with other efforts toward developing a market orientation, lead Italian farms to seek success not only by focusing on product quality but also on the most efficient competitive position.

The proposed model and the development of software adaptable to all wine farms provide a cost-accounting tool that aims to strike a balance between informative detail and the costs associated with this task. The model adopts a learning-by-doing approach, with a circular verification of the data inputs with respect to the outputs. Because of this process of verification, the model, starting with elementary extra-accounting information, identifies the most tractable drivers related to indirect costs as a priority, or, when this is not possible, provides an estimation of them. In the results obtained, the model highlights the most relevant costs in terms of input typology and production phase, giving useful indications for the validation of the estimated drivers employed: thus, the farmer is able to evaluate the possibility of collecting more detailed data only for the most relevant costs (per cost typology and per production phase).

Cost accounting represents an important innovation for those wine farms that are willing to improve their competitiveness in the global market. The implementation of such a tool helps in defining internal critical elements, the consequences of organizational choices, and the margins in relation to customers and competitors. Such an innovation, immaterial in nature, has to be introduced in a receptive managerial environment; thus, the future of wine companies relies heavily on their ability and capability to invest in skilled human resources.

Teaching Notes

1. What is the correct detail of analysis for cost accounting in a wine farm?

   The cost of the implementation of an analytical accounting tool must not be higher than the benefits deriving from its implementation. Thus, there is not an absolute ideal detail but optimal levels depending on each case and each managerial and organizational issue facing the wine farm.

2. How can a correct detail be identified in the analytical accounting for each farm?

By a reiterative process, with increasing levels of detail about the most critical points. Once the critical elements of the productive process are detected, further elaborations are possible, primarily improving the detail of the drivers to be adopted for the repartition of the most relevant indirect costs and just for the critical phases of production. As an example, in the case study critical costs are related to depreciation charges and thus imply that significant attention should be paid to the use of machineries, the cellars, and the equipment. If the cost apportionment for each of these aspects is performed simply using the surface area or production drivers, the information regarding the cost of the adoption of a specific agronomic technique is completely invalid. In general, farmers know the effects that modifying the technique would have on final product quality, but they do not know how much this change will affect final production costs. In this case study, the labor cost and the depreciation shares for grape production account for more than 77% of the total for the phase and 32.6% of the final cost per bottle of the examined label. Because the farm does not have a system to document the use of labor and machineries separately for each product, the information that it can obtain is an average cost of these cost elements for this productive phase. For this reason, this cost could be over- or underestimated and would not allow, in any case, for an evaluation of the possible effects of modifying the productive technique, because the higher costs or savings will affect the farm's overall production costs but not those of a given product.

3. If the total production cost of a wine bottle is higher than its market price, is it correct to assess that it is solely the symptom of production inefficiency?

   No, it is not, because it could depend on a condition of marketing inefficiency. However, if this is the case, cost accounting enables the assessment of an inadequate selling price; thus, before operating to adjust production costs, it is necessary to verify the market positioning of the product and, particularly, the efficiency of distribution choices.

4. What should a wine farm do when production costs are too high?

   There are two different solutions:

   a. Reducing the total production costs of the farm, without knowing the detail for each product. However, if such an action is undertaken, this could lead to the penalization of those products that show higher margins.

   b. Analyzing through cost accounting the total cost for each product and detecting the critical one: with this detail it is possible to verify which phase and, in terms of priority, which input has to be modified. The analysis may also consider whether the issue is related to fixed or variable productive input, thus implying short- or long-term choices.

5. The production cost of a specific phase is particularly high. What should the wine farmer do?

Verify if the higher cost of production coincides with a higher quality perceived by consumers:

a. If so, the critical situation is not the phase but the capability of the producer to emphasize that aspect in the attributes considered relevant by the consumers; moreover, the producer could consider the opportunity to adapt the entire process to the level of the specific phase, repositioning the final product on a higher level.

b. If not, the producer should improve the efficiency of the phase, reducing the costs.

6. Indicate, in the short term and for a single product, the correct typologies for the following costs:

COSTS	Fixed	Variable	Direct	Indirect	Implicit	Explicit
Depreciation charges						
Family labor						
Energy						
Interest on land assets						
Fertilizers						
Nonfamily labor						
Marketing						
Tanks						

ENDNOTES

1. However, this was once a little-perceived need by the farmer because the technological conditions were stable and allowed the plants to have a very long economic duration if ordinary maintenance was performed accurately.
2. This was according to an efficiency objective inspired not only by the maximization of farm income but also the satisfaction of other extra-economic objectives, such as the maintenance of a certain level of employment, safeguarding specific productive traditions, and so on.
3. GIs are divided into DOCG (Controlled and Guaranteed Designation of Origin), DOC (Controlled Designation of Origin), and IGT (Typical Geographical Indication).

Dominio del Plata Winery

KEEPING COMPETITIVE IN A RAPIDLY GROWING WINE MARKET

Javier Merino, Área del Vino Cosulting, Argentina

SUMMARY

Dominio del Plata is a small modern winery located in Argentina that offers a special focus on ultra-premium wines and aims to sell to external markets. The winery was founded in 2002 and has enjoyed a very strong growth since its beginning. Nowadays it sells more than $10 million of wine per year. The winery must decide how to continue its previous success in a market that is getting more competitive and saturated worldwide.

INTRODUCTION

Similar to other markets in the past few years, the world wine market has undergone profound changes because of globalization. A greater reach has been achieved because of a global supply and demand of products, going considerably beyond previous national boundaries and generating a great mobility of goods and services all over the world.

However, this globalization has caused a significant breakdown of traditional trends for a great number of variables in the world wine market. Among them stand out five that have been carefully observed by industry companies and organizations in the development of their business strategies. In some cases, the trends should be adapted, whereas others are useful to consider in creating differentiation:

- Greater global market share of wines with a more modern style
- Growth of consumption in the highest price ranges
- Expansion of nontraditional wine retail chains
- Communication of the distinctive attributes of wines and regions
- Development of competitive advantages by companies, regions, and wine-producing countries

New market opportunities have arisen from the breakdown of previous market patterns, and those companies or regions that can quickly capitalize can gain ground in the world wine market.

GREATER GLOBAL MARKET SHARE OF WINES WITH A MORE MODERN STYLE

Up to the beginning of the 1980s, there was a strong worldwide leadership of the so-called old producers, which generally intended their production for domestic and neighboring countries' consumption. International trade was not developed and less than 20% of global consumption was marketed.

Then international development of so-called new world wine began by countries that in general destined their production to exportation, led in this first stage by the United States, Australia, and to a lesser extent Chile.

At the same time, there appeared on stage a group of countries whose emerging wine consumption was propelled by better economic conditions of the population and an increased opening of their economies. Other countries, also experiencing good economic conditions and driven by anti-alcohol regulations, started to replace beverages with higher alcohol levels in their markets, benefiting the distribution of wine.

New consumers showed different cultural patterns, not adhering to the traditional wine-consumption patterns that prevailed in the oldest wine-drinking countries, and started to consume wine like other drinks, highly regarding the accessibility of the new world's products. Nonetheless, consumers evolved and matured and started appreciating attributes of more complex wines, granting old world wines a greater competitiveness. New wine-producing countries have responded by also offering very complex and competitively priced wines.

Therefore, the new direction of the wine business is clear in the globalization process of the world's economies as well as the important role that economic prosperity plays in the development of these new markets.

A significant variable in these wine-consumption trends has been the growth of interest in wine by the youngest generation. Among their preferences, red wines stand out, though some sweet, aromatic, and fresh whites have had great success. In addition, this generation also prefers sparkling and rosé wines.

According to many international studies, when choosing what to eat and drink, modern consumers are influenced by three megatrends: health, convenience, and premiumization. These trends are propelled mainly by young consumers and have a great impact on wine consumption.

The more visible effect of these new behaviors and synthesis with previous wine-drinking ways was the substantial change seen in wine styles all over the world. In the 1980s, this change started to be observed in the numbers of varietals or "young" wines being offered, and it quickly became a way for winemakers to differentiate the wines. This expansion was propelled by the emergence of new countries whose consumption had not been part of a previous wine culture.

Therefore, the style of wines made by the new world may be characterized as more sweet and sparkly, with a lesser astringency and acidity, and displaying more fruity and spicy aromas, instead of vegetable or animal tones. The more inclusive definition may be "young and easy-to-drink wines." These preferences have affected the development of varietal wines since the 1980s as opposed to terroir wines.

GROWTH OF CONSUMPTION IN THE HIGHEST PRICE RANGES

As international wine markets become increasingly competitive, wineries' profit margins have eroded. Therefore, companies have focused their businesses on more profitable segments. Bottled wines of medium and high price ranges have higher profit margins than entry-level products. However, as margins decrease, the modality of bulk wine exports has significantly increased because it allows a considerable reduction of transportation costs and enables the sale of higher-quality wine at lower prices.

Globally, the wine market is divided into three sectors:

High-priced wines (sold at over $10 a bottle) represent 11% of world wine consumption. This range includes some very successful, well-regarded examples with positive international reviews.

Mid-priced wines (between $6.50 and $10 per bottle) account for 18% of global consumption. This is a very dynamic segment. It encompasses the varietal wines fashionable since the new millennium such as Pinot Grigio and Riesling, partly Malbec, and low-priced sparkling wines.

Low-priced wines are sold at under $6.50 a bottle and represent 72% of global consumption.

The growth since 2000 has concentrated in mid-priced and high-priced wines, whereas those within the low-price segment have shown a decline in sales.

Moreover, high-priced wines enjoy a larger share of imported wines to consume, whereas lower economic segments consume wines that are distributed locally.

Here, there is profound change because of the incorporation of new countries that consume wine. Many of these countries, because they do not have local production or it is not very developed, import most of the globally consumed wine, which provides a great opportunity for exporting countries, especially considering that the share is larger in the highest-priced segments.

Taking into account the share of imports and consumption growth rates, the most attractive markets are the medium- and highest-price ranges.

Figure 1. Price pyramid of 2011 global wine consumption (MM cases 9 liters), Area del Vino's estimate.

	CONSUMPTION	GLOBAL SHARE	ANNUAL GROWTH	
High-priced wines Sold at over USD10 a bottle	286 MM Cases	11%	*3.8%*	32% Local production 68% Imported bottled wine
Mid-priced wines Between USD6.5 and USD10 per bottle	489 MM Cases	18%	*1.4%*	39% Local production 61% Imported bottled wine
Low-priced wines Sold at under USD6.5 a bottle	1.949 MM Cases	72%	*-0.4%*	72% Local production 22% Imported bulk wine 6% Imported bottled wine
GLOBAL CONSUMPTION	2.715 MM Cases	100%	*0.3%*	62% Local production 16% Imported bulk wine 22% Imported bottled wine

EXPANSION OF NONTRADITIONAL WINE RETAIL CHAINS

The search for new products gave rise to the development of retail chains such as supermarkets into the wine-selling business. This expansion has been considerable in the past few years, and today these wine retail chains account for over 40% of the global wine retail market.

This strong growth has resulted in the following consequences in the world wine market: on the one hand, there has been a benefit of a greater reach and visibility and an ability to obtain new customers, because trade was previously concentrated in specialized shops of more limited reach.

On the other hand, this wine-promotion benefit creates a disadvantage for producers: an increased bargaining power by new retailers that has affected the profitability of the producers. Therefore, smaller producers started to migrate to countries with less development of these retail chains and made a foray into direct sales or on-trade channels. Today, large-sized companies are the ones with greater competitive capacity in the face of this type of expansion.

COMMUNICATION OF THE DISTINCTIVE ATTRIBUTES OF WINES AND REGIONS

Communication has become a fundamental element for success in the wine world. Since the 1990s, more than 35 promotional organizations from different wine regions and countries have emerged, the aim of which is to promote wines of certain geographical locations, hoping for some kind of differentiation in such a competitive wine world.

Although at first the primary promotion was of a "country brand" as wine producer, recently the sector has observed a trend toward greater specificity. Besides, new regional organizations have emerged, even organizations of varietal wine promotion.

The messages and communications mechanisms used by these organizations have changed from the beginning. At first, the purpose was just to spotlight the quality of wines from the region, but then this concept of quality diversified. Nowadays, these campaigns market other distinctive attributes highly appreciated by consumers, such as the style and sustainability.

Another change experienced in the wine world has been the emergence of wine critics. The fast incorporation of countries and brands into the world trade entailed a strong need for differentiation, giving rise to the opinion of "experts" who enjoy public respect and have the power to push or make difficult sales of certain wine brands. At first, these critics were wine specialists who mainly came from the trade. Now, due to the horizontality provided by the Internet and the fact that the younger generation bases its recommendations on their peers, wine bloggers have arrived on the scene. They are just consumers with a great interest in wine, who share their experiences and recommendations on the web.

Nonetheless, perhaps the most important change in wine communications in the media is the movement from traditional media to the Internet. Within this new channel, there have been developments, too. The use of web pages and advertising has changed to more interactive formats, based mostly on the use of social networks.

DEVELOPMENT OF COMPETITIVE ADVANTAGES BY COMPANIES, REGIONS, AND WINE-PRODUCING COUNTRIES

The development of competitive advantages has occurred through constant improvement of the quality-price relationship, entailing developments along the value chain that raise the value perceived by customers in relation to profitability levels.

The concept of productivity in the wine world was introduced by new world countries. It was not incorporated into the winemaking of the old world, where price had little to do with costs, and in certain cases the quality and productivity had been understood as opposing concepts.

Technological modernization and research to improve the productivity of vineyards were established in Australia and United States in the 1990s. Through this, those countries paved the way for global wine exportation.

Figure 2. Change in revealed comparative advantage between 2002 and 2011, Área del Vino's estimate.

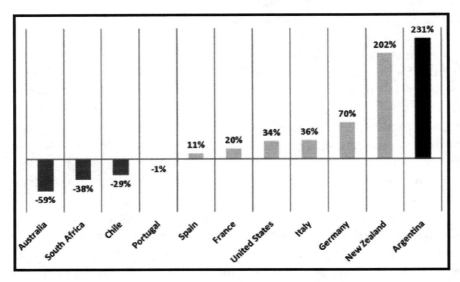

The rate of revealed comparative advantage (RCA)[1] helps to understand the exporting specialization of a country. RCA is defined as the quotient between the share of a product in the exports of a country and the share of the product in global exports. Comparing the evolution of the RCA for wine exports in the world's leading rival wine-producing countries, it is observed that Argentina is the country experiencing the fastest growth from 2002 to 2011. In the comparison, all countries start from a value equivalent to 1 in 2002 and in 2011 Argentina had reached 2.31 (see Figure 2). Three groups of countries with different behaviors are clearly shown in the figure. First, Argentina and New Zealand enjoyed a very significant growth, over 300%. Second, the group of countries with moderate or zero growth includes old world countries and the United States.

The third group consists of countries that are experiencing a downturn in their RCA during this period: Australia, South Africa, and Chile. Australia, the worst-positioned in this comparison, has had big problems in past years due to diverse factors such as a sustained delay of the exchange rate and an overproduction of lower-quality wines. This has caused a great loss of share in the leading markets. Moreover, Chile has also suffered a delay of the exchange rate because of the great capital inflow to the country, whereas South Africa, for its part, has gone down in share in its main market, United Kingdom.

According to the exhaustive analysis of the situation of these countries, we can conclude that the sources of the RCA in the global wine trade can be grouped as follows:

- Competitive prices (due to exchange rate or high productivity)
- Successful or "fashionable" varietal wines
- Proximity to very attractive markets

- Increase of productivity derived, to a large extent, from the investment in research, development, and innovation
- Tariff agreements with other countries

In the case of Argentina, a very favorable exchange rate at the beginning of the decade, together with an emblematic varietal (Malbec), well adapted to the demand of the top markets, especially in the United States, were decisive factors in its better positioning.

Dominio del Plata Winery

Dominio del Plata winery is part of a group of modern companies that started during the last decade in Argentina and whose strategic focus tallied with the new global trends. We will show precisely through this case how this company followed these trends, managed to consolidate, and became highly competitive in order to face future challenges within this context.

Technical data

Vineyards

Owned by the company: 20 hectares

Owned by independent growers under contract: 340 hectares

Vineyards location: Salta: Cafayate—Mendoza: Luján de Cuyo, Tunuyán, Tupungato, Maipú, San Carlos

Varieties: Malbec, Cabernet Sauvignon, Torrontés, Chardonnay, Sauvignon Blanc, Merlot, Bonarda, Cabernet Franc, Petit Verdot, Syrah

Winery

Crush capacity: 4,000,000 kilos

Total Vat Capacity: 4,435,000 liters

Storage Capacity: 3,200,000 bottles

Bottling lines: 2,500 bottles per hour

Standards: ISO 22.000, SA 8000, ISO 14.001 in progress

Sales

Turnover: $10.8 million (2012)

Export brands: Anubis, Crios, Zohar, Dominio del Plata, BenMarco, Susana Balbo, Susana B., Nosotros

Export destinations: United States, United Kingdom, Canada, Brazil, Mexico, Puerto Rico, Peru, Colombia, Australia, Japan, Hong Kong, Taiwan, China, Switzerland, Germany, Belgium, Sweden, Russia, Spain, Portugal, Ireland, and other European countries

Brief History

The idea of creating Dominio del Plata was born in 1999 when Susana Balbo and Pedro Marchevsky decided to embark on a project of their own. Susana had started her career in the industry as a winemaker with many companies and then performed different duties in her family-owned winery, Balbo. It was her wish to make high-quality wines as opposed to the strategy of the family winery, which produced basic wines. For this reason, she decided to start a consultancy firm that assessed several wine companies. Then she was hired by Catena Zapata to design and lead the construction of a new winery, in which she also performed as export manager.

Pedro started his career in 1972 as technical advisor for different wine companies. One of those companies was Catena Zapata in which he worked full time beginning in 1975. His goal was to optimize production management, and he played a leading role in the transformation process of the winery's wines.

At the beginning of their own project, Susana and Pedro were faced with their first dilemma: where would they put in their efforts when they had only limited financial resources? Would they first work on production or trading channels? At first, many small companies focus on production and sell to big wineries that already have developed distribution channels and popular brands, and only marginally develop their own trading channels and brands. Susana and Pedro decided to focus on marketing and make use of all the contacts they had made through their time in the wine business.

They rented Dolium winery to develop ultra-premium wines, specifically adapted to the US and British markets. They used a small part of the grape production from their own vineyards in Agrelo, one of the best regions in Mendoza. Additionally, they had access to a group of selected growers whom they advised to produce high-quality grapes. The two of them designed a strategy based on a single premise: connection between the marketing and the technical departments.

Because high-end winemaking requires long periods to mature, Dominio del Plata needed a product that would generate immediate revenues. In 2000, the company was ready to put its first super-premium wine named Anubis on the market. Thanks to an old friendship with the Italian consultant Alberto Antonini, they were able to get into the British market. The volume of sales was small and the winery needed to increase its revenue, so they moved from the off-trade to the on-premise (bars and restaurants). This channel brings advantages because British consumers consider the wines sold in this channel better than those sold in supermarkets. Based on good value and quality, Anubis started to win consumers over. A few years later, it was sold in wine shops in the $9 to $15 price range.

In September 2001, Susana and Pedro started their own winery, and made their first wine in 2002. The investment was high for a small company. However, its expansion did not take long because the depreciation of the country's currency in 2002 increased sales three times over. For a winery that exported 95% of its production, the generated profits enabled the expansion to work.

Moreover, Chile, Australia, and Europe currencies, in relation with the US dollar, made those countries' wines lose competitiveness compared to Argentine wines.

Macroeconomic conditions benefited Dominio del Plata between 2001 and 2002, and also helped in terms of production and marketing. The wines in the ultra-premium segment were ready: BenMarco and Susana Balbo.

Selling these wines in the United States and United Kingdom was not yet possible. The wines needed more time in the barrel to meet Americans' taste and the British preferred more fruity wines. Besides, they still had to develop trading channels. Susana and Pedro got in touch with Nick Ramkowsky and Ed Lehrman, who both worked for Catena Zapata's importer and were starting their own import company: Vine Connections. This company would focus on high-priced wines from boutique wineries. They proposed that Dominio Del Plata join their efforts to give its wines high visibility in the United States that the importer in the United Kingdom could not afford because his focus was on volume and high turnover. BenMarco and Susana Balbo penetrated the US market with high prices ($20 to $25 for BenMarco and $25 to $30 for Susana Balbo).

The wines started to gain recognition. In 2002, *Wine Spectator* gave them scores of over 90 points. However, sales grew slowly and the United States was going through a recessionary period that negatively affected the demand of ultra-premium wines. At the same time, the lower segment was growing steadily.

The company began suffering the disadvantages of being highly positioned in a specific segment. Vine Connections suggested introducing Anubis into the US market and the winery decided to adapt this wine to the US taste by adding a touch of oak. This is how Críos was born: a young, fruity, and delicate wine made for consumers of the super-premium segment ($15 a bottle). This wine allowed Dominio del Plata to maintain its export volumes until sales of higher-priced wines got better.

The good performance of the strategy in the United Kingdom and United States created an impact on other markets. These two markets, apart from generating great sales and profits, opened the door to other countries, because specialized publications have global reach and are read by consumers of many different countries. These media channels are important because they set trends. Dominio del Plata obtained positive results in Canada, Switzerland, Denmark, the Netherlands, Brazil, and other countries.

Figure 3. Sales volume (thousands of cases). Source: Dominio del Plata Winery.

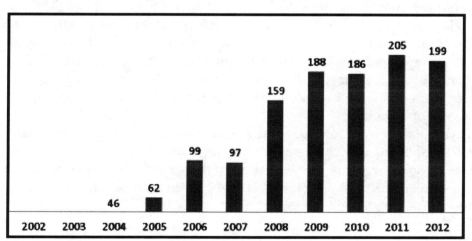

Figure 4. Annual turnover (thousands of dollars). Source: Dominio del Plata Winery.

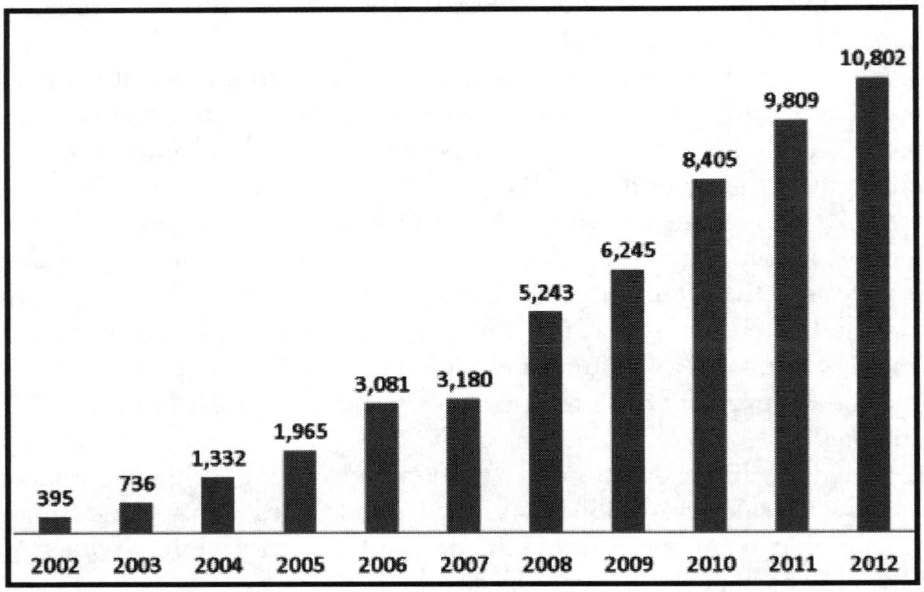

In 2005, the firm began establishing in other countries. Brazil seemed like a good market. Its geographical location and preferential tariffs of Mercosur[2] made it look like a good opportunity.

Asia was also in the winery's plans. This market needed extra efforts because consumers were not used to drinking wine; it had been considered exotic and unknown to Asian consumers. In Japan, consumers spend a lot of money, and consumption in various segments was growing fast. The Chinese market is complicated, but huge.

In the mid-2000s, growth slowed down. Tesco, one of the biggest supermarkets in the United Kingdom, made an offer to buy 70 to 100 thousand cases a year of Anubis in 2006-2007. In addition to sales, there was an opportunity to promote the brand and the winery. However, this proposal implied increasing investment in the winery's working capital. Sales volume looked attractive, but supermarkets ask for special prices when dealing with large volumes so the winery would operate on tight margins. Dominio del Plata's shareholders were willing to take risks, but they had to think about this opportunity carefully and analyze it in depth. US importers also needed to increase wine volume in the premium segment. They ran into some difficulties accessing different distribution channels because some consumers asked for complete product portfolios. Additionally, logistic costs were high and the company needed greater volumes to generate economies of scale.

In 2010, Pedro Marchevsky sold his shares to an investment group, with Susana Balbo holding 50% of them. This change was associated with a new investment plan that allowed picking up the rate of growth in sales. At the same time, in this new stage, the company's management areas were reinforced, and Susana's children, both having a solid professional training, joined the firm.

THE COMPANY'S FIGURES

In 2012, sales amounted to over $10 million, showing the firm's ability to place itself among the 25 biggest export companies of the Argentine wine industry, competing against companies with a long-standing reputation, some of them major multinationals.

Results are positive for the company. It has reached a period of maturity in the business and boasts a solid financial position and a low debt level.

Since 2009, the development of sales volume (thousands of cases) is at a standstill (see Figure 3) and there is a strong growth in turnover (see Figure 4). The reason for this is the price increase policy on some product lines and a change of portfolio based on the brand's good reputation. Between 2009 and 2012, the average price went from $33.20 per case to $54.30 (see Figure 5).

Figure 5. Average sales price ($/case). Source: Dominio del Plata

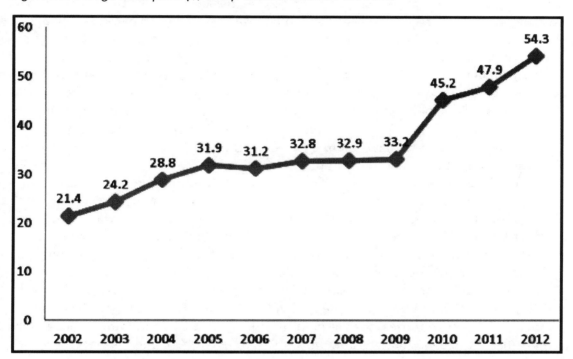

Markets

In 2012, the company operated in 21 international markets and in the domestic market, though its presence was still small there. In the long term a growth in the number of countries can be seen up to 2011. It then decreases in 2012 due to the clear introduction of a market-focused policy in search of global efficiency in the business.

The most important market for the company is the United States with a total share of 60%, followed by Canada, Brazil, and the United Kingdom. These four markets represent 86% of the company's international turnover and are identified as new-consuming countries (see Table 1).

Table 1. Destination of Exports ($ thousands).

REGION	Turnover 2007 (USD thousands)	Turnover 2012 (USD thousands)	CAGR 2007/2012 (%)	Growth in 5 years (USD thousands)
North America	1,705	7,715	35.2	6,010
Latin America	530	1,227	18.3	697
Europe	924	1,105	3.6	181
Asia	21	755	104.3	734
TOTAL	3,180	10,802	27.7	7,621

Following international trends, the winery started in 2009 to research and develop markets of long-term attractiveness such as some European and Asian markets that import high-price products. The biggest examples are Hong Kong, with its significant growth, and Switzerland, with a great potential to seek wine in high-price ranges.

An analysis by region shows the strategy. North America is the main market, presenting a growth above the global average due to Canada's boost in recent years. Latin America grew less than the average, with a strong focus on Brazil, which grew at rate of 26% although the rest of the region had substantially lower rates. In terms of Europe, the company decided to disinvest in this region, though it focused on some markets. For example, Switzerland grew at annual rate of 33% and the rest of European countries had lower or even negative rates. In the case of the United Kingdom, the fourth most-important market, the firm focused on high-price ranges, changing the strategy with distributors. Last, the growth in Asia has been outstanding, showing that a new business approach toward the more attractive regions in the world is successful at the moment.

The company's focus on these markets is one of the factors that contributed to raising the average price of sales, and, therefore, the global profitability equation.

Furthermore, though still small in relation to the total, there are five markets with significant growth in terms of value and volume: Hong Kong, China, and Thailand among the Asian countries; Switzerland in Europe; and Chile in Latin America (see Figure 6). In 2012 these markets amounted to $900,000 (8.3% of international turnover), but showed a growth rate above the global average, and, except for China, all of them have a higher purchasing average than the general average.

Figure 6. Growth by market

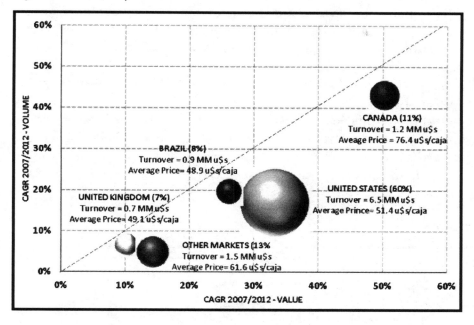

PRODUCT PORTFOLIO

Dominio del Plata has a rather limited product portfolio, which is in accordance with the type of companies that have more control over their costs. In spite of having a restricted range of products, the winery boasts several brands that meet the demands of specific markets.

Average sales prices go from $32 per case, classified as super-premium category, to the firm's icon wine (Nosotros), which has an average price of almost $600 per case. The portfolio can be divided into three big groups: up to $40 per case, between $40 and $60, and more than $60 (see Figure 7).

Figure 7. Portfolio prices ($/case).

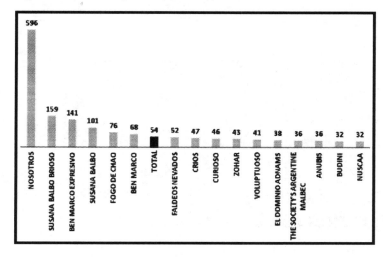

The business-refocusing policy has been marked not only by a change in markets but also in products. A company of such magnitude can be successful only in the relatively high price ranges, and as a result, it has to sell its wines to high-end consumers. This has been achieved thanks to a good brand positioning in consolidated markets and the search for countries that import at higher average prices.

The annual average growth of sales volume since 2007 to 2012 has been 15.5% and the average price grew 10.6%.

The Críos brand represents 46% of turnover and its growth has been greater in value than in volume. It can be clearly seen in Figure 8 that the brands BenMarco and Susana Balbo experienced the greatest growth, because those wines are part of the highest profit categories. On the other end, the lowest-priced wines are showing a growth rate below average.

Figure 8. Growth by brand.

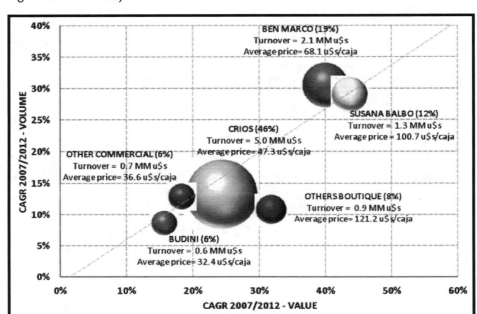

Table 2. Changes in prices (in cases).

Prices	Volume 2007	Share 2007 (%)	Volume 2012	Share 2012 (%)	CAGR 2007/2012 (%)
More than USD60/case	12,116	12.5	47,841	24.0	31.6
Between USD 40 and 60/case	60,819	62.7	111,739	56.1	12.9
Below USD40/case)	23,258	24.0	35,743	18.0	9,0
TOTAL	**97,024**	**100.0**	**199,112**	**100.0**	**15.5**
Growth in average price					**10.6**

Dominio del Plata's competitive advantages

As was said before, Dominio del Plata winery is a clear example of a modern company that has been able to grow successfully by basing its management on the five trends that have changed the global wine market. The following section explains how the winery performed in each of these trends and how it created and developed competitive edges that made it stand out from the average wine producer.

Greater global market share of wines with a more modern style

Since 2002 international penetration of Argentine wine has been based on value wines, reds, and Malbec. Dominio del Plata has focused on these same goals.

From its start the winery has concentrated on making a modern style of wine. The clearest example is Críos, a wine that targets young people of different countries and recognizes the worth of young, expressive, and value wines. It is precisely for this attribute that the winery has put in a great deal of effort. Since 2004, it has received very good scores in the main international magazines and publications for its quality. Additionally, wine critics have praised Críos as "best value" several times, and some consider its Malbec and Torrontés the epitome of Argentine modern wines.

The other varietal wine that makes the competitive difference is Torrontés. Dominio del Plata concentrates almost 14% of exports on this product, which gives an excellent competitive edge for Torrontés because it is a highly dynamic wine, especially considered so in the United States.

The wine's quality and good price give a competitive edge to those who market it and extra satisfaction to those who consume it. To achieve this, the company carries out blind tastings to confirm that the product is able to compete against other wines of the same quality but are 30% more expensive.

In a characterization of the wines consumed in the Unites States, the portfolio of Dominio del Plata fits perfectly, and it is this market where the company directed its product policy.

Growth of consumption in the highest price ranges

The strategy of the company and its reason for success can be clearly seen. Although the annual rate of world consumption in the range where the winery operates went up 2.8%, Dominio del Plata's sales grew 15.5%, taking advantage of the trend with products adapted to these markets.

In the highest-price range, world consumption had an annual growth of 3.8%, and the winery's average rate increased 18.5%, precisely in the range where it sells the most. Finally, the lowest range where the firm operates has shown an increment of 9% whereas world consumption grew 1.4%.

Expansion of nontraditional wine retail chains

The expansion of consumption and import to new countries, and the development of new trading channels, required special strategies for companies to take advantage of the new trends and avoid the threat of the increased bargaining power of retailers. In the five most important markets for Argentina, Dominio del Plata concentrates almost

87% of its efforts, quite superior to the 61% of the total exports of Argentine bottle wines. Likewise, in the main Argentine market (United States), Dominio del Plata's share is 60%, whereas for all exports the total is 28%.

Beyond a market strategy, the company boasts a special feature that allows it to work in line with the channel and avoid a permanent struggle for commissions, which spoils commercial performances. Susana Balbo herself visits every market, which allows her to design wine styles. It also helps to easily adapt wines to the change in consumption trends and to make decisions in advance that can reach the consumer as soon as the change is established.

Communication of the distinctive attributes of wines and regions

The adaptation to markets is a consequence of the way the company was promoted. The marketing strategy is based mainly on making the product known through good scores and reviews by the specialized media.

Direct promotion in different occasions has also worked, for example, showing in specialized fairs and those venues intended for consumers, tastings, and participation in prestigious contests, among others. This awakens consumers' curiosity about tasting a product that they have heard of in the specialized media.

In some markets, as is the case in the United States and Canada, the opinion of the specialized media is decisive for business success. As mentioned previously, there is a small group of publications whose conclusions have international reach, for instance, *Wine Spectator, Wine Advocate,* and *Decanter.* In all these publications, Dominio del Plata enjoys an excellent reputation.

In the last few years, the active participation of the winery owner as president of Wines of Argentina[3] has attracted the attention of the global specialized media and consequently has benefited the image of her wines.

Development of competitive advantages by companies, regions, and wine-producing countries

From the point of view of the Argentine economy, Dominio del Plata has enjoyed the same opportunities as it did during the first decade of the new century: a depreciated currency that has benefited exports through its impact on the price-quality relationship. Furthermore, Malbec's mark on the international scene generated a lot of press and created new consumers of Argentine wine.

Except for established wine brands, there is no stopping innovation in this industry; once introduced in the market, innovations are inevitably imitated if they result in success. The best strategy is to create entry barriers based on constant innovation and redesign the product and the style every one to two years. It also helps to keep the core business active by launching novelties, that is, to take seriously that leading is reinventing over and over and if possible, before competitors do so. In this sense, specialized critics have pointed out this attribute as one of the Dominio del Plata's strongest.

Moreover, the company has been working for years on a productivity program: applying precision viticulture techniques and keeping a strict cost control that allows it to face successfully a new stage in Argentine viticulture in which the exchange rate will not be the main tool to maintaining the right price-quality relationship.

Dominio del Plata's key points to achieve growth and consolidation

- Produce wines that adapt well to market trends and stay in a price range with high profitability.
- Target young consumers with high purchasing power, which contributes to long-term soundness.
- The market share protection policy is based on a permanent presence at promotional occasions (specialized fairs, contests, and attention to specialized media).
- Maintain a high price-quality relationship by comparing its product with wines of the same quality which are more expensive, and maintain strict cost control.

QUESTIONS TO THE READER

- Do you believe the company will maintain its competitive level with this strategy if it grows in size?
- Do you think that the company's dependency on its founder becomes a weakness and that it needs to be changed?

AUTHOR'S CONSIDERATIONS

Many new countries have grown considerably from very low wine consumption to levels averaging today similar to several traditional wine-drinking countries. However, wine consumers in these countries have not shown the same taste preferences as traditional wine-drinking countries, which have imposed changes in the kinds of wine produced. So the most dynamic wineries have adapted to new kinds of tastes and marketing. This was positive, to a large extent, for producers from new wine-producing countries in the market.

Many of these new wine-consuming countries have looked abroad for supply and they found a series of new providers ready to do business. New world wine-producing countries appeared on the scene and gained ground through exporting. They generated a market expanded beyond the traditional limits of Europe. In just a couple of decades, the international wine trade has almost trebled its size, and exports are the focus in the strategy of most wine companies of the world in search of the expansion that their domestic markets fail to provide.

New world countries do business more freely than European countries, which are more strictly controlled, and quickly adapted products to new consumer needs, based mainly on more efficient productions and scales. This way, they started out on a stage marked by higher productivity than traditional wine producers.

After some time, traditional wine-producing countries also exhibited new behavior patterns and searched for higher productivity. The coexistence of two viticultures, to an extent, has begun: one more traditional and the other more modern, the latter with a significant orientation to the international trade. What has happened in Spain and, more recently, France are clear examples of this phenomenon. These countries are developing new regions that are having international success with modern production and marketing systems similar to those in the new world.

Greater competitive rivalry of wineries in the global market created an intensive drop in profit margins. In the face of this, a search for scale to remain or grow in the market became the most-used strategy. In this way, companies like Constellation, Foster's, Concha y Toro and Gallo started to grow in the global market on the basis of aggressive pricing policy and better levels of productivity. Expansion, merger, alliances, and other business behaviors also were found in the wine market. Additionally, there was a need for stronger bargaining power because of the growth of retail chains. The launch of global brands was a natural process that took place with great intensity.

In terms of demand, in the 1980s and before, the presence of traditional food and beverage retail chains was a very small part of the wine market. Due to the attraction of the business, the trade was developed little by little and today has become the world's leading wine retail channel. The consequence has been a huge increase in bargaining power, which led to pressure to drop profit margins. The positive side of the development of the world wine market has been higher visibility of the product, which is no longer aimed just at expert consumers, but also to a more general public.

New wine-producing countries and a great number of newly created companies and brands have led to the need to create distinctive attributes to keep market share. Thousands of wine brands require a large promotional budget to stimulate sales to consumers, who generally opt for a small group of popular brands or who are sometimes driven by discounts. Additionally, experts and critics review and rate wines, which helps to create a path to success or failure of many brands. Finally, promotional organizations developed very aggressive policies worldwide in order to consolidate country brands.

The direct consequence of this dynamic business sector is the appearance and fast deterioration of strategic windows for wineries to move toward in search of expanding their business. There is also increasing competitive rivalry and a very short space of time in which margins can be maintained. This also takes place in a context of great macroeconomic volatilities that have generated strong needs for strategic plans and capital.

A thorough review of these developments in the world wine market seems to suggest that the success or individual expansion of companies, regions, or countries has been closely related to what we may call modern trends or breakdown of traditional trends.

The most important trend arose from the demand by emerging countries and young generations and as a reply from producers, mainly those of the new world, who gave the global market a greater share of wines with more modern styles.

In the past few years, the wine sector also has observed a clear appearance of new competitive behaviors and communication styles from private companies and public organizations. The first one led to a pursuit of competitive advantages and the second to a communication of attributes appreciated by consumers.

Between supply and demand, there are retail and distribution channels, as in any market. And here, there appeared a strong trend toward an expansion of nontraditional retail chains.

As a result of the heightened competitive rivalry and constant search for more profitable spaces, an increasing share of the highest price ranges was observed in the world wine market during the last few years.

DOMINIO DEL PLATA WINERY: DECISIONS FOR THE FUTURE

Some initiatives could quickly be developed by the winery:

- Design a business model in which the first stage develops the market and once consolidated, incorporates fixed assets.

- Participate in Endeavor Foundation[4], which enables the acquisition of the formulation of a business plan and the design of a balanced scorecard.

- Open and expand markets with the help of the excellent reviews achieved. In few years, the company went from 12 markets to 25. Probably in the future this growth will be more selective.

- Establish quality policies and the ISO 22.000 standard dealing with food safety because this practice is well considered in the world market. Maintain high innovation standards. The company's managers have attended the most important technical conferences in the world (especially in the United States and Australia) for more than 20 years. Additionally, Susana Balbo's children studied at enology and business universities with excellent reputations.

- Permanently invest in knowledge of markets through an annual program of trips that in the past ranged from 120 to 160 days a year. This enables those in charge of the winery to get to know markets' level of development and technologies.

- Plan and project sales that allow generating incentives for every goal achieved.

- Provide strong support for the winery's sales force in the entire world.

ENDNOTES

1. Balassa, Bela (1965), "Trade Liberalization and Revealed Comparative Advantage," The Manchester School, 33, pp. 99-123.
2. Mercosur (Spanish: Mercado Común del Sur) is an economic and political agreement among Argentina, Brazil, Paraguay, Uruguay, and Venezuela; with Bolivia becoming an accessing member on 7 December 2012 to be ratified by the Member State's legislatures. It was established in 1991 by the Treaty of Asunción, which was later amended and updated by the 1994 Treaty of Ouro Preto. Its purpose is to promote free trade and the fluid movement of goods, people, and currency.
3. Wines of Argentina is the Argentinean wineries´ association that is in charge of promoting the Argentine wines worldwide.
4. Endeavor Foundation is a global organization whose mission is to lead the global movement to catalyze long-term economic growth by selecting, mentoring and accelerating the best high impact entrepreneurs around the world.

CASE 9

The Great Cork Debate 2012

CORK STAGES A COMEBACK

Tom Atkin, Sonoma State University
Duane Dove, Sonoma State University

SUMMARY

The product development dilemma presented here boils down to a choice between the technical superiority of one closure (screw cap) versus the greater consumer acceptance of natural cork. There is still a risk of tainted wine due to corks, but the cork industry has substantially reduced the defect rate over the past decade. Readers are immersed in the decision process at Rodney Strong Vineyards, whether to use natural corks or metal screw caps on their wines.

Analytical tools recommended include Total Cost Analysis, the Weighted Point System for evaluating suppliers, and Cost of Quality. The case is very appropriate for advanced undergraduate and MBA level classes. The case is designed to be taught in one hour of class time with one hour of outside preparation by students.

INTRODUCTION

Closures are the hot topic this year as consolidation of producers has raised the bar on quality and led to greater price competition. John Leyden, the Vice President of Packaging and Distribution at Rodney Strong Vineyards, must decide whether to stick with natural corks, switch over to screw caps, or use one of the new alternatives. He has wrestled with this issue before and he mentally reviewed his information from previous years. Historically, there had been a big issue with cork taint—a widespread quality problem that ruins a significant percentage of wine. To their credit, cork suppliers have made huge progress toward reducing the incidence of the taint. This cork taint gives the wine a moldy, musty aroma and can alienate customers, leading to lost sales.

The closure decision is not clear-cut. On the one hand, screw caps and synthetic closures possess some superior performance characteristics and cost advantages over natural cork. From a quality viewpoint, screw caps are a good solution because they offer a durable, long-lasting seal that will not produce taint. The problem with changing to more effective closures is that many wine consumers love natural corks. Consumers have rejected screw caps in the past because cork is perceived as a high quality closure while screw caps are associated with cheap jug wines.

The Rodney Strong Vineyards

Rodney Strong Vineyards was the 20th largest wine company in the United States in 2012 (Penn, 2012). With its headquarters and winery in Sonoma County, California, sales at Rodney Strong were about 800,000 cases per year (Dugan, 2012) and revenues were between $50 million and $100 million (ZoomInfo, 2012). The winery was originally built by Rodney Strong in 1969 and was technologically a state-of-the art facility at the time it was constructed. Tom Klein purchased the winery in 1989, when sales were $3 million per year. He has been the Chairman and CEO since 1989. He established a lofty goal for the company. "I would like to be perceived as the finest super-premium winery in Sonoma County," he informed the *Wine Spectator* (Marcus, 2001). "We have the land, the people, the focus, and the commitment."

Rodney Strong wines compete at a variety of price points. Its Sonoma County brand varietals sell for $15 to $18 per bottle, while vineyard designated wines such as Alexander's Crown and Rockaway are priced at $75.

The Cork Taint Problem

John remembered the old days all too well. In the past, industry estimates of the percentage of cork tainted wine ranged from 2% to 10% of all bottles sold (Chehalem, 2004). The main culprit was a compound known as 2,4,6–Trichloranisole, or TCA, which can be found in natural cork.

TCA is one of the strongest aromatic substances in the world. High levels cause wine to smell like moldy old newspapers. Lower levels, with only a few parts of TCA per million parts of wine, can strip a wine of its fruitiness and flavor. These off flavors associated with the use of cork alter the character of the wine from what the winemaker had originally intended.

Cork taint is a serious economic problem for wine makers because it ruins a substantial percentage of wine. In 1997 the consensus placed the incidence of cork taint at least above 5% according to Murray and Lockshin (1997). So prevalent was the problem of faulty corks that some commentators believe that cork problems cost the global wine industry as much as $10 billion per year (Fuller 1995). "It is Russian Roulette," John said, referring to the odds of buying tainted corks back then (Leyden, 2004).

How does the cork get contaminated? The original contamination probably occurs in the forest when freshly cut slabs of cork bark are cured on the ground. Batches of cork planks are then boiled in large tanks at processing plants to prepare them for grading and punching. This boiling may actually spread the contamination from batch to batch if the water is not changed. If the cork has been contaminated in the forest or during production, it can ruin the wine that it comes into contact with. Natural cork isn't the only source of taint, however. TCA has been found in winery equipment, oak barrels, building materials, and even winery air conditioning systems.

Initially enjoying a virtual monopoly, cork producers denied the problem existed and dismissed the problem as a cost of doing business (Patterson, 2010). The introduction of synthetic corks and screw caps that eliminated the cork taint problem changed the game. The winery would probably even save money as well as better protect the quality of the wine with these types of closures. Although they were slow to respond to the problem, the cork industry has greatly improved its quality over the last twenty years.

REDUCING TCA CONTAMINATION

Reducing the incidence of TCA contamination has been a long and expensive process. For John Leyden, the effort started many years ago: "I have been going to Portugal since 1992. Conditions were deplorable then compared to now. I am not sure they ever changed the water during the boiling process. I went back to Portugal in 1996 and was told they change the water once per week. We asked what day they changed the water."

"Monday," they replied.

"Give us corks boiled on Monday," John requested.

Since then, cork producers have made heavy investments to improve the quality of the corks they sell in the U.S. The main supplier at Rodney Strong, M. A. Silva, opened a new production plant in 2004 in order to implement new processes that reduce the level of TCA in cork. The new plant cost about $3.5 million and featured major new technology to reduce taint.

At the new facility, cork planks are stacked on a concrete slab for drying instead of being piled on the ground. Traditionally, the cork planks were stacked to dry on bare earth in the open air for about 6 months, which allowed them to be contaminated by fungi in the dirt. The use of concrete slabs prevents contact with the soil. Cork planks are then carried into the plant on stainless steel pallets.

The centerpiece of the plant was a new type of boiling system called the Dynavox Pressurized Boiling System (M.A. Silva, 2012). The cork planks were pressure boiled for about one hour in a closed tank and the water was continuously cleaned to remove contaminants. This eliminated the possibility of one load of cork planks contaminating another load. Stainless steel pallets were again used to move and store the planks after boiling, also reducing the chance of contamination. The results of tests performed by M. A. Silva indicate that the new boiling process has markedly reduced the incidence of TCA.

The finished corks are subsequently disinfected and cleaned using the Maszone washing system. A combination of ozone and hydrogen peroxide is used to wash the corks. Average TCA levels are now found to be below the threshold of human sensory capabilities.

Such large capital expenditures have led to a consolidation and better quality control in the industry. The cork industry in Portugal has moved from a fragmented, cottage industry with 500 producers to a vertically integrated industry where 10 companies produce 70% of the world's cork closures (Dugan, 2012). Producers have used a combination of research, quality control and investment to reduce the occurrence of taint. A steady reduction in TCA levels over the last nine years has resulted in TCA levels that are 82% lower (Cork Quality Council, 2012). Only 3% of incoming lots were considered unacceptable.

Have these efforts eliminated TCA completely? Almost. Complete absence cannot be guaranteed, but the occurrence of tainted corks reaching wine producers is now about 1% (Arora, 2012). Leyden has found that a new technical cork, the MicroAgglo, is not showing any TCA at all (Leyden, 2012). Christian Butzke of Purdue University has declared that "TCA is no longer a major problem for the American wine industry" (Butzke, 2009).

Natural Cork and Alternatives—Competitive Analysis

The purpose of any wine closure is to prevent oxidation and leakage of the wine. Oxidation is one of the main causes of spoilage of wine, and closures prevent oxidation by providing a seal that allows a minimal amount of air into the bottle. In Roman times, a layer of olive oil was floated on top of the wine to protect it. Natural cork has been the closure of choice for wine since the 1600s, when Dom Perignon, a French monk, began putting cork stoppers into sparkling wine bottles. The first cork factory was opened around 1750 in Spain.

About 18 billion wine closures are produced annually, of which slightly less than 13 billion are made from natural cork (Quackenbush, 2010). The global cork industry has been growing at a rate of 8% to 9% for the last two years (Dugan, 2012). Despite this recent improvement, a substantial loss of market share has occurred. Cork closures, including both natural and technical cork, have fallen from about 90% of all wine closure sales in 2003 (McKenna, 2003) to their current market share of 69% (Quackenbush, 2010). The most common types of closures and their current worldwide market shares are listed below:

> **Natural Cork:** Natural cork, which is harvested from the bark of the cork oak, is the most popular closure for wine bottles. Whole corks are punched from treated bark and graded on their appearance. Natural cork now claims a 28% market share worldwide (Aeppel, 2010).
>
> **Technical Cork:** Technical corks are made from natural cork materials that have been reworked in some way. One popular type is the twin top. The body of the closure is made from ground-up pieces that are left over from the making of natural corks. The top and bottom of the closure consists of natural cork discs to provide a high quality barrier. Technical cork holds a 41% share (Aeppel, 2010).
>
> **Synthetic Corks:** Synthetic closures accounted for about 9% of sales. Synthetic corks are made from food grade thermoplastic elastomeric materials. These plastic corks function in a fashion similar to natural corks and are available in a variety of colors. These represent 20% of the market (Aeppel, 2010).

Screw Caps: The remaining 11% of wine bottles are sealed with screw caps made from aluminum, with a liner specifically designed for wine. The screw cap is removed by twisting it counterclockwise. Screw caps have been used most often on lower-priced wines, while the closure of choice for expensive wines has typically been natural cork.

Zork: The Zork is a soft re-sealable wine closure invented in Australia. It can be removed by hand but still makes a "pop" sound when opened. About 2% of North American wineries use the Zork (Phillips, 2011) but sales figures are unavailable.

Glass (Vino-Seal): This is an elegant glass stopper that has a plastic, non-reactive O-ring that provides an airtight seal for the wine. About 4% of North American wineries use Vino-seal (Phillips, 2011). Actual sales figures are unavailable.

QUALITY CONTROL AT RODNEY STRONG

In 2004, John knew that the TCA problem had not been solved completely. Obviously, each winery had to protect itself by instituting some sort of inbound inspection and quality assurance program. "The more you can control right from the beginning, the better it will be at the end" (Leyden, 2004).

"Here is how quality testing works at Rodney Strong. For each lot of 500,000 corks, we ask for a pre-purchase sample of 250. We visually inspect 100 of them. We also soak 150 of them individually in small jars containing a small amount of neutral white wine. They soak for 24 hours and we then perform a blind tasting with staff members. The supplier is also invited to participate, but not to vote. If less than 2% show signs of taint, the lot is accepted. If the taint level is above 2%, the lot is not considered for purchase. A similar testing process takes place when the shipment actually arrives. This has worked pretty well and constitutes a big improvement over the old days when the taint level was from 4% to 8%."

Of course there is a cost for these efforts. Simpson and Veitch (1993) estimated the cost of sensory appraisal of 1,000,000 corks to be $1,600 to $3,200 (or 2–3 cents per case). Alternatively, a local laboratory can perform the sensory evaluation for $35 per lot. It is typical to pull a sample from every lot of 10,000 corks, so this amounts to about 4 cents per case.

COST ANALYSIS

There are several grades of natural cork, based primarily on appearance, and the prices vary according to the grade level (Cork Quality Council, 2004). In 2012, John expected to pay about $400 per thousand for an acceptable natural cork, although lower cost corks are available. Capsules can add from 4 to 30 cents to the cost per bottle.

In order to save money, many wineries have turned to technical corks. A technical cork is essentially a cylinder of ground-up cork with a disk of natural cork at each end. It is the least expensive option, but it has the same taint problem as natural cork.

Acceptable technical corks cost about $130 per thousand. These have a very consistent shape and few surface defects. Furthermore, technical corks also allow the cork makers to use material that may have been thrown away previously. The new, cleaner Micro-Agglo technical corks run about $180 per thousand due to more extensive processing.

Synthetic corks are basically made out of plastic. One type has an inner core that is manufactured from Low Density Polyethylene (LDPE) foam designed to offer the elasticity of a natural cork and a long-term seal. There is rarely any taint with synthetic corks but sometimes they give a bit of a plastic taste. They have been known to be somewhat difficult to pull out of the bottle. They will not break, however, and they are guaranteed not to crumble, as sometimes happens with natural cork (Wilson and Lockshin, 2003).

Suitable synthetic closures can be obtained for about $120/M each. Suppliers assert that consumers are accustomed to synthetic closures and that customer reaction is now one of indifference; many do not even seem to notice (Pitcher, 1999). Synthetics work well for wines consumed within twelve months of bottling. "But how do you know that the wine will get sold and consumed within twelve months?" John asked.

An alternative that has recently received greater attention is the screw cap. It is constructed of aluminum and it has an inside liner where the closure contacts the bottle rim. Testing has been very positive. The Aussies have accomplished some long-term testing that shows the screw cap preserves the quality of the wine better than either synthetic or natural cork. The Australian Wine Research Institute (AWRI) results show that, after three years in the bottle, screw caps provide the best protection against oxidation and there is no TCA taint. The next best performer was the synthetic cork (Godden, 2002). Still, John felt that, "The jury is still out on wine requiring several years of bottle aging."

The unit price for screw caps is about $160/M, so they cost less than natural cork but more than synthetics and technical corks. There are some additional production costs, however. The Production Department estimated that it would cost about $90,000 to purchase the capital equipment needed to utilize screw caps on the filling line (Mironicki, 2012). That capital expenditure could be avoided by using a contract packer or the mobile bottling line for screw caps. The bottling fee at a contract packer was about $.20 per bottle or $2.40 per case. There was no additional expense for screw cap compatible bottles and they are readily available. The leading screw cap product is the Stelvin cap, manufactured by Pechiney Corporation of France, with cap manufacturing facilities in nearby Napa County. While not widely employed in the U. S., screw caps are very popular in Britain and Switzerland. Consumer resistance to the screw cap has been strong in the United States for wines priced over $10. "The biggest thing against the screw cap is consumer perception," John said. John used the following spreadsheet to perform a Total Cost Analysis evaluation (Exhibit 1).

Exhibit 1.

Exhibit 1	Total Cost Analysis Model				
Suppliers:	**Supplier A**	**Supplier B**	**Supplier C**	**Supplier D**	**Supplier E**
	Natural	Natural	Technical	Synthetic	Screw
	Cork	Cork	Cork	Cork	Cap
Price per 1000					
Other Costs (per 1000)					
Capsule					
Transportation/Receiving					
Inspection/Quality Assurance					
Accounts Payable					
Capital Equipment Investment					
Total per 1000 (Price + Other Costs)					

MARKETING CONSIDERATIONS

The wine industry is unique. People who work in the industry frequently speak of their passion for wine making. The word "romance" is likely heard more often in this industry than any other. Consumers are caught up in the mystique of wine. The customers have a great fondness for the ambience and sensuality provided by the cork. The cork is a major essence of the wine experience. The ritual of opening the bottle and hearing the cork pop is very dear to customers. John Leyden summarized it this way, "It's like the Japanese tea service. People just love the ceremony."

In 2003, *Wine Business Monthly* found that a majority of wineries were using natural corks, even though industry insiders gave natural corks less than favorable ratings on price and risk of cork taint. Natural cork scored extremely well on consumer acceptance and proper aging of the wine. Ratings of synthetic closures and screw caps received low marks on consumer acceptance (Wine Business Monthly, 2003). The tension between closure performance and consumer acceptance was shown by the fact that screw caps received the highest marks when it came to wine protection attributes, but natural cork was far and away the leader in consumer acceptance.

The impact that consumer acceptance has on winery decisions was confirmed by research of Atkin and Garcia (2004). When wineries were asked to rank the issues that prevented them from using screw caps, the most frequent answer was consumer reluctance to accept screw caps. Wineries listed uncertainty about product quality and cost of equipment as the secondary reasons for not using screw caps

Fast forward to 2011. According to *Wine Business Monthly,* natural cork still remains by far the most popular closure, but there is an increasing perception in the industry that are accepting screw caps. Over 75% of wineries reported using at least some natural corks, while 34% use screw caps, up from 5% in 2004 (Phillips, 2011). Figures add up to over 100% because many wineries use more than one type of closure.

Others in the wine industry echoed Leyden's opinion about the romance of the cork. Here is what John Souter, Sales and Marketing Manager at Casella Estate Wines, had to say: "Screw caps for wines resold quickly would be ideal: however, in my opinion, the consumer still enjoys the experience of opening a bottle of wine with a corkscrew in the traditional way. I think the investment in the education process to convince consumers their wines are far better in screw caps would be more than my budget could afford."

COMPETITIVE ASSESSMENT

For the time being, most wineries have elected to stay with natural cork. An industry poll by *Wine Business Monthly* in 2011 found that the vast majority of wineries (78 percent) utilized natural cork (Phillips, 2011). As stated earlier, natural cork accounted for 90% of all closures employed. The popularity of technical corks has held steady, with about 30 percent of wineries applying technical cork. A smaller proportion of wineries are using synthetic closures, but their usage is concentrated in larger wineries and brands so they still represent a sizeable market share. Screw caps are used at 34% of wineries and miscellaneous closure like Zork and glass are used at about 6% (the numbers add up to more than 100 percent because many wineries use more than one type of closure).

Bonny Doon and Plumpjack are two wineries that have bottled some excellent wines under screw caps. Other wineries preferring screw caps are Fetzer, which used them on wines exported to Europe, Sonoma Cutrer on top-of–the-line Chardonnay, and Murphy-Goode on the line of wines called Tin Roof (Prial, 2003). Clos du Bois announced a change over to synthetic closures in 2001 on the bulk of their Sonoma County Classic wines. They have not switched to 100% synthetics, however.

On the international scene, Tesco, the biggest wine retailer in the U.K., has had almost no customer resistance to the introduction of large numbers of screw caps to its shelves. The chain has been selling up to a million bottles of high quality screw cap wines per week (Joseph, 2003).

CONCLUSION

"Pop! It's a sound every wine lover knows—that of a cork being pulled from a bottle of wine. But more than that, it is the music of wine itself, an echo that evokes a world of history and culture and a pleasure that touches all our senses. Some may argue that twist-offs help to demystify wine, but wine is not a commodity in the manner of mineral water or milk. Wine represents civilization; reducing it to the level of mundane, everyday beverages and condiments with twist-offs erodes its core, its very essence" (Suckling, 2005).

Thus spoke senior editor James Suckling of *Wine Spectator* in the March 31, 2005 issue devoted to the "Great Cork Debate." In Suckling's statement one finds the passion that forms consumer resistance to switch from natural cork, a flawed historical solution to the preservation of wine, to a modern reliable solution, the twist-off screw cap. While the screw cap solves a costly quality problem, it is vehemently resisted by legions of wine aficionados.

The rational side of the debate is well represented by another senior editor at *Wine Spectator,* James Laube "For wine drinkers, faulty corks lead to frustration and annoyance far too often. A bad cork is more than just a spoiled wine. It is hard-earned money down the drain."

Until recently, only natural cork had been used for all Rodney Strong wines since its founding. A new production line has the ability to apply screw caps, however. Consumer surveys still show that the customers strongly prefer natural corks. Customers have reported that screw caps cheapen the image of the wine, although they are becoming increasingly acceptable. John summed it up this way as he reviewed the current situation: "It is a perception situation. People associate the natural cork with quality. Unfortunately, sometimes it is tainted. When cork is clean, it is our number one choice. Our number one concern is to protect the wine and deliver to the consumer as the winemaker intended."

Questions and Teaching Suggestions

John Leyden presents the goal of the Rodney Strong Vineyards in the last paragraph of the case: "To deliver the wine to the consumer as the winemaker intended." Students should read the textbook chapter on Quality Management, Product Development, or Supply Chain Management prior to discussing the case, and prepare responses to the following:

1. Identify the customer requirements for the product. What features define quality in the wine business?
2. What are the tradeoffs involved in the closure decision?
3. What are the quality-related costs caused by cork taint?
4. Which product development and/or quality management techniques can be used to assess this situation?

Author's Perspective

1. Identify the customer requirements for the product. What features define quality in the wine business?

   This is where the voice of the customer becomes apparent. Characteristics of the wine itself include alcohol content, flavor, aroma, complexity, and appearance. Price is certainly a factor. The actual product includes the wine, bottle, label, and closure. Things like the ritual of opening the bottle, swirling the wine in the glass, and the story behind the wine are part of the product bundle.

2. What are the tradeoffs involved in the closure decision?

   The basic tradeoff in the cork issue is the risk of tainted wine versus consumer resistance to the use of screw caps and synthetic closures. Synthetic closures and screw caps provide a higher level of protection from taint but they are associated in the mind of the consumer with poor quality, no doubt the result of these types of closures having being used on the cheapest brands of wine for decades. They do not provide the same romance and sensory appeal that natural cork does. Screw caps and synthetic closures are less expensive than natural cork.

A complete list of advantages and disadvantages of each type of closure (from a student assignment) appears in the Appendix as Exhibit 6 (Golden, 2012).

3. What are the quality-related costs caused by cork taint in wine?

Cost of Quality is a system developed to assess all the costs associated with defective products. Exhibit 3 shows an itemized list of total quality costs of cork-related defects presented in the Cork Sensory Quality Control Manual developed by Butzke and Suprenant (1997).

As Exhibit 3 suggests, the costs of poor quality can be very high. First, there is the cost of inspecting incoming corks. Extra inventory of corks has to be maintained in order to have coverage in case lots are rejected. Once a tainted bottle reaches the consumer, it really becomes expensive. A refund has to be given to the customer and this credit has to be tracked back up the distribution system from retailer to distributor to winery.

The most difficult cost to assess is the damage to customer loyalty. Some customers will be happy with a replacement bottle, but others may just think that the chosen brand simply tastes bad. In the worst-case scenario, the winery will lose a customer. Wineries spend a large portion of their budget on marketing in order to create a customer. Each time a customer is lost, that money has to be spent again to create a new one.

4. Which product development and/or quality management techniques can be used to assess this situation?

The winery can attempt to reduce the occurrence of cork taint by working with the suppliers. The QC procedures in the case are methods to push suppliers to reduce TCA contamination in corks. Strict specifications were developed to insure acceptable levels of TCA and establish criteria for rejecting bad lots of cork. Supplier Certification can be used to assure that the supplier uses specific quality techniques during manufacturing. Specifications can also address harvesting, storage and cleansing practices, as well as shipping procedures, and quality control practices, such as Statistical Process Control. Pressure can be applied to suppliers, because wineries have sufficient choices among suppliers because cork is no longer the only option.

READINGS

Atkin, T. and Garcia, R., (2004), "A study of the diffusion of a discontinuous innovation," Decision Sciences Conference, Boston, Nov. 2004

Butzke, C. (2009), "TCA no longer a major problem for the U. S. wine industry," *Vineyard and Winery Management*, accessed online on October 12, 2012, from www.corkqc.com

Chehalem, (n. d,), "Cork, going from stopper to show-stopper," retrieved on January 18, 2004, from www.chehalemwines.com

Cork Quality Council (2004), "Cork industry worldwide and U. S. production estimates," retrieved Feb. 22, 2004, from www.corkqc.com

Cork Quality Council (2002), "Cork distributors see dramatic improvement in recent cork shipments," retrieved October 10, 2004, from www.corkqc.com

Cork Quality Council (2012), "CQC audit results," June 2012, retrieved October 10, 2012, from www.corkqc.com

Dugan, B. (2012), "Closure market's shifting currents sort out leaders," *Wine Business Monthly*, June, pp. 26–31

Fuller, P., (1995), "Cork taint—closing in on an industry problem," *Wine Industry Journal*, 10 (1), pp. 58–61

Godden, P., (2002), "Update on the AWRI trial of the technical performance of various types of wine bottle closure," *Australian Wine Research Institute Technical Review*, No. 139

Joseph, R., (2003), "Show stoppers," *Wine International Magazine*, retrieved on September 10, 2003, from www.wineint.com

Leyden, J., *Personal Communication*, August 2004

Leyden, J., *Personal Communication*, October 2012

M. A. Silva USA (2012), "A higher standard," accessed online on October 8th, from www.masilva.com

Marcus, K. (2001, April), "Revival at Rodney Strong," *The Wine Spectator*, retrieved from www.winespectator.com

McKenna, C., (n.d.) Zork, "The wine closure that seals like a screw cap and pops like a cork," retrieved October 15, 2004, from www.zork.com.au

Mironicki, J. of Collopack "Solutions" (2012), *Personal Communication*, October 2012

Murray, W. and Lockshin, L. S. (1997), "Consumer acceptance of synthetic corks," *International Journal of Wine Marketing*, 9, (1), pp. 31–52

Patterson, T. (2010), "Closure wars," *Wine Enthusiast Magazine*, accessed online on October 8th, from www.winemag.com

Penn, C. (2012), "Review of the industry," *Wine Business Monthly*, February. p. 59

Prial, F., (2003), "Popping corks: A sound bound for oblivion?" *The New York Times*, May 14, 2003

Phillips, C. (2011), "2011 closure survey report," *Wine Business Monthly*, June. Accessed online on October 9, 2012, from www.winebusiness.com

Pitcher, S., (1999 Nov–Dec), "Cork—essential stopper material or wine's last affectation," *Vineyard and Winery Management*, pp. 34–41

Quackenbush, J. (2010), "Cork, other closure makers adjust to cost issues," *Northbay Business Journal*, July 26, accessed online on October 10, 2012, from www.northbaybusinessjournal.com

Simpson, R. E. and Veitch, L. G., (1993), "A protocol for the assessment of the incidence of cork taint," *Australian and New Zealand Wine Industry Journal*, 8 (1), 89–96

Suckling, J. and Laube, J., (2005, March 31), "The great cork debate," *The Wine Spectator*, pp. 44–53

Wilson, D. and Lockshin, L., (2003), "The communications issues for producers of alternative closures in the wine industry," International Colloquium in Wine Marketing, University of South Australia, Adelaide, Australia

Wine Business Monthly, (2003, June), "Winemaker closure survey," *Wine Business Monthly*, pp. 58–61

ZoomInfo (2012), "Rodney Strong Vineyards Company Profile," retrieved on October 10th, from www.ZoomInfo.com

CASE 10

Dark Horse Ranch Vineyard

A Mendocino County, California, Biodynamic Winemaker Explores Future Directions

Liz Thach, PhD, MW
Sonoma State University Wine Business Institute, U.S.A.

Summary

Paul Dolan, considered California's "godfather of sustainable winegrowing," faces a crossroad of decision making concerning his future plans. He has had a full career including serving as CEO of Fetzer Winery, President of Mendocino Wine Group, LLC, and partner in several other businesses. His passion, however, is Dark Horse Ranch Vineyards, a 70-acre organic and biodynamic property that he owns jointly with his family. At this time in his life he is trying to decide on potential future directions for the vineyard. Should he expand, follow a stability strategy, sell, or start a new wine business? Whatever direction Paul takes is likely to be fruitful considering his previous successes.

Introduction

As soon as Paul Dolan, the CEO and owner of Dark Horse Ranch Vineyard, crossed the Golden Gate Bridge he let out a sign of relief because he knew it was only two more hours of driving before he arrived back in Mendocino County. The steering wheel of his biodiesel pick-up truck felt secure in his hands as he headed north on Highway 101 and he thought about his upcoming meeting with the wine business consultants, wondering what they would suggest regarding future strategic options for Dark Horse Ranch Vineyard.

The Old River Road exit appeared sooner than he expected, so Paul decided to take the longer and more meandering road to Dark Horse Ranch Vineyard rather than the more direct route through Ukiah. Besides, the October afternoon was bright and sunny, and Old River Road was far more scenic. The arching branches and dark green leaves of oak trees intermingled overhead and pear orchards spread on both sides of the road. Soon these were replaced by vineyards filled with old vines, heavy with purple and navy grape clusters, and showing the first yellow and orange leaves of autumn. Every mile or so a farmhouse dotted the hillside, and in the distance the Mayacamas Mountains were etched against the blue sky.

Eventually Paul saw the small but distinctive sign with its wooden depiction of a horse face with one-half dark brown and the other side cream-colored, signaling the entrance to Dark Horse Ranch Vineyard. He turned up the steep narrow road to the 160-acre ranch with its seventy acres of Demeter-certified biodynamic vines. The grenache block appeared first on his left, and then he saw the wooden outbuildings, horses in the corral, and chickens pecking around the yard. The old farmhouse that was used as an office and wine tasting room came into view, and then the house of his son, Jason, who was in charge of vineyard operations.

Paul parked the truck and then looked at his watch. One hour before his meeting with the consultants. Just enough time to pull together the financial and organizational paperwork they had requested as part of this first strategy session.

At his desk, Paul logged onto his computer and printed several documents. They included financial information on the costs, revenues, and other data regarding the operations of Dark Horse Ranch Vineyard. Paul has had many discussions with his family regarding the future of the vineyard. Should they expand and put in more vineyard acres, stay the course with a stability strategy, start a new wine brand, or even consider selling? Based on his prior experience as a CEO, Paul knew the benefit of seeking objective third-party advice on occasion. This was why had decided to call in some wine business strategy consultants. He was curious to hear what they would recommend after reviewing the situation.

OVERVIEW OF CALIFORNIA AND THE US WINE INDUSTRY

The United States is the fourth largest wine-producing nation in the world, with 90% of production coming from California. According to the Wine Institute (2012), there were 3,540 bonded wineries in California, with more than 4,600 vineyard operations producing a total of 3.35 million tons of grapes in 2011. In 2011 there were a total of 256.6 million cases of California wine sold to all markets, which was an increase of 5.6% from the previous year. In the United States alone, the value of all California shipments was $19.9 billion, whereas exports were approximately $1.25 billion. California global wine shipments and revenue have increased every year since 2000 (Table 1).

Table 1: California Wine Shipments to All Markets (Source: Wine Institute, 2012).

Year	California Wine Shipments (in millions of nine-liter cases)	Retail Value (in billions of dollars)
2011	256.6	$19.9
2010	242.9	$18.5
2009	237.1	$17.9
2008	239.8	$18.5
2007	233.5	$18.9
2006	227.1	$17.8
2005	224.1	$16.5
2004	219.4	$15.0
2003	207.6	$14.3
2002	195.2	$13.8
2001	188.9	$13.4
2000	187.5	$13.0

Wine is produced in all fifty US states. According to Fisher (2012), the total number of wineries in the United States reached 7,116 in 2011, showing a 9% increase from the previous year. Of these, 6,027 are produced by bonded wineries with a physical location, whereas the other 1,089 are created by virtual wineries. California currently accounts for a 61% volume share of the US market (Wine Institute, 2011) with 26% of total volume from imports. The remaining 13% is produced by other US states, the next largest after California being Washington, Oregon, New York, Virginia, and Texas, respectively.

In 2010, the United States became the leading wine-consuming nation at 330 million cases (Halversen, 2011). This equates to Americans drinking 3.96 billion bottles of wine in comparison to France's record of 3.85 billion bottles. According to the *Wine Spectator* (2010), Americans spent more than $40 billion on wine in 2010, and US wine consumption recorded its 17th annual increase.

CALIFORNIA GRAPE PRODUCTION AND PRICING

California wine grape production is cyclical in nature because of weather and climate issues as well as new vineyard plantings and pulling out old vineyards, referred to as "grubbing up." Some years the climatic conditions provide a bountiful harvest, and other years, such as 2010 and 2011, crops are low. Due to this, tonnage prices for wine grapes fluctuate based on market supply and demand. In 2011, California crushed 3.3 million tons of wine grapes (see Figure 1). From this, chardonnay was the largest grape varietal harvested, at 14.4%, followed by cabernet sauvignon at 9.9%.

Figure 1: California Wine Grape Production (Source: USDA NASS, 2011, in millions of tons).

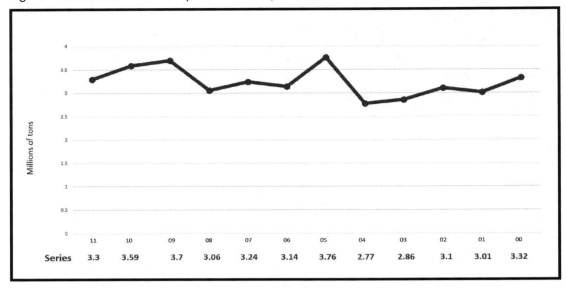

| Series | 3.3 | 3.59 | 3.7 | 3.06 | 3.24 | 3.14 | 3.76 | 2.77 | 2.86 | 3.1 | 3.01 | 3.32 |

In terms of wine grape prices, in 2011 the average price per ton for all California wine grapes was $543. The highest-priced region was Napa at $3,389 per ton, followed by Sonoma at $2,081. Mendocino County averaged $1,284 per ton (USDA NASS, 2011).

The average annual cost to maintain an existing vineyard in California depends on the region and in many cases is determined by labor costs. Average annual costs in the San Joaquin Valley were $5,400 in 2012 (Verdegaal et al., 2012), whereas annual vineyard production costs in Napa can range from $6,000 to $12,000 (Ashby, personal communication, December 2011), and in Sonoma from $4,000 (Frey, personal communication, January 2012) to $11,000 (Low, personal communication, October 2011).

WINE CONSUMERS IN THE UNITED STATES

Of the more than 313 million inhabitants in the United States, approximately 35% drink wine at a per capita rate of 3.03 gallons, or 11.5 liters (Wine Market Council, 2012). In terms of demographics (Silicon Valley Bank, 2012), wine drinkers are 69% white, 14% Hispanic, and 11% African American, with the remaining 9% from other races. The average age of the US wine consumer is 49, with millennials, or those who fall between the ages of 21 and 34, making up 26% of wine consumers, 19% of ages 35 to 44, 21% of ages 45 to 54, and 34% of those over 55. College degrees are held by 24% of US wine consumers. Consumption rates are growing among millennials and men.

Preferred varietals in terms of sales are chardonnay, which holds first place in the United States at a 21% market share, and cabernet sauvignon, in second place at 15% (Nielson, 2012). Though sales are decreasing, merlot still holds third place, with pinot gris and pinot noir as fourth and fifth favorites, respectively. The fastest-growing categories are moscato, malbec, riesling, and sweet red blends. The most popular price point in 2011 was the $9 to $11.99 category. Some of the best-selling brands include Sutter

Home Moscato, Cupcake Chardonnay, Barefoot Pinot Grigio, Gnarly Head Zinfandel, Menage a Trois Red, and Gallo's Apothic Red.

Americans also enjoy drinking imported wine, with one out of every four bottles sold from a foreign country. In 2010, the top imported wine countries were Italy (30%), France (24%), Australia (14%), Chile (7%), Argentina (6%), and Spain (6%) (ITA, 2011). These accounted for 87% of the total value of wines imported to the United States.

Dark Horse Ranch Vineyard Operations

Dark Horse Ranch Vineyard is located in Mendocino County, California. The name Mendocino is derived from a Spanish explorer named Mendoza who explored the coastline of current day Mendocino County. Composed of 3,878 square miles of land (Appellation America, 2007), Mendocino County borders the Pacific Ocean to the west, Sonoma County to the south, and Lake and Napa Valleys to the east. It is part of the North Coast wine region of California, and has 15,000 acres of planted vineyards (see Figure 2 on page 162).

Vineyards were first planted in the area in the 1850s during the California Gold Rush. The oldest winery is Parducci Winery, established in 1932 toward the end of Prohibition. Today there are more than ninety wineries in Mendocino County, with ten American viticulture areas, or AVAs (Mendowine.com, 2012). Mendocino County is known as a leading producer of organic and biodynamic wines, with more than 25% of its acreage using these farming methods (Appellation America, 2007).

Dark Horse Ranch Vineyard is located in the eastern foothills of the Ukiah Valley in the Mendocino AVA. Originally it was called the Twining Ranch and was planted with own-rooted, dry-farmed grey riesling vines in the 1960s. Paul Dolan and his family purchased the 160-acre property in 1998 and renamed it Dark Horse Ranch Vineyard, replanting seventy acres of new vineyards. "In racing circles," explains Paul Dolan, "a dark horse is one that comes from behind and wins. We are competing with Napa and Sonoma, so in Mendocino County we are using organic and biodynamic viticulture to help propel us ahead." The harvest from the vineyards is sold to wineries in Napa, Sonoma, and other parts of Mendocino County.

Terroir, Varietals, and Trellising Systems

The soil is of the "red vine series" composed primarily of red clay and small rocks (fines and silica), and is part of the Mayacamas mountain range. According to Paul, "If you dig down six to eight feet you will find a lot of rock, clay, and organic matter in the soil, which helps it to be well-draining and demonstrates it is healthy and alive."

The vineyard sits at a range of elevations from 600 to 1,250 feet. Some vineyard blocks are on the valley floor and others are planted on hills and terraces facing the southwest and west. The climate is ideal for wine grapes, with average summer temperature ranges from 55 to 90 degrees F. However, there is only 30 to 35 inches per year of rainfall.

When planting the seventy acres of new vineyards, Paul and his son Jason, the director of vineyard operations, took time to study the soil, slope, drainage, and sun

Figure 2: Map of Mendocino County American Viticulture Areas (AVAs)

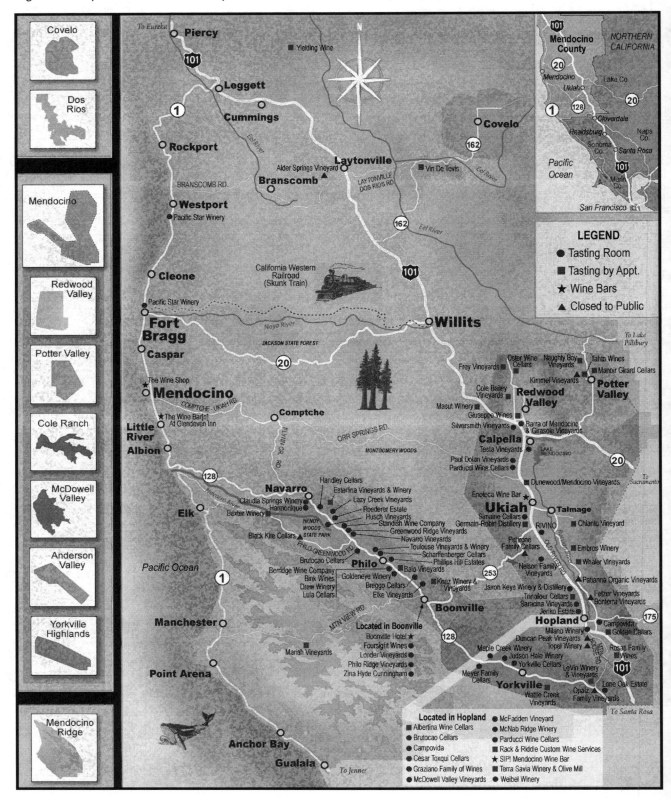

exposure of the ranch in order to determine which varietals to plant. Due to the warmer climate, they elected to plant all red varietals, with 22 acres of cabernet sauvignon, 17 acres of zinfandel, 10 acres each of syrah, petite syrah, and grenache, and 1 acre of mouvedre. These rich, bold varieties thrive here.

According to Paul, they use a combination of different rootstock and clones. "For rootstock we primarily use 110R, St. George, and 1103. We like 110R because it is drought-tolerant and deep-rooted. Clones vary by varietal and block. For example, we like the Durrell clone for syrah because it has an extremely flavorful profile. Cabernet sauvignon clones include 4, 8, 15, and 337. With zinfandel we have clones from Italy, Dry Creek, and the heritage California clone from the DuPratt Vineyard, and we are pleased to have the Beaucastel clone from Paso Robles for our grenache."

In terms of spacing and trellising, the most common system is VSP (vertical shoot position) with bilateral cordon, spur-pruned vines on eight-by-seven spacing. Most of the vineyard is positioned on an east-west line, with the exception of the terrace blocks, which are north-south. This allows the tractor to pass easily through the vineyard to mow weeds and disk the soil. However there are also ten acres of zinfandel and six of petite syrah, which are on the traditional head-pruned trellis system with eight-by-eight spacing. Paul admits these are more difficult to prune and harvest but feels they provide a unique flavor. "With the head-pruned zinfandel we generally prune to eight spurs per vine, which produce about sixteen bunches per vine. This way we get the perfect balance of fruit for each vine" (see Figure 3).

Figure 3: Photo of Dark Horse Ranch Vineyard's Rows

Farming Practices—Demeter-Certified Biodynamic

The choice to plant the ranch according to biodynamic principles and pursue Demeter certification was very deliberate and strategic. "I'm a fan of Rudolf Steiner, the father of biodynamics, who was born in Austria in 1861. He believed that in order for humans to be truly creative they needed food with great nutritional value," says Paul. "Steiner was concerned that conventional farming was stripping nutrients out of the soil and so he advocated biodynamic farming, which attempts to put life back into the soil and air so that it moves through the plant and thereby contributes to the nutrition of the fruit. Our goal at Dark Horse is to integrate the life-giving principle of biodynamic farming so as to create great wines.

"We call this a 'farming company' rather than a vineyard. It is not just a site for growing grapes, but has wide diversity of life forms such as chickens, horses, cows, and sheep that we have added along with the natural diversity that the native woodlands provide in the form of beneficial insects, birds, and wildlife. We work to farm in such a way as to integrate all these life energies. In this way the vineyard is like a living organism. I like to describe it as having a circulatory system—water flowing from the mountains into the valleys and down through the soil to the vine roots. It has a respiratory system—the wind and air circulating through the trees and vine canopy. The soil breathes in at night and out as the morning warms. Additionally the leaves inhale CO_2 and exhale oxygen. It has a digestive system, found in the cows and sheep, because when they graze they digest the grass and spread fertilizer back in the ground. Most farming today is exploitive in that we are removing nutrients from the soil every time we harvest. We farm so that we replace the nutrients with natural practices, composting and animal grazing. In this way the vineyard rewards us with high-quality fruit year after year. I like to refer to this as regenerative agriculture. The farm is actually 160 acres with a mixture of woodlands, pastures, orchards, and vineyards. We like to look at the farming from the standpoint of developing a self-regulating system. Each of the different elements of the farm contributes to the balance of different predator-prey dynamics. Owl boxes attracts owls to manage the gophers, blue bird boxes attract the birds to manage unwanted insects, and the chickens in the vineyard eat problem insects in the springtime while root tilling and fertilizing as they cruise through the vines. Additionally we are trying to put art back into farming. In order to do this we look at each block of grapes as requiring its own unique farming regimen of fertilization, cultivation, and training. No cookie cutter approach here."

Demeter Certification: According to the Demeter Biodynamic Trade Association (2012), Demeter is a not-for-profit organization established in 1985 with the mission "to enable people to farm successfully, in accordance with biodynamic practices and principles," and a vision "to heal the planet through agriculture." Based on the work of Rudolph Steiner, a biodynamic philosophy views each vineyard as a living organism that can maintain itself if the soil and environment is nursed back to its natural condition before people intervened with chemicals and other unnatural systems. Viewed by some as an extreme form of viticulture, it goes beyond the organic certification requirements of no synthetic pesticides and fertilizers, and advocates practices such as planting new vines or pruning when the moon is descending. Biodynamics also includes preparing and administering field sprays made with cow manure, ground quartz, and herbs to bring the soil back into balance, and using beneficial insects.

In order to become certified, a farm must show documented proof they have been using Demeter principles for a minimum period of three years. A Demeter-certified inspector examines the farm, soil, and paperwork, and if found acceptable, the property can be certified and the resulting crops can use the Demeter label for marketing and sales purposes (see Table 2). The certification fee in the United States ranges from $3,000 to $4,500, and the property must be reinspected on an annual basis for an additional fee ranging from $450 to $500. There are additional certification requirements for winemaking, such as the use of SO2 being limited to 100 ppm and no additions of acid, sugar, water, or commercial yeast (Beaman, 2009).

Table 2: Farming Definitions from the Demeter Biodynamic Trade Association Website (Source: Demeter Biodynamic Trade Association, 2012).

Biodynamic®: The Demeter label was one of the founding food certification agencies that started in Europe in 1928. It predated certified organic agriculture and follows many of the same guiding principles as organics under the National Organic Program. Demeter Certified Biodynamic agriculture has major philosophical differences from organic agriculture. Viewing the farm as a whole organism, increasing farm biodiversity, and limiting off farm inputs are just a few examples.

Organically Grown: This farming method avoids the use of synthetic chemicals in favor of natural methods, such as crop rotation, tillage and natural composts, which help to maintain soil health and control weeds, insects and other pests. Independent agencies certify farms using organic methods.

Sustainable Agriculture: These practices are interpreted and implemented differently from farm to farm, but the idea is to approach agriculture in a way that is environmentally responsible, socially equitable and economically feasible. However, with no third-party certification for sustainable farming, there is no accountability nor are there measurable goals associated with this method. The term has become increasingly meaningless, as conventional farm operations have adopted the term without actually using appropriate practices.

Conventional: This approach to farming is primarily concerned with production yields rather than product quality or environmental impact. Usually chemical inputs such as herbicides and pesticides are used.

Industrial: Here, agriculture is large-scale, with machine- and chemical-intensive farming. This method erodes the natural ecosystems of the land and treats the harvest as a commodity.

Fertilization: Dark Horse Ranch Vineyard has developed natural compost for fertilizing the vines, which is created on the property and is a combination of cow manure, straw, grape pumice, and biodynamic preps. Vineyard workers put this natural fertilizer on the vines after harvest, usually in November. The soil then receives its cover crop seeds of clovers, purple vetch, and bell beans, which are allowed to grow naturally through the winter and spring.

In addition the two standard biodynamic preps are applied according to the seasons with the 500 prep (buried in cow horn for six months) applied to the ground and the 501 prep (silica) sprayed in the air over the vines. The compost preps are composed of six natural sources: nettle, oak bark, yarrow, dandelion, chamomile, and valerian. Finally, sheep and chickens are allowed to roam through the vineyard at certain times of the year, which assists with fertilization along with some soil cultivation.

Paul cites university research studies proving the viability of biodynamic preps: "There was an interesting experiment conducted with the biodynamic preps by UC Davis. They took two piles of compost and added a biodynamic prep to one but not to the other. After six months they measured the nutrients in the two compost piles and the pile with the biodynamic prep had 30% more nutrients. This shows the power of biodynamics."

Weed Control and Thinning: One issue with biodynamic farming is the need to control weeds, but synthetic weed control products such as Round-up are not allowed. Therefore, the vineyard workers need to pass through the rows to either pull weeds or hand hoe in the earlier years of the vines' development. Eventually the weeding is maintained with tractors. In addition, if needed, workers will thin leaves and remove suckers (unwanted new vine growth) and extra clusters from the vines – usually in the late spring and early summer months (May and June), all with the intent to keep the fruit in balance with the vigor of the vine.

Disease and Pest Control: In terms of disease control in the vineyard, powdery mildew can be an issue during some years. Therefore, both wet and dust sulfur are applied to the vines, usually three times per season. Demeter allows the use of sulfur and copper sulfate in the vineyard because they are organic substances.

Pests are rare because of the natural balance of the environment through the biodynamic practices. However, sometimes small insects such as mites and hoppers can be an issue. These insects are managed by the predator insects that have been attracted by the diverse flora throughout the property. The property is deer fenced so the deer do not eat the tender young leaves. Paul states that birds and gophers are not a problem, most likely because of the owl boxes and hawk perches that are placed around the property. This encourages birds of prey to frequent the vineyard, and they are a natural predator of gophers and small birds.

Irrigation and Vineyard Technology: In general, Dark Horse Ranch Vineyard tries not to use irrigation, but a drip-irrigation system is installed as well as weather stations as a back-up option. According to Paul, "We irrigate primarily when the vines are young and wean the vines off the water as they develop their root system. Additionally we watch the phases of the moon. If the moon is rising that means the moisture is rising; whereas if the moon is waning the moisture is leaving the soil and vines. Therefore, we like to harvest the crop when the moon is waning because there is more concentration of flavors." Weather stations are the only other technology in the vineyard and are used to monitor temperature and rainfall.

Harvest Measurements: As is found in many high-quality vineyards throughout the world, the decision when to harvest the fruit is critical. If they are picked too soon, the grapes will not have achieved ideal flavor profiles as well as acid, pH, tannin, and sugar levels. However, if picked too late, the fruit can be overly high in sugar and alcohol, and deficient in other areas. "We mainly decide based on taste and don't rely on sugar tests as we did in times past," says Paul. "Also winemakers who purchase our grapes set their own farming expectations and visit the vineyard often to observe and taste. Since we are producing all red varietals, for us the most important issue is tannin and flavor ripeness. In general, our ideal is a Brix of 26 or under, with a pH of 3.5 to 3.6."

ORGANIZATIONAL STRUCTURE AND FINANCIALS

Dark Horse Ranch Vineyard has seven full-time employees, as illustrated in Figure 4. Paul Dolan serves as CEO, with his son Jason managing vineyard operations and four full-time workers who live on the property. During harvest and pruning, part-time seasonal workers are hired. Heath Dolan, Paul's other son, manages the marketing and sales aspects of the vineyard. Accounting and legal functions are outsourced.

Figure 4: Organizational Structure of Dark Horse Ranch Vineyard

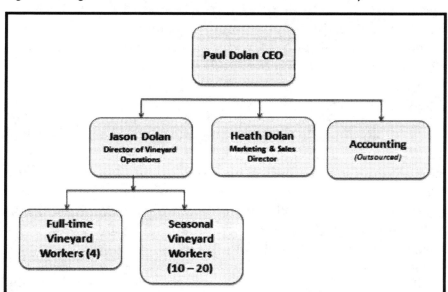

ECONOMICS OF THE VINEYARD

Vineyard Costs: The cost to install the vineyard was $10,000 per acre for the VSP blocks and $12,000 per acre for the head-pruned blocks on terraced land. Average maintenance **cost per year per acre ranges from $3,500 to $3,600.**

Labor Costs: Labor is included in average maintenance costs and is $10 to $15 per hour plus 30% extra for benefits. There are four full-time vineyard workers who are given housing on the property, and funds are set aside to pay for their children's college tuition. During harvest, families of workers arrive and the pay is increased to $15 to $20 per hour.

Tons per Acre: The vineyard averages 4.5 tons per acre.

Revenue: Dark Horse Ranch Vineyard is sold to a variety of wineries in Napa, Sonoma, and Mendocino Counties. The average price ranges from $2,000 to $3,000 per ton.

Economic Viability: Because the money to purchase and install Dark Horse Ranch Vineyard was borrowed, it took a number of years to reach a position of economic viability. According to Paul, "The vineyard has always created revenue, but it took us thirteen years to reach a cash flow positive position."

BIOGRAPHY OF PAUL DOLAN

Paul Dolan is a fourth-generation California winemaker, with his family's involvement in the wine industry extending back through the Rossi and Concannon families. Growing up in Oakland, Paul spent a month each summer in Asti, Sonoma County, where his grandfather – Edmund Rossi – ran Italian Swiss Colony. "During the rest of the year, Granddad visited us in Oakland every weekend," remembers Paul. "At our family table you could always count on great food and wine, and stories of the old days." As an undergraduate at Santa Clara University, Paul studied business and finance. Shortly before he graduated, he wrote a paper on the wine industry (advised by his winemaking uncle, Ed Rossi), and Paul's family legacy came alive. In 1975 he enrolled in the enology program at California State University, Fresno, ultimately receiving a master's degree with honors.

In 1977 Paul joined forces with the Fetzers, becoming the company's first winemaker from outside the family. Together they grew the business to two million cases a year, regularly earning acclaim and awards for their wines. After the Fetzers sold their family business, Paul became president of the company under its new ownership. While at Fetzer Winery, he helped to create the organic wine brand Bonterra, and published a book describing the company's adoption of sustainable winegrowing practices entitled *True to Our Roots: Fermenting a Business Revolution* (2003).

In 2004 Paul Dolan and the Thornhill family formed Mendocino Wine Group, LLC to acquire the Parducci Wine Cellars winery, vineyards and brands. Paul served as President of Mendocino Wine Group until January 2012.

Today, Paul is a partner in several other business ventures including Truett Hurst Winery and VML, Virginia Marie Lambrix Wines in Sonoma County, as well as Wine Spies, an online wine retailer. He is also involved in a wine packaging and design company, and produces third-party customized wines for Safeway. With his family, he has recently purchased two new vineyards near Ukiah, with plans to convert these to organic and biodynamic ranches. Additionally, the family has interest in animal husbandry and a small olive orchard.

Paul continues to be an advocate of green farming, and is called by some "the godfather of sustainable winegrowing in California." He knows that sustainability is an economic asset and a competitive advantage as well as an imperative for healthy life on this planet. He is spreading the word—for the good of business, the community, and the environment:

> A sustainable business should be a whole business, like a whole person. It must have integrity. It must have a moral center. It must be connected to its values and the greater world. It must aspire to do what is right, not just for the bottom line, not just from a legal standpoint, but from a moral and ethical standpoint. It's not only accountable, it's responsible. (Paul Dolan, *True to Our Roots, Fermenting a Business Revolution*, 2003, p. 167)

Paul resides in Healdsburg, California, with his wife, Diana, and daughter Sassicaia. He spends leisure time in his Mendocino County vineyards and on horseback at Dark Horse Ranch Vineyard. "Dark Horse Ranch is my family's home, where my sons and their children are fifth- and sixth-generation winegrowers in the mountains of Ukiah," says Paul. "We're rooted here. I am part of the fabric of this place: the water, air, wine, and food are part of me."

Strategic Options

Assume you are a member of the wine business consulting team visiting Dark Horse Ranch Vineyard to meet with Paul Dolan. Based on the information in this case, perform the following calculations and analyses in order to make a recommendation on which strategic options Paul should consider for his vineyard operation.

Financial Calculations

Based on the information provided in the financial section, determine the following:
- Total cost to install the vineyard
- Annual cost of operating the vineyard
- Annual revenue produced by the vineyard
- Annual profit

Porter's Five Forces Analysis

Using Porter's five forces analysis, developed by strategy expert Michael Porter, examine the competing forces in the business environment of Dark Horse Ranch Vineyard and determine whether they are weak, moderate, strong, or fierce (see Table 3). If all five forces appear to be very strong or fierce, it is probably not a good business environment in which to enter. However, if just one or two of the forces are strong, and the others are weak or moderate, chances for success and achieving attractive profits are higher (Thach, 2008).

Table 3: Analyzing Dark Horse Ranch Vineyard through Porter's Five Forces Analysis

Force	Indicators of Strong Force	Situation at Dark Horse Ranch Vineyard	Your Rating
1. Rivalry among competitors	Many competitors Very aggressive price cutting and discounting of wine Slow market growth Heavy acquisition activity		
2. Entry of new competitors	Many new candidates Low entry barriers (doesn't cost much to start a new business) Rapid industry growth Profit potential is high. Existing industry members have a strong incentive to expand into new geographies.		
3. Substitute products to wine	Many good substitutes available at lower prices Low switching costs for consumer High-quality substitute available		
4. Supplier power	Only a few suppliers in market High cost in switching to alternative suppliers Supplier provides a differentiated input to enhance the quality. Some suppliers threaten to integrate forward.		
5. Buyer power *In this case, buyers are wineries and winemakers.*	Only a few buyers Buyer-switching costs to competing brands are low. Buyers can demand discounts. Buyer demand is weak or declining. Buyers can wait to buy. Buyers threaten to buy wineries. Identity of buyer adds prestige to list of customers.		

MAJOR STRATEGIC OPTIONS ANALYSIS

Using the strategic options shown in Table 4, identify the advantages and disadvantages of each major strategic option for Dark Horse Ranch Vineyard. If possible, identify one or two additional options and evaluate them. Then select which you believe to be the best choice and provide justification for your decision.

Table 4: Strategic Options for Dark Horse Ranch Vineyard.

Strategic Option	Advantages	Disadvantages
Growth Strategy: In Same Business Expand Dark Horse Ranch Vineyard by adding new vineyard acres and/or buying additional vineyards.		
Growth Strategy: In New Business Expand Dark Horse Ranch Vineyard by adding a new business line, for example, build winery, wine brands, establish a resort or ecotourism location, and so on.		
Stability Strategy: Continue to operate in same fashion.		
Exit Strategy: Sell Dark Horse Ranch Vineyard.		
Other Option _____		
Other Option _____		

Author's Perspective

Although there are a variety of strategic directions Paul Dolan can consider for Dark Horse Ranch Vineyard moving forward, following are the author's perspective regarding potential answers to the case study issues presented.

Financial calculations

> **Total cost to install the vineyard:** Paul stated it was $10,000 per acre for the VSP blocks and $12,000 per acre for the head-pruned blocks on terraced land. Because there are a total of 70 acres, of which 16 are head-pruned, the total cost to install the vineyard was $732,000 (70 − 16 = 54 acres × $10,000 per acre = $540,000 plus 16 acres × $12,000 = $192,000 = $732,000). This is actually quite inexpensive because new vineyards in California today can go as high as $40,000 to $80,000 per installed acre.

Annual cost of operating the vineyard: Paul stated the average maintenance cost per year per acre ranges from $3,500 to $3,600. This includes all labor costs. Therefore, with 70 acres the total annual cost of operating the vineyard ranges from $245,000 to $252,000. Again this is rather inexpensive compared to other regions, such as Napa and Sonoma, which can cost as much as $6,000 to $14,000 per acre for annual maintenance costs.

Annual revenue produced by the vineyard: Because the vineyard averages 4.5 tons per acre and the average price received is $2,000 to $3,000 per ton, estimated annual revenue for Dark Horse Ranch Vineyard is $630,000 to $945,000 (4.5 × 70 acres = 315 × $2000 to $3000 = $630,000 to $945,000).

Annual profit: If revenues range from $630,000 to $945,000 and annual maintenance costs average $245,000 to $252,000, the rough annual profit of Dark Horse Ranch Vineyard ranges from $205,000 to $700,000. The wide swing in profits primarily has to do with the negotiated price per ton for the wine grapes. In years when the price of grapes is higher, obviously profits to grape growers increase.

Porter's Five Forces Analysis

Table 5 provides an example of how to fill out Table 3.

Table 5: Analyzing Dark Horse Ranch Vineyard through Porter's Five Forces Analysis (Sample)

Force	Indicators of Strong Force	Situation at Dark Horse Ranch Vineyard	Your Rating
1. Rivalry among competitors	Many competitors Very aggressive price cutting and discounting of wine Slow market growth Heavy acquisition activity	*There has been a grape glut in California in past years, which has made rivalry among competitors quite fierce including some grape growers electing to not even harvest their grapes. However, starting in 2013, the California grape supply situation is in balance, and the Organization International de Vin (OIV) predicts fewer wine grapes being produced around the world. Therefore, it is possible that there will be a shortage of California grapes in the future (2013–2015), which will cause rivalry among competitors to decrease from its current state. Therefore, the current rating has moved from fierce to moderate.*	*Moderate*

2. Entry of new competitors	Many new candidates Low entry barriers (doesn't cost much to start a new business) Rapid industry growth Profit potential is high. Existing industry members have a strong incentive to expand into new geographies.	*Because of the forecasted need for more California wine grapes, it is predicted that new vineyards will be planted. Though cost is high to install a new vineyard and there is a three-year lag time before grapes can be harvested, it is possible that there will be new competitors to this arena. Therefore the current rating has moved from weak to strong.*	*Strong*
3. Substitute products to wine	Many good substitutes available at lower prices Low switching costs for consumer High-quality substitute available	*Substitute products are always strong to fierce in the wine industry. Beer and spirits are highly competitive with much more sophisticated marketing campaigns and larger advertising budgets than wine. Therefore, this rating will continue to be fierce.*	*Fierce*
4. Supplier power	Only a few suppliers in market High cost in switching to alternative suppliers Supplier provides a differentiated input to enhance the quality. Some suppliers threaten to integrate forward.	*Supplier power to vineyards is usually weak to moderate. Major suppliers are vineyard development consultants, vineyard set-up and maintenance supplies (trellises, irrigation, shears, etc.), grapevine nurseries and grafters, vineyard applications (sprays, fertilizers, pesticides, etc.), vineyard IT equipment (sensors, GPSs, etc.), vineyard equipment and tractor manufacturers, vineyard labor contractors, and vineyard consultants. At this time, there are many suppliers and not that many new vineyards. Therefore, supplier power remains weak. However, the wine grape grower as a supplier to wineries may move into a highly competitive position with the predicted shortage of global wine grape supply.*	*Weak*
5. Buyer power *In this case, buyers are wineries and winemakers.*	Only a few buyers Buyer-switching costs to competing brands are low. Buyers can demand discounts. Buyer demand is weak or declining. Buyers can wait to buy. Buyers threaten to buy wineries. Identity of buyer adds prestige to list of customers.	*Because the buyers of wine grapes are wineries and winemakers, during times of excess grapes on the market, buyer power can be fierce. However, as we move into this cycle of predicted shortage of wine grapes from 2013-2015, buyer power becomes moderate.*	*Moderate*

Major strategic options analysis

Table 6 presents an example of how to fill out Table 4.

Table 6. Strategic options for Dark Horse Ranch Vineyard.

Strategic Option	Advantages	Disadvantages
Growth Strategy: In Same Business Expand Dark Horse Ranch Vineyard by adding new vineyard acres and/or buying additional vineyards	*Because it is predicted that California is moving into a cycle of grape shortage, expanding Dark Horse Ranch Vineyard and/or buying additional vineyards makes financial sense. In fact Paul is currently doing this.*	*The downside is that grape supply in California has always been cyclical with huge swings in grape prices. If too much debt is taken on by expanding vineyards and a down cycle hits, financial distress may occur.*
Growth Strategy: In New Business Expand Dark Horse Ranch Vineyard by adding a new business line, for example, build winery, wine brands, establish a resort or ecotourism location, and so on.	*Paul has strong experience in managing wineries and creating new wine brands so it is highly likely he would be successful in adding a new business line to the vineyard. He has also held short boot camps for wine distributors to teach them about biodynamics. He could expand this concept to tourists. By diversifying he could also protect himself financially during oversupply cycles of wine grapes.*	*The cost of establishing a new business can be quite high – especially purchasing equipment for a new winery or opening a tasting room. It could be many years before Paul reaches a break-even point. It may be more feasible to expand slowly or to use a custom crush facility if he wants to launch new wine brands.*
Stability Strategy: Continue to operate in same fashion.	*A stability strategy for the next few years will probably result in success as wine grape prices are predicted to increase. It will also be less stressful for Paul and his family to continue to operate the business in the same fashion.*	*By doing nothing, Paul could lose the window of opportunity to purchase more vineyards, which could allow him to expand revenues. With wineries in Napa and Sonoma Counties currently seeking to purchase existing vineyards in Lake County, by buying more vineyards in Mendocino County he may benefit by predicted price increases for both grapes and vineyard land. A stability strategy would not allow for this.*
Exit Strategy: Sell Dark Horse Ranch Vineyard.	*After having built the vineyard to be so successful, Paul could probably make a decent profit by selling it now or in the next couple of years when grape prices increase. He could then relax and spend more time with his family or travel the world.*	*Selling the vineyard is not in Paul's plans. He wants to build a family legacy that future generations can inherit and take care of. The vineyard is very close to his heart and selling it is currently not an option for him.*
Other Option _____		
Other Option _____		

References

Appellation America (2007), "Mendocino County: Appellation description." Available at http://wine.appellationamerica.com/wine-region/Mendocino.html

Beaman, M. (2009), "Drink living wine: The nuts and bolts of biodynamic winemaking." Available at www.demeterbta.com/files/BDwine.pdf

Demeter Biodynamic Trade Association (2012), "Media and trade: Important definitions." Available at www.demeterbta.com/media.html

Dolan, P. (2003), *True to our roots: Fermenting a business revolution*. Princeton, NJ: Bloomberg Press.

Fisher, C. (2012), "U.S. wineries up 5% to 7,116," *Wine Business Monthly*, Available at www.winebusiness.com/wbm/?go=getArticleSignIn&dataId=96717

Halverson, N. (2011), "U.S. now the largest wine market in the world," *Press Democrat*. Available at www.pressdemocrat.com/article/20110315/BUSINESS/110319663

ITA (2011), "The US wine industry 2010." Report by International Trade Administration, US Government. Available at http://ita.doc.gov/td/ocg/wine2011.pdf

Nielson (2012, December), "52 week wine market report," *Wine Business Monthly*.

Silicon Valley Bank (2012), *State of the wine industry 2011–2012*. Annual report published by Silicon Valley Bank. Available at http://www.svb.com/2012-wine-report

Thach, L. (2008), "Wine business strategy," in L. Thach & R. Matz (Eds.), *Wine: A global business*, New York: Miranda Press.

USDA NASS. (2011). "2011 final grape crush report." Available at www.nass.usda.gov/Statistics_by_State/California/Publications/Grape_Crush/index.asp

Verdegaal, P. S., Klonsky, K. M., & de Moura, R. L. (2012), "2012 Sample costs to establish a vineyard and produce winegrapes," UC Davis Cooperative Extension Report. Available at http://coststudies.ucdavis.edu/files/GrapeWineVN2012.pdf

Wine Institute (2011), "Record high 2010 wine shipments make U.S. the world's largest wine-consuming nation." Available at www.wineinstitute.org/resources/pressroom/03152011

Wine Institute (2012), "2011 California and U.S. wine sales." Available at www.wineinstitute.org/resources/statistics/article639

Wine Market Council (2012), "Wine consumer research summary for 2011." Available at http://winemarketcouncil.com/

Wine Spectator (2010), "Big wine brands lead growth in U.S. market." Available at http://www.winespectator.com/webfeature/show/id/44261

Cru Bourgeois Médoc

WILL JOINING A WINE ALLIANCE IMPROVE QUALITY AND SALES? IN VINO VERITAS

Tatiana Bouzdine-Chameeva, Philippe Barbe
KEDGE Business School, France

SUMMARY

The owner of a newly inherited vineyard in the Médoc region in France contemplates whether she should rejoin the wine alliance her father had belonged to some years before. Recently the alliance has put in place a qualitative selection procedure in collaboration with Bureau Veritas, the world's leading certification body. This is a totally new approach for Bordeaux winemakers, and requires a fair amount of financial and time investment. The owner must decide whether the marketing opportunities for her winery that could result from the membership would outweigh the added burden associated with quite a heavy wine-quality assessment and fulfilling membership requirements.

The authors would like to express gratitude to Mrs. Frédérique Dutheillet de Lamothe, director of the Alliance des Crus Bourgeois du Médoc, and Mr. Vincent Fabre, a former president of the Union of Wine Producers of Médoc and Haut-Médoc, for their advice, remarks, and useful comments.

INTRODUCTION

Valerie Forgeron looked out at the gorgeous sunny vineyard landscape. She felt tired after a long weekend being involved with the Médoc marathon. She did not run this year but was among the 3,450 volunteers who worked hard to help organizers with the event. The Médoc marathon is ranked second in *Runner's World* after the New York marathon for the quality of its organization, but it requires so much effort! Valerie's mind focused on issues more practical and urgent. She just received a letter requesting her membership in the Alliance des Crus Bourgeois du Médoc for the next year. Did she need to join the association? Eight months ago Valerie inherited a wine property of 33 hectares in the Haut-Médoc area (see Figure 1) from her father, who passed away in a car accident the past winter very suddenly. Valerie has not yet gotten used to the idea that she must make all these decisions on her own.

Figure 1: Bordeaux wine regions (https://www.bordeauxprof.com).

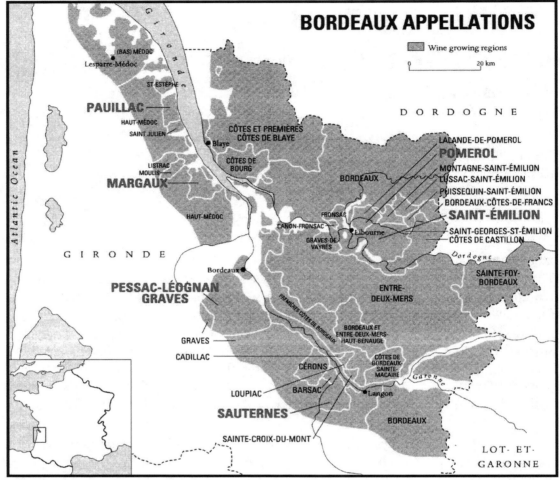

Valerie turned away from the brilliant view and sighed. The harvest period would start in about a month; by mid-October she will spend much time indoors in the cellar making wines, and then time will move quickly, pushing her to focus more on sales. Valerie's wine is a traditional blend of cabernet sauvignon, merlot, and petit verdot, priced between US$6 and US$12 a bottle. Her father had been a member of the previous Union of Cru Bourgeois du Médoc and even once won the Cru Bourgeois du Médoc Cup (a regional wine competition). He stopped his membership in 2004 when the union members contested the 2003 classification to the courts. Valerie's father had hesitated to renew his membership during the ensuing three years because he was considering whether it was worth it. The label "Cru Bourgeois" had revolutionized externalization of the certification process and seemed to be flourishing. However, it required winemakers to make significant investments into their wine monitoring and quality. In a couple of years from now the alliance could move from an annual selection of best wines to an annual classification scheme, which could be valid for two to three years. What benefits could this bring? Yes, Valerie needs to gather all the documents of the Alliance des Crus Bourgeois, call her father's friends for advice, and reconsider a membership because it directly affects the future success of her vineyard.

CONTEXT AND TRENDS IN THE BORDEAUX WINE CLASSIFICATION SYSTEM

All French wines are distinguished according to the location where they are grown and the production control of their creation. The AOC system (Appellation d'Origine Controlée), which applies to high-quality French wines, goes beyond simple classifications. It refers to precisely specified regions and on the specific constraints and rigid controls stated by the Institut National des Appellations d'Origine et de la Qualité (INAO). These rules include the allowed grape varieties, maximum yield, density of vine planting, minimum alcohol level, cultivation methods, winemaking techniques, and quality controls.

Bordeaux's glamorous wine reputation has been in large part due to the classifications of the grands crus classés. They provide the consumer with information about prestigious wines, representing about 5% of the 9,000 wine producers in the region, "the cream of Bordeaux wine scene." The classifications serve as an indication of the potential for the quality of the wine, but most of them had been determined initially on a price evaluation. There are currently five classifications in Bordeaux (seeTable 1 and Appendix 1 for more information about Bordeaux wines).

Table 1: The essential information on Bordeaux wine classifications.

Title	Year	Regions concerned	Number of classes	Number of wine estates indicated	Revision
Médoc and Graves Grand Cru Classification	1855	9 AOC (8 AOC of Médoc and Graves)	5 classes	61 wine properties	Minor revisions in 1856 and 1973
Sauternes and Barsac Classification	1855	2 AOC	3 classes	26 wine properties	No revision
Cru Bourgeois du Médoc	1932	8 AOC	3 classes (initially)	444 wine properties	Annual selection without classification
St. Emilion Grand Crus	1955	1 AOC	3 classes	82 wine properties	Revised every 10 years
Cru Artisans du Médoc	1994	8 AOC	1 class	44 wine properties	New revision in 2006

THE ORIGINS OF CLASSIFICATIONS

Everyone who knows French wines has heard of the Bordeaux Grand Cru Classification of Médoc dated 1855. More than a century before, in 1740, the Chamber of Commerce in Bordeaux issued a document outlining the wine prices for each rural community. In

Médoc and Graves, regional brokers ranked the wines according to a chateau's reputation, which mainly depended on the trading price that the wines were bringing in the market at that time, which was directly related to quality. Certain regions in Bordeaux were not enthralled with the opportunities afforded by classification. For example, the Pomerol region has never had a classification.

The famous Bordeaux Grand Cru Classification of 1855 was created at the request of Napoleon III to be presented at the first Exposition Universelle de Paris showcasing agricultural products, industry, and fine arts, which lasted from May to November 1855. France's best Bordeaux wines were to be on display for visitors from around the world (see Figure 2).

Figure 2: "Exposition universelle de 1855, vue de la grande nef du Palais de l'Industrie," by Provost.

The wines were divided into five categories, known today as growths. The classification ranked 60 top Bordeaux red wines: 59 from Médoc and one from Graves (today this is called the Médoc and Graves Grand Cru Classification of 1855). The fourteen finest sweet whites from Sauternes and Barsac also were listed separately in their own Sauternes Classification of 1855. The first change in ranking occurred in 1856, when Cantemerle was added as a fifth growth (having been either omitted originally by oversight or added as an afterthought, depending on which of the conflicting accounts is correct). A more significant change occurred in 1973, with Chateau Mouton Rothschild being promoted from second-growth to first-growth status after decades of intense lobbying by the powerful Philippe de Rothschild. The other original rankings stand more than 160 years later. The classified chateaux are responsible for nearly 25% of the wine produced in the Médoc region.

The Existing Classifications and Their Roles in Imports and Exports

The desire to give a hierarchy to wine properties in the Bordeaux wine region goes back centuries. The goal is to establish preferences and help the consumer in a puzzling choice among more than 10,000 wines produced in the region. Soils, technical processes used, and aging periods differ; for example, Médoc grand cru is not equivalent to Saint-Emilion's grand cru.

The classification attempts to emphasize certain merits of wine quality, though Bordeaux wines have frequently been criticized for the heterogeneity of their quality. It is not clear whether classifications further complicate the picture or really help the consumer to choose: do they really serve as a sign of quality, particularly for those wine estates that are too small to have their own recognizable branding, financial reserves, and human resources, especially for developing exporting opportunities?

Long before the classification of 1855 wine brokers introduced the hierarchy of Crus. In their conversations they talked about a good 3rd, a 3rd and a half, or a 4th. Certain brokers referred to four classes, while others used five. If they had created 6th, 7th and 8th classes there would be no term used in Médoc area other than Cru Classé (Classified Growth). Thus the tradition regarding the differentiation between Crus Classés and Crus Bourgeois has evolved with no formality; a certain number of crus were classified differently or not classified depending on their price evolution or brokers' personality.

The classification of Cru Bourgeois du Médoc, first established in 1932, recognized the quality and value of red wines produced in the eight appellations of the Médoc region (Médoc, Haut-Médoc, Listrac-Médoc, Moulis, Margaux, Pauillac, Saint-Julien, and Saint-Estèphe). The term Cru Bourgeois goes back to medieval times during English rule, when wine merchants in the "bourg" of Bordeaux city were an affluent and influential class in their own right. They had numerous privileges, such as being exempt from paying the high taxes levied on wine from their vineyards, having priority when exporting their wines, and selling before other producers. Such privileges gave them an advantage commercially and enabled them to invest early on in land, to plant vineyards, and to create large wine estates. Bordeaux's prosperous bourgeois class acquired Médoc's best parcels; the wines they produced were the "cru" wines of the Bourgeois and often noted to be of a superior quality. Wine brokers used this term for the wines from the Médoc appellation that were not included in the 1855 classification (see Appendix 2 for more information on this classification).

In 1932, Bordeaux wine brokers, under the joint authority of the Bordeaux Chamber of Commerce and the Gironde Chamber of Agriculture, officially classified 444 wines from Médoc appellations by three classes: 339 Crus Bourgeois, 99 Crus Bourgeois Superior, and 6 Cru Bourgeois Exceptional Superior (see Figure 3). That list served as a reference point for commercial use for more than seventy years. A new version was presented in 2003 (with government homologation) and banned in 2007; it was re-established with new rules in 2010 by the Alliance des Crus Bourgeois du Médoc.

Figure 3: Example of wine labels mentioning different ranks of Cru Bourgeois classification.

A stand-alone classification of Graves wines—red and white wines of the Graves region in Bordeaux—was not put together until 1953 by a jury appointed by INAO and approved by the minister of agriculture. Six years later, in 1959, the selection was revised with a few additions. All these classified chateaux belong to the appellation Pessac-Léognan, which came into effect in 1987. Since 1959 the top of this classification remains unchanged.

The classification of wines in the Saint Emilion region was first established in 1955. There were ten premier grands crus classés and 63 grans crus classés included in the initial list. Unlike other existing classifications in Bordeaux, this one is revisited every tenyears. The fifth edition, released in 2006, was challenged by unsatisfied producers who had been demoted. After several legal applications the edition was announced invalid, and the classification of 1996 remained in place until 2012. Ninety-six wine estates of Saint Emilion have applied for classification in the 2012 edition, and the newly revised classification scheme comprises 18 premier grands crus classés and 64 grands crus classés.

A traditional classification of Crus Artisans du Médoc, including the 44 small family-owned wine estates in the eight Médoc appellations that often own less than fivehectares, has existed since 1868. It was officially recognized by the European Union in 1994 and classified as Crus Artisans in 2006. To belong to this classification you have to be a family-owned estate that grows, produces, and markets wine, and the owner has to be self-employed and work on his own estate. In total there are 340 hectares of vines under this classification, mainly in Médoc and Haut-Médoc AOC.

ALLIANCE DES CRUS BOURGEOIS DU MÉDOC (SOURCE: ALLIANCE DES CRUS BOURGEOIS SITE)

The creation of the Cru Bourgeois Union, renamed Alliance des Cru Bourgeois du Médoc in 2004, goes back to 1962, when about a quarter of the wine producers in the Médoc area whose wines were classified Cru Bourgeois in 1932 decided to unite their forces for promoting their wines on the international wine scene (see Figure 4). Full of enthusiasm and new idea,s the union provided the dynamism, economic weight, and innovations to contribute to the stronger recognition worldwide of Cru Bourgeois.

Figure 4: The logo of the Alliance des Crus Bourgeois du Médoc, the Cru Bourgeois label, and the sticker of authentication with a hologram and a traceability number that will be required on each bottle starting with the 2010 vintage.

The alliance organized an internal classification in 1966 and 1978 to promote a competitive spirit within the Crus Bourgeois. In 1979, the European Community labeling regulations approved the traditional term Cru Bourgeois, provided that the conditions for its use were specified by French law.

In 1985, there was a substantial increase in demand for Crus Bourgeois wines. As a result, the members organized a tasting tournament, the Cru Bourgeois du Médoc Cup, which further enhanced their reputation. This cup was extremely successful and was held every year until 1999. Many other initiatives have been undertaken by the alliance that focused on the promotion of Cru Bourgeois wines.

In 2000, the minister of agriculture stipulated the rules for the organization of the Crus Bourgeois classification, with the purpose of establishing a quality hierarchy of Crus Bourgeois for the eight AOC wines in the Médoc area. Carrying on the traditions of the 1932 Cru Bourgeois classification, three quality categories were suggested: Crus Bourgeois Exceptionnels, Crus Bourgeois Supérieurs, and Crus Bourgeois.

The classification was established by a jury of 18 professionals recognized by the Place de Bordeaux, who had to judge the wines on the basis of seven criteria: the nature of the terroir, the grape variety, the cultivating techniques, the winemaking process and the bottling conditions, the management and general presentation of the property, consistency in the quality of the product, and the wine's reputation and organoleptic qualities of the wine.

On June 17, 2003, a ministerial order finally approved the first official classification of the Crus Bourgeois du Médoc, which recognized 247 chateaux out of 490 candidates. Some of the chateaux that were not included in the classification denounced it as unfair. Even some chateaux that were unsatisfied by their ranking denounced it. The judging panel included the president of the Union of the Crus Bourgeois du Médoc at that time. This fact became an argument for the Administrative Court of Appeal of Bordeaux to cancel the classification of 2003: "One cannot judge something in which one has an interest." The classification was therefore banned.

It was amazing how wine producers of Médoc mobilized around the alliance after this dramatic quake. Because the Médoc winegrowers were not ready for a new classification, the alliance had to inspire the wine growers to commence the project "Revival and Reconnaissance of the Cru Bourgeois," and a rigorous quality assurance procedure was put in place by the union in 2009. They also set up specifications that formed the basis for an annual selection of wines.

Frédérique Dutheillet de Lamothe started working as communications director for the Alliance des Cru Bourgeois du Médoc in January 2007, five days before the 2003 classification was annulled. "One month later," she explained in an interview with *Guilbert & Gaillard* magazine, "the Saint-Emilion classification of 2006 fell, too, but rather than being cancelled totally as was our case, the classification reverted to the 1996 one. We have had to start completely from zero and create a system that did not exist before, on the quality of an individual wine. We had a dark period of three years between 2007 and 2010 when we had no official existence. We had to find our way in the dark and over the past years we have fought alongside the wine producers to protect the valuable heritage that is the Cru Bourgeois."

The collective approach of the alliance has enabled the traditional name of Cru Bourgeois to be saved, and moreover it proposed a form of quality assurance recognized by public authorities. In 2009, the ministerial order authorized a qualitative selection procedure for the Crus Bourgeois du Médoc. Since September 2010 the Crus Bourgeois du Médoc Official Selection has been published every year.

The Quest for Quality and Excellence

Cru Bourgeois is not a brand: "It is a traditional mention and we need to give a community [a] figurative mark, a sign of recognition," explains Frederique de Lamothe. By definition, recognition means that there is an acknowledgment of achievement, a quality of merit. "The goal of the Cru Bourgeois is however to represent our wines in a foreign country, in European and distant markets, to promote and communicate. It is a sign of recognition, which, existing since 1932, was known and eligible. All that was missing was a formal classification system for rewarding, promoting, and communication."

The alliance started searching for new ways to renew the assessment process. Six fundamental values have been highlighted by the members of the alliance: innovation, humanity, accessibility, exigency, impartiality, and authenticity. The characteristic of Cru Bourgeois has always been related to the acknowledgment of the wine owners' efforts in improving their wine and continuing the quest for quality, innovation, and, above all, excellence. The idea of working with an independent organization specializing in quality certifications was born. Previously, the main focus of the certification process had been centered only on wine quality assessment.

By the 2009 the system put in place had become a bit clearer. "The difficulty was in finding the criteria which are transversal for eight different AOC wines. For example, some technical procedures, like aging period, differ in the appellations. A set of specifications must find the criteria common for all wines eligible for Cru Bourgeois recognition, and this took time. We were inspired by the AOC new organization ('ODG'). Bureau Veritas has helped to write them down and deal objectively and impartially so that they will be able to control and verify each stage. That was a four-handed writing effort with a person from the Bureau Veritas, which allowed us to move on as quickly as possible," emphasized Frederique de Lamothe.

For both Bureau Veritas and the alliance, it was a learning process: characteristics of wines on the one side, using a certification approach that lacked experience with classifications and with the sector itself on the other side. "I believe that we surfed a bit on the wave of a new organization form of the sector; it is clear that it is a revolution for winegrowers." The exchange was mutually enriching; each part has taken a few small steps forward to find a solution. "They [Bureau Veritas] impose the rules and regulations to ensure that the results are impartial and just. They advised that an annual classification was the most reliable way of ensuring the quality of a product that changes each year, in accordance with the vintage. This annual system is time-consuming but it is representative and a good way to start."

The following eight main points summarize what is new in the classification system proposed by the alliance:

1. During the first stage wine properties are checked for eligibility.
2. Cru Bourgeois has become a single-tier classification, although initially (in 1932) the wines were ranked in importance in three categories.
3. An annual quality assessment considers the wines' quality and not the property or terroir.
4. The selection process takes place from March to July by an independent panel of professional tasters.
5. All procedures are carried out by an independent organization, Bureau Veritas France.
6. Wines are sampled after being uniformly blended.
7. There is a selection of a representative benchmark wine each year that serves as the reference for the tasters.
8. Wines are classified two years after the harvest.

Each of these points attests to a continual quest for wine quality and excellence.

MEMBERSHIP AND TERMS OF REFERENCES

One of the main reasons for becoming a member of the alliance is to join a community of people who share similar interests, similar problems, and support each other in finding solutions. "It is a true alliance and our members are consulted before any decisions are made. We like to see ourselves as one big family, which helps in terms of visibility in export markets. We are open to improvements, we are flexible, and we try to listen and take on board the suggestions and reactions of our wine producer members."

The objective of the alliance, as with other wine unions, is to represent and defend the interests of their members, owners, and wine producers, as well as investigate frauds and counterfeiting. The Alliance of Cru Bourgeois has gone forward to save the Cru Bourgeois mention, which was condemned to disappear. For certain members the selection process is seen as a burdensome task. Since the introduction of the AOC system in 1935, winemakers have gotten used to numerous AOC control procedures, and they don't want to add more. Alliance members think that Bureau Veritas should assist in the selection process to avoid having several organisms doing the same work. Therefore the new assessment process has two different objectives, improving wine quality and increasing traceability of the whole process.

Traceability starts from the parcel of vineyard, continues right through the production process, and finishes with specific attention paid to the taste of all lots presented by a member of the alliance to attain a Cru Bourgeois Official Selection. "They [winegrowers] considered the system partly as a license to buy, while our objective was tracking down the quality of the product. The quality presented in tasting by a property must be exactly the same throughout the entire volume presented for the label. That is a key driver in every phase of our modernization approach."

The members of the alliance who want to opt for the Cru Bourgeois mention must meet the terms of the two following commitments:

- Ensure the specifications of a quality assessment of cultivating and winemaking, for example, designating vineyard parcels for each wine presented, carrying out regular on-the-spot control, taking notes on each procedure performed on each parcel, and so on
- Participate in a number of selection-sampling processes for the wine

At the beginning, in particular during the first year, the assessment is time-consuming for a winemaker, who must get used to the approach and constantly create written assessment of the everyday activities in the vineyard.

"The quality control started in February 2010 and staggered through July 2010. They did not expect that; they had their reputation and years of experience. We had 323 members in 2008, and in 2009 when the specifications of the assessment were finalized, there were many reversals. However, we had 290 candidates. The same person from Bureau Veritas visited all the candidates. She did only that for three months. There were 243 accepted candidates selected for the 2008 vintage; they represented about 30% of the total Médoc production.

There were about forty members rejected during the process, which represents an 85% success rate. Moreover, between February and July, any chateau that failed could present a sample for tasting. Except for logistics constraints, there were no limits; those who started in February could present three or four times. At one tasting, there could be random differences of appreciation; one cannot erase a candidate on the first campaign."

The process of complete traceability of wines must become routine for a winemaker. Keeping timely and accurate data, summarizing key information on different conditions and risk factors, comparing the parcels on a long term, and so on will then facilitate the winemaker's work. A meticulous approach to observing and controlling the vines and the winemaking process will allow detection of problems likely to alter the quality of the wine, and enable implementing preventive measures to avoid and eliminate such risks. To some extent, this type of constant quality assessment could make it possible to avoid costs linked to errors and to increase the performance of a vineyard.

COMMERCIAL ACTIVITIES AND DEVELOPMENTS IN THE INTERNATIONAL MARKET

Since its creation in 1962, the purpose of the alliance has been to promote wines in the international arena. Therefore the alliance has undertaken networking and communication activities to facilitate the recognition of the Cru Bourgeois status. It is essential that information and its dissemination be widely placed to concentrate efforts to reinforce the position of Cru Bourgeois wines abroad.

According to Frédérique Dutheillet de Lamothe, "Depending on the markets, having Cru Bourgeois on your label adds value; according to wine merchants, prices can be increased by 10–20%. Retail prices in France vary from €8 to €30 and up. There is the need for a classification system for the wines that fall between Cru Classé and Cru Artisan. With today's climate and increased competition, the Cru Bourgeois classification is a tremendous chance to 'stand out from the crowd.' We organize many press and trade events for our members see [Figure 5], the presentation of the new vintage in Bordeaux, les primeurs, for example, and most recently with many of our Cru Bourgeois chateaux in China. In emerging markets such as these, any sign of authenticity is reassuring for the new wine consumer."

Figure 5: Cru Bourgeois tasting in Bordeaux, 2011.

The alliance's innovation in its wine-selection process has received abundant attention from local and national media. Since 2010, the impact of the quality procedure has grown. There has been an increase in active communication abroad (particularly in Belgium, the United Kingdom, Germany, China, Hong Kong, and the United States), increased organizing and participating in official tastings, and the creation of salons for wine professionals (more than 70 promotional activities per year).

In 2011, the alliance reinstated the Cru Bourgeois Cup award with a new version in partnership with *Le Point* magazine and Jacques Dupont, a famous wine writer. The competition was organized at VinExpo in Bordeaux. Out of more than 150 Crus Bourgeois du Médoc challenging in the 2008 Official Selection, the specially selected jury identified ten top wines. The overall winner was then determined at a blind tasting of a special jury.

The alliance also created fan clubs on Facebook and Twitter and organized several successful games for their fans, which served as a viral marketing tool for educating and attracting a younger generation of consumers.

There are no exact statistics on the impact of the Cru Bourgeois label on wine commercialization in international markets. "At the level of the Alliance there is no common database on sales' financial statistics. Most of the transactions are usually made via wine merchants (trading houses), and even wine producers themselves do not have complete statistics of the sales of their own wine. What I do request from journalists of different countries whom I meet is whether Cru Bourgeois wines are present in their market and, if so, at what price. They each have their own commercial strategy. Even if the Cru Bourgeois wines are being sold in their country, there is not necessarily information on market sales volume. Our members may sell via wine merchants, distributors, wholesalers, and other distribution channels. The Alliance does not interfere with wine sales. We have neither a central purchasing body nor a trading house."

Nevertheless, the first results of the revised Cru Bourgeois selection confirm that the labeling impact is not homogenous and depends on the distribution channel and the markets where Cru Bourgeois wines reach. At first glance, HSM (hyper- and supermarkets) in France are attentive to the label; the Belgium market strongly appreciates the whole concept of labeling. In Germany supermarkets accept the distinction of Cru Bourgeois wines. The UK and US markets are in the process of learning about the official selections but still are quite neutral in valorizing the Cru Bourgeois mention. In the United Kingdom, famous names of the press follow the official selection and attend annual tastings. The growing Chinese market, which became Bordeaux's largest importer in terms of volume in 2011, is starting to understand the notion and perceives more adequately the value of Cru Bourgeois wines. This is due to strong efforts and numerous events organized especially by the alliance in about five cities across China and in Hong Kong.

FUTURE OF THE ALLIANCE

Definitely, since the earthquake of 2007, the Cru Bourgeois name has made good progress. After a period of disarray, the new formula has been implemented and contained within a comprehensive set of legal and technical procedures. The new system has been in place since 2010 (for a 2008 vintage), and is a valid and original recognition focused on quality and excellence.

Other Bordeaux regions, fascinated by the system developed by the Alliance des Cru Bourgeois du Médoc, have started thinking about joining the process and creating Cru Bourgeois in Sauternes. The president of the ODG (Organisme of the AOC Défense and Management) Sauternes-Barsac has emphasized that it will necessarily require agreement with the alliance: "We should accept the same set of restrictions. The properties should be subject to the same controls to provide the verification of methods and means used, with a mandatory post-adoption visit of each wine property and annual certification of results by blind tasting. For certain winemakers of Sauternes this approach seems to be too cumbersome and restrictive, but it is necessary to know what we really want!"

However, from a commercial point of view, putting a wine back into play annually is not easy to manage, particularly because the alliance communicates with clients in international markets. There is a need to move toward a multi-annual recognition system, which could have a different format—either a chateau can maintain its label for several consecutive years or it could be updated every few years. This project is under study by the Alliance des Crus Bourgeois du Médoc, and the decision could be made soon, though there remain several legal points to address in the meantime.

Another important possible development concerns a one-tier approach. Today the Cru Bourgeois du Médoc annually presents the official selection with no categories or ranking. The annual classification is closer to a label concept than to traditional bordelaise hierarchies. "The fact that the current system is a one-tier classification has caused some criticism. We wanted to securely build the ground floor of our castle, if you like, before adding five or six floors. The historic Cru Bourgeois classification is a precious tool and worth fighting for!" So another decision to make within the same time frame is whether to establish hierarchy as in previous versions of the classification. Again there is no simple, legislative solution for the moment on this issue. The wines of 2013 vintage, for example, which will be selected in 2015, could be thus ranked.

THE PROS AND CONS OF THE CRU BOURGEOIS MEMBERSHIP

Valerie shifted away from the documents she studied and focused on the previous year's sales figures. Her father had sold about 45% of the produced wine abroad, mainly to Germany and the United States; sales in the United Kingdom had dropped significantly in the previous year (from 15% to 5%). She remembered how happy her father was to sell the rest of the stock via wine brokers thanks to the long-standing relations with Société Bonnet Gapenne. In 2011, almost 40% of the wine went to French supermarkets, but the three-year contract was coming to its end quite soon. There were some loyal clients whom her father knew personally for years and maintained warm relations with. He was introduced to a Japanese importer just before his death, though they did not sign any agreements. Valerie recalled that the Japanese client insisted on an exclusivity of sales which was a tricky constraint for her father to accept. Several of her neighbors had started selling wine to China, though they still questioned whether they could rely on the importers, whether demand would continue growing, and whether the investments made would be paid off. Valerie thought that she was not ready yet to explore this option just on her own.

Valerie thought back to discussions with some of her father's friends on the membership in Alliance des Cru Bourgeois du Médoc. The following represents some of their thoughts:

Ludovic and Julien Meffre, joint directors of Chateau du Glana (Saint-Julien), Chateau Lalande (Saint-Julien), and Chateau Bellegrave (Pauillac): "We have the chance to be in very prestigious appellations and have made the choice since the 2009 vintage to communicate under our own brands and opt out of the Cru Bourgeois classification. We feel that too few of the criteria are concerned with the production of quality (for example, in terms of grape sorting after harvest, barrel aging). There are too many heavy administrative procedures, particularly in terms of labeling and technical constraints. We work with Denis Dubourdieu to bring out the wonderful differences of our wines and their terroir. The idea of a benchmark wine that our wines are compared to seems to be working toward the opposite—standardization. The absence of any hierarchy within the classification means that there are no quality distinctions among the different Cru Bourgeois, which removes the desire for healthy competition. For us, the classification has become the equivalent to being awarded a medal.

Our distributors have confirmed what we feel, namely, that Cru Bourgeois for us represents little interest in traditional distribution. We prefer to respond to the actual demands of our customers, which correspond to the real demands of the market today. We are not alone. In Saint-Julien there are no more Cru Bourgeois remaining and many of the former elite of the Cru Bourgeois Exceptionnels, such as Poujeaux, Chasse Spleen, and Siran, have chosen to do the same and focus on their own brand following. What this does mean is that we have to organize our own communication with the world press and trade. For the last primeurs we organized tastings here at Chateau du Glana with the other ex-Cru Bourgeois chateaux of Saint-Julien. There is much work to be done to build our individual brands on the world markets."

Bruno Segond, Chateau Lousteauneuf (Médoc): "At our level, a family property of 28 hectares, we do not have the notoriety of estates such as Poujeaux to be able to promote our wines on our own. Being part of the Cru Bourgeois is a good trampoline for Lousteauneuf. For example, for the Primeurs we have the same visibility as the Crus Classés. The Alliance organizes a tasting for these three days for the thousands of buyers and press from around the world. My press book is filled with press from such events organized by the Alliance. There is a real visibility and exposure that I would not otherwise have. I am involved in the practical aspects of growing and making wine so I have no time to dedicate to press and general communication.

There is a market for Cru Bourgeois; it is a brand in its own right. In markets such as China I have found that to have Cru Bourgeois on your label is a marker, an assurance of a certain level of quality. The new Cru Bourgeois classification is a beginning. It is important that as members, the wine producers continue to communicate with the Alliance about ways to improve the system. There are many opportunities to speak out, but sometimes there is more speaking in the corridor once the meeting is over than during it!

I do not find the labeling requirements restrictive. In this climate you need to anticipate, to be equipped to the minimum before it is required. You get nothing for nothing."

These three winemakers' views are quite contradictory. The process for being selected seems to be quite arduous, though rewarding because it does seem to improve the wine quality.

Valerie then checked other financial documents. The entry fee for alliance is €600, the contribution fee to the alliance per cru including union membership is €15, and then there is the financial contribution to participate in all the activities, including promotion and quality control (see Table 2).

Table 2: The wine alliance fees for participation in Cru Bourgeois selection process (depending on the volume of wine production presented for certification).

Hectoliters 2010 vintage recognized indicated in the first declaration received	Total contribution in € (including VAT)
Less than 500 hl No volume recognized in 2010	3,000
Between 500 and 1000 hl	3,900
More 500 and 1000 hl	4,500

After turning over in her mind a hundred times the question of whether she should become a member of the alliance, Valerie decided to write down all the points she's considering:

- Is there a synergy between her inherited company's marketing strategy and the Alliance des Cru Bourgeois du Médoc membership? What are the benefits and limitations of Bordeaux classifications in the international market from the consumer and distributor points of view?

- It is true that the alliance annual membership fee is not that much (see Table 2), though the participation cost of the certification process ranges from €5,000 to €10,000 per year, and there will be recurring additional labor and overhead charges because of the paperwork necessary for tracking the wines. Does precise tracking improve the quality of the wine production? It is clear that disorder in your winery definitely means a loss of time and quality. But is the opposite true?

- Will Valerie gain advantages from alliance membership in the markets where her wine is well known? Will she need to develop strategies for new markets? The alliance will not take care of her sales but they will take care of promotion. Even so, the label brings benefits in certain export markets ,but the impact is not uniform.

- By the time Valerie will be eligible to present her wines in a selection process (the 2012 vintage) the classification should become multi-annual. What happens if her wine will be classified for three years and then does not get on the list?

Valerie considers drawing a comparative table on classification and assessment to analyze the managerial implications. This should help her to make up her mind concerning Alliance des Crus Bourgeois membership. The outcome of this decision will affect the future of her company.

Authors' Perspective

A new Cru Bourgeois classification on a quality assessment with an external certification body independent of the wine sector is innovative for Bordeaux wines. The case suggests three levels of discussion and questioning. The first relates to the role of classifications, the complexity of wine classifications in Bordeaux, and their impact on sales.

The second includes the analysis of the classification procedure put in place – the heavy legal and technical specifications and their difficulties and advantages for wine producers: benchmarking versus standardization, using an annual versus multiannual approach, and considering the ultimate benefits of classification for wine export versus the heterogeneity of international market reaction.

The third refers to the synthesis that students need to perform in order to suggest a strategic decision for the heroine of the case, the young entrepreneur who inherited a wine property in Médoc.

Complexity of Wine Classifications

Similar to all old vineyards in the world, the Bordeaux wine sector is extremely complex, similar to the Italian DOCG and the French Burgundy region, although the total surface of Burgundy is smaller than the Médoc area and contains about 100 different AOC. Classified growth wines easily maintain their strong position on the market, but other classifications struggle to find and improve their place, particularly in exporting success. Nevertheless, the Pomerol region of Bordeaux has no classification and does not seem to miss it.

In contrast to other wine regions in the world, the Bordeaux wine sector is extremely dispersed and small wine estates are less competitive in external markets because of being alone. The example of the Alliance des Crus Bourgeois du Médoc illustrates that winemakers could create stronger possibilities for wine promotion and communications. Classification is not a guarantee of increased sales, but a sign of recognition that is important, and sometimes even crucial, for a consumer.

Classification via a Quality Assessment with an Independent Agency

We witness that competition for competition's sake is rejected by wine sector actors and there needs to be a greater focus on quality. Since 1998, the AOC system controls the process from the vineyard to the bottle. The Alliance des Crus Bourgeois initiated the idea to develop a selection system centered on wine quality and complete traceability. Several initiatives on wine quality have been proposed recently in Bordeaux; Quali Bordeaux is a good example. Nevertheless, it is different from what the alliance proposed because Quali Bordeaux's purpose is to check the compliance of its member wineries with standards set out in the AOC specifications. The quality assessment concept of the alliance goes further, with traceability and security issues and an objective selection process, a merit of being selected as a Cru Bourgeois.

The recognition of customers comes partly through reinforcing quality. The presence of an independent body, such as Bureau Veritas, assures the customer (in the case of Bordeaux wine, a customer is a wine merchant or wine distributor) of the wine's quality. Richness of the Cru Bourgeois classification is also diverse, with eight AOC represented with different norms and restrictions.

To refer to a benchmark in wine tastings has a double effect: on the one hand a guarantee of the average high quality of the Cru Bourgeois wines, and on the other hand it could bring a homogeneity of tastes, though the bench is given a level, not a wine profile.

The correlation of price to quality is another aspect to consider. It has been shown and proven in numerous academic studies that superior quality typically commands higher prices; the price-quality correlation rises with an increase in information for the consumer. A Cru Bourgeois designation brings reliability and consistency in wine pricing, which can reassure intermediate players (e.g., wine merchants, wine brokers, importers, distributors, e-commerce agents, etc.) on the wine scene.

The highly innovative approach of the alliance is unique and definitely merits further development.

STRATEGIC DECISION MAKING

Well-known decision-making tools (e.g., causal mapping, a strategy map, or issue tree) could be used at this stage by students to enhance the understanding of the benefits and challenges Valerie will face with eventual membership in the Alliance des Crus Bourgeois du Médoc (see Figures 6, 7, and 8).

Figure 6: Example of a causal map.

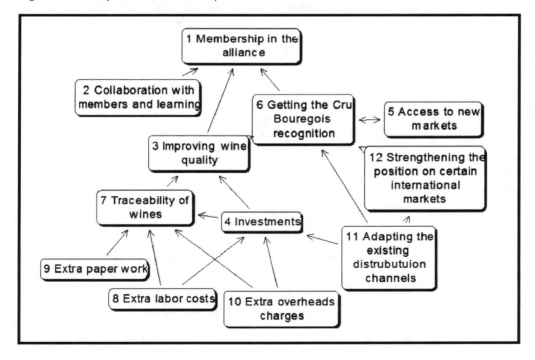

Figure 7: Example of a strategy map

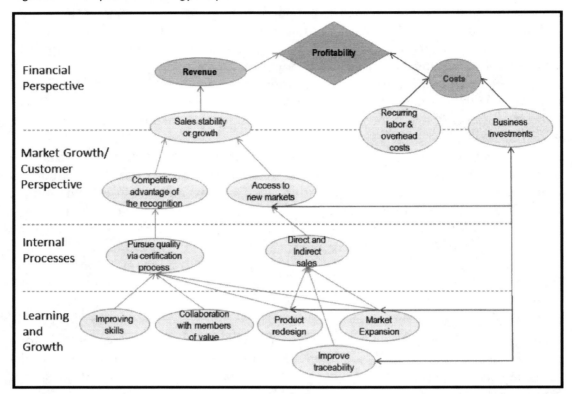

Figure 8: Example of an issue tree

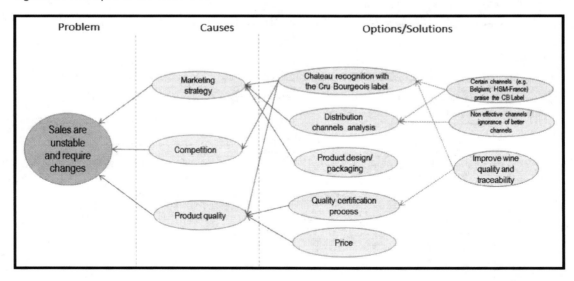

The discussion should consider the marketing strategy of the company, distribution channels, and the selection of countries where Valerie's wines are imported. The Cru Bourgeois official selection brings certain advantages to particular markets where the wines are sold (Germany or the United Kingdom, for example, or China, where there are cases of counterfeiting).

Through these three levels of analysis, what becomes clear is how confusing these existing classifications are, how hard it is to put in place a transparent classification process, and how difficult it is to make a decision about investing in the membership and further classification process, because it is a long-term, multi-stage game in a heterogeneous international wine environment.

APPENDIX 1. BORDEAUX WINE SECTOR DATA

The Bordeaux region of France is the second largest wine-growing area in the world. There are 57 AOC, more than 8,500 wine-producing chateaux, about 40 cooperative cellars and unions of producers, 400 houses of trade (negociants), and about 130 wine brokers (courtiers).

Appendix Table 1: The evolution of Bordeaux wine export from 2000 to 2010.

Source: CIVB (2011) Customs report.

	Volumes in thousands of hectoliters				Value in millions of euros		% BDX in imports of still wines. Volume
	Average 01-05	Average 06-10	2010	1-year trend (%)	2010	1-year trend (%)	
Germany	378	292	264	+5	111	-7	2.0%
China	6	100	229	+67	164	+121	8.1%
Belgium	355	273	222	-5	118	-4	8.5%
United Kingdom	299	241	208	+5	227	-3	1.6%
Japan	137	134	141	+22	95	+4	8.3%
United States	141	143	123	+6	99	-28	1.4%
Hong Kong	15	39	71	+68	251	+130	18.5%
Canada	75	71	66	-4	47	-10	1.9%
Netherlands	144	82	65	+11	41	+10	2.0%
Switzerland	88	69	62	+5	93	-4	3.5%
The 10 main dest.	1 746	1,465	1,449	+13	1,247	+16	2.8%
World	1,979	1,772	1,768	+14	1,514	+17	2.2%

APPENDIX 2. FACTS AND FIGURES ABOUT THE CRU BOURGEOIS

Appendix Table 2: The data on Bordeaux vineyards per region (for the eight AOC represented in the Cru Bourgeois). Source: CIVB, 2011.

	Vineyard surface area (in hectares)	Production (in millions of bottles)	Vineyard information
Bordeaux region	110,000	850	~8,500 wine producers
Médoc	4,900	40	~650 wine growers
HautMédoc	4,270	36	~400 wine growers
Margaux	1,300	9.5	80 wine estates
Saint Estephe	1,200	9	155 wine growers
Pauillac	1,100	8.5	115 wine estates
Saint-Julien	900	6.5	26 wine estates
Listrac	700	5	90 wine estates
Moulis	550	4.2	42 wine estates

Appendix Figure 1: The Cru Bourgeois du Médoc timeline.

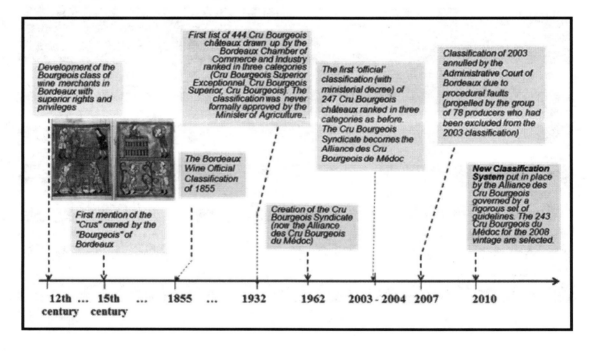

Appendix Table 3: Synthesis of the official selection results 2010-2012.

Vintage year	Selection year	Number of the alliance members	Numbers of classified properties	Total surface of vines (in hectares)
2008	2010	323	243	3,500
2009	2011	304	246	4,300
2010	2012	272	260	4,400

CASE 12

Mouton Cadet

A BRANDED WINE IN THE UNIVERSE OF FIRST GREAT GROWTHS

Jacques-Olivier Pesme
KEDGE Business School, France
Wine and Spirit Management Academy

SUMMARY

Mouton Cadet is a singular story. No other Premiers Grands Crus has ever tried to develop a branded-wine since such endeavor might jeopardize their excellence and scarcity, which are the strength and essence of these prestigious wines. The case examines some marketing strategy aspects of a premium wine brand built upon a venerable history and the vision of Baron Philippe de Rothschild during the 1929 crisis. It pays specific attention to issues such as brand creation, notoriety, distribution channels strategy, and brand portfolio in a recently changing international market environment.

SPECIFICITIES AND MARKET ORGANIZATION OF THE BORDEAUX WINE BUSINESS
1. The "Négoce" based on the estates—brokers—merchants scheme

The first group of wine merchants was created during the 11th century in Bordeaux in response to the expansion of the wine sector resulting from the trade with England, which started after the marriage of Alienor of Aquitaine and Henry II Plantagenet.

Soon Bordeaux actors realized the necessity of protecting and organizing the trade of their wines. Wine brokers (courtiers) and wine merchants (négociants) became intermediaries between wine growers and customers. They created a unique wine trade organization referred to as négoce. The city was deeply influenced by this organization even in its physical development, with the "Chartrons" district entirely devoted to wine trade. Its geometrical architecture responding to trade needs, with the creation of long streets with wine storehouses, was mainly built during the 18th century and designed to ease the transport of barrels and the wine exports through the Garonne River. Over the years, brokers and wine merchants had a major influence and impact on the evolution of wine growing. They were the first to understand and consequently emphasize the importance of the soils (terroirs). They often initiated new methods of production, such as aging in barrels, in view of responding to the customers' specific and evolving tastes. They clearly played a key role in the promotion and the quality enhancement of Bordeaux wines.

At the turn of the last century, the wine industry went through a crisis, due to fraud and a downwards trend in prices. Reacting to this situation, Bordeaux wine actors initiated a national legislation on wine origin, which first designated areas of wine appellations. A national regulating body called Institut National des Appellations d'Origine (INAO) was established in 1936, with the creation of AOC labels (Appellations of Controlled Origin). Since then, INAO has continued to ensure the control and protection of labels, requiring producers to strictly observe the rules. The AOC label originally regulated only wines and brandies, but due to the system's popularity and economic success, INAO's area of competence was extended in 1990 to dairy products and processed foods. On 119,000 hectares , Bordeaux wine industry counted in 2012 around sixty AOC.

Today, the Bordeaux wine sector is made up of 8,000 wine-producing estates, more than 400 wine merchants and approximately 100 brokers. While a great diversity prevails among producers and growers, the 400 wine merchants market more than 70% of Bordeaux production in about 170 countries. Small merchants handle the trade of bottled wines, while larger négoce companies trade bottled wines as well as bulk wine. In such cases, they handle the blending and bottling. Some of the biggest négoce houses even have their own trading brands. Brokers are involved in most of the transactions. Their role is to advise producers on vintage production, select wines for merchants and ensure the proper performance of contracts. They also have a key role in price-setting, which is based on the evolution of the market and is easily predictable for most of the wines, except for the greatest, which stand beyond any economic logic.

Bordeaux château (or estates) might be divided in two main categories. On the one hand, there are about 3,000 small château accounting for more than 95% of Bordeaux region's production, and on the other hand are the most prestigious wines, or Grands Crus (Great Growths), among which around fifty great names stand as flagships of Bordeaux production.

In Bordeaux, small wine producers either trade their wines through négociants and cooperatives, or through direct selling to customers, as for many producers in other wine regions. For the great names, there is no direct sale. The Grand Cru estates trade is entirely handled by the négociants of Bordeaux marketplace.

2. The key role of premiers grands crus

The first official classification of the red and white wines of Bordeaux dates back to 1855. It was established by Bordeaux Brokers Union (Unions des courtiers de Bordeaux) upon a request of the Emperor Napoleon III for a list which could serve as reference in view of the organization of the Universal Exhibition in Paris. Based on more than two centuries of tradition and unofficial ranking, a classification aimed at directly reflecting the quality of the wines was established. In this official classification, published in April 1855, the château were listed according to three criteria: their size, experience and soils. Red wines were listed in a ranking going from first to fifth growths (premiers to cinquième crus), while white wines, limited to Sauternes and Barsac, were divided into three categories. The 1855 list contained 88 château, among which 61 produce red wines, and 27 white. Since 1855, and despite massive changes regarding notably the size of vineyards, this ranking was revised only once. This change occurred in 1973, with Château Mouton Rothschild upgrading from second to first cru.

The sale of these great wines also follows a specific system, called en primeur sale or vente en primeur, which should not be confused with the sale of young wines, referred to as primeurs wines. This sale system is specific to the Bordeaux region. The Vente en primeur only concerns best growths of Bordeaux and is based on the expectation that the prices will increase over time. En primeur sale is articulated around three key moments: tasting, evaluation and pricing. According to this system, wines of the latest vintage are sold during the spring following the harvest. The en primeur sale involves owners and merchants of the region, through brokers. After the transaction, wine nevertheless stays under the responsibility of the estate, which handles its growing and bottling, about 18 to 24 months later. As such, the 2012 vintage is to be sold en primeur in spring 2013, for an actual delivery starting during the first semester of 2015, at the time when the wines will be bottled. The concept can be described as "buying futures," and indeed these wines are made in the perspective of becoming cellar wines for aging. This system of en primeur sale comes from an old tradition of sale between Bordeaux estates, brokers and merchants, based on oral contracts between gentlemen. Lately, these informal deals were partly replaced by a more formal system. In the '70s, price quotations started to be more organized, followed by the holding of important tastings in the '80s. In the '90s, speculation surfaced with Japanese buyers, and it has further increased and intensified since 2000. With the apparition of the Chinese buyers on the market, 2005 and 2008 were two decisive years for speculation intensification, to the point that the greatest estates sell their production in less than thirty minutes, during the spring en primeur sale.

This recent evolution partly results from the creation of the Union des Grands Crus de Bordeaux (UGCB) in 1973. A little less than forty years ago, almost all the Grands Crus decided to gather under the frame of an union, which currently has 132 members. Its core mission is to organize the communication and marketing strategy of these great houses. Each spring, UGCB organizes a primeur tasting week, which soon after its creation became an institution, and was attended in 2012 by 6,000 people from more than 68 different countries. In addition, UGCB organizes about sixty events each year, in France and abroad. In 2011, 35,000 wine professionals and 11,000 amateurs participated in the UGCB events. Despite criticisms over the gap hence created between small estates and Grands Crus, this specific sale system, together with the related communication and marketing campaigns, has had a positive impact on Bordeaux region as a whole and eventually benefits all the wine industry actors.

Over the years, with the critical price increase of the wines belonging to the 1855 classification and their massive export abroad, average customers have turned to less prestigious and more affordable wines. This trend has notably benefited the category of Crus Bourgeois wines. The classified great estates then decided to engage the wine market at a lower level and notably compete with the Crus Bourgeois with the trading of their second wines. The practice related to the production of a second wine goes back at least to the 18th century but was only generalized in the '80s, and is currently the rule. By definition, second wines are made with plots located on their premium growth estate, but not selected for the composition of the first wine blend. Second wines blending often results from the premium wine vats' "leftovers," which did not meet the extremely high level of quality expected for the blending of the great growth. Even though resulting from different vine plots and blends second wines share many common characteristics with their first wines. They usually are less concentrated, and intended to be drunk sooner than the first label. The second wines are usually made from younger vine plots and aged in lower quality barrels. They are bottled with a separate label. Nonetheless, second wines produced by the Grands Crus estates are high quality wines. Recently their prices increased significantly, especially for the second wines of the Premiers Grands Crus (or First Growths), with prices more often above 150 euros, which make them even more expensive than famous 2nd Grands Crus (or Second Growths). Some of the great estates even define a second wine as "another" wine, a wine on its own, with its own character. Other Grand Cru estates, more in line with tradition, see their second wine has a blend enabling them to devote a very limited selection of their production for the first wine. All the great growth château capitalize on their names and distribution channels to trade their second wines, which are of great value to them and have become major assets. Notably since the emergence of Chinese buyers on the market who are desperate for first Crus, or a second wine if they cannot obtain the first wine. These second wines are hence rapidly sold at high prices, and stand as instrumental ambassadors of their château by popularizing the label among a larger audience.

Table 1. Bordeaux place price (euro, €), second wines. September 2011

Châteaux	2009	2008	2007	2006	2005	2004	2003	2002	2001	2000
Carruades (Laffite)	305	350	360	375	375	375	350	375	375	370
Pavillon Rouge (Margaux)	155	135	138	140	145	130	147	140	142	165
Petit Mouton (Mouton Rothschild)	130	135	126	170	145	150	135	140	150	NC

BARON PHILIPPE DE ROTHSCHILD S.A.

In the mid-19th century, Baron Nathaniel de Rothschild, one of the sons of Baron Nathan, the founder of the English branch of the family, settled in Paris, where he hosted prestigious dinners for Paris' greatest personalities. In 1853, he bought Château Brane

Mouton, which was located in Pauillac (Médoc). The estate was renamed Château Mouton Rothschild, hence fulfilling his wish to serve his own wine to his guests. Two years later, it was ranked first of the second classified Grands Crus of Bordeaux. After his death, the estate was ruled by his son James and after him, his grandson Henri, who showed limited interest for wine making. The youngest son of Henri, Philippe de Rothschild, took the head of Mouton in 1922, at the age of twenty. Under his leadership, which lasted more than sixty years, the family estate drastically expanded and evolved. Some of his management strategies and choices even modified some rules of Bordeaux traditional négoce. Among Baron Philippe's greatest achievements are the revolution of the bottling at the château, the creation of Mouton Cadet and the 1973 classification of Mouton Rothschild among the first Grands Crus. Over the years, the company has also considerably expanded the scope of its activities by purchasing other estates, creating new wines and establishing partnerships. Baron Philippe de Rothschild died in 1988, and since then his daughter Baroness Philippine de Rothschild has been chairing the family company.

Today, Baron Philippe de Rothschild S.A. is a public limited company, with four subsidiaries:

- Baron Philippe de Rothschild, Maipo Chile ;
- Baron Philippe de Rothschild, Orient ;
- Baron Philippe de Rothschild, France Distribution;
- La Baronnie, France.

With a €6.25 million capital, the company total sales accounted for €233 million in 2011, with the selling of 35 million bottles. The company activities are divided into two separate businesses: château wines and branded wines. From Pauillac, where its headquarters are located in the Centre Baron Philippe, the company fully owns and manages three classified great growths on a total surface area of 200 hectares : Château Mouton Rothschild, the flagship of the company (First Growth); Château d'Armailhac (Fifth Growth); and Château Clerc Milon (Fifth Growth). This group also contains the two second wines of Château Mouton de Rothschild: Le Petit Mouton de Mouton Rothschild and Aile d'Argent. These estates annually produce a total of 700,000 bottles, bottled and aged at their respective estates. Three other growths situated outside of the Bordeaux region, also belong to the companys: Opus One in California (in association with Robert Mondavi Winery), Almaviva in Chile (in association with Concha y Toro) and Domaine de Baron'arques (Languedoc, France). Furthermore, Baron Philippe de Rothschild S.A. is the exclusive distributor of three other premium wines which it does not produce: Château Coutet (First Growth Sauternes-Barsac) and its second wine, La Chartreuse de Coutet, as well as Dry White of Château Coutet.

Besides premium wines, Baron Philippe de Rothschild S.A. produces each year twenty million bottles of branded wines. The company's branded wines produced in France come from vineyards located either in the Bordeaux Region or in the Pays d'Oc . After harvesting, branded wines are grown, blended and bottled at Saint-Laurent-Médoc Winery. This was built in 1993 to gather on a 40-acre site all the needed facilities and equipment to blend, age, bottle and package the branded wines produced by Baron Philippe de Rothschild S.A. The other branded wines of the company are made in Chile by one of the company's wholly-owned subsidiaries, Baron Philippe de Rothschild Maipo Chile. One of its latest achievements was the launching of the Escudo Rojo branded wine in 2003.

Exports account for 80% of the company activity. Baron Philippe de Rothschild S.A. has maintained overseas regional agencies and partnerships in each of the following great trade areas: Asia, the Americas and Europe. The United States, France, Great Britain, Canada, Germany, Belgium, Switzerland, Netherlands, Scandinavia and Japan are its most important markets. Baron Philippe de Rothschild S.A. is present in 150 markets thanks to its 140 agents and partners, and stands as Bordeaux AOC wine's leading export company.

According to Bordeaux tradition, the trade of the Rothschild premium wines is partly handled by Bordeaux négoce houses, with which the company maintains closed links. Each year, the company offers Bordeaux négociants its premium wines in the frame of the en primeur sale. Another part of these wines export is supported by the company's exclusive and strong distribution network abroad. One of the company's key success factors has been to totally separate and differentiate the distribution channels of its premium wines and branded wines, with its two lines of business using distinct distribution channels, a selective one for its premium wines and a large-scale one for its branded wines.

The distribution of the company's branded wines in France, which accounts for 20% of revenues, is indeed entirely handled by Baron Philippe de Rothschild France Distribution (R.F.D.), another fully-owned subsidiary of Baron Philippe de Rothschild S.A. Overseas branded wines are distributed through agreements with partners and agencies.

HISTORY OF MOUTON CADET

Mouton Cadet was born in 1930 thanks to a bold and brilliant idea of Baron Philippe de Rothschild. It was originally created as the second wine of Château Mouton Rothschild, but this successful wine soon became a branded wine with its own personality, blended from wine plots located outside of its original estate domain to cope with a growing demand. The year 1930 was marked by a difficult harvest which resulted in a poor quality wine that Baron Philippe found not worthy of being traded under the Château Mouton Rothschild label, but still good enough to be sold. This wine was named Mouton Cadet, after Baron Philippe, who was the youngest son of his family, the cadet in French.

Mouton Cadet soon proved successful, due notably to the tough economic context. In 1930, people were affected by the dire economic situation and thus attracted by this new wine from Rothschild sold at an affordable price. Production stopped during Second World War, before resuming in 1947, which was also marked by Mouton Cadet classification as a Bordeaux AOC. In France, Mouton Cadet owed its fast success to a network of leading French restaurants' chefs, who liked this quality wine and hence favored its popularization. Afterwards, Mouton Cadet distribution expanded abroad, thanks to an active marketing strategy, first in Great Britain during the '50s and during the next decade in the United States. Mouton Cadet then enjoyed an extremely fast expansion, mainly backed by its tremendous popularity on the North American market. In response to this increasing demand, Baron Philippe de Rothschild created a Mouton Cadet white in 1972, which soon became popular and further reinforced the idea of a Mouton Cadet brand range. A rosé wine, Le Rosé de Mouton Cadet, was eventually added to the range in 1993.

In 1975 Mouton Cadet sold three million bottles. This figure reached a record high less than ten years later, with seventeen million bottles sold. The success was overwhelming in North America, with 4.7 million bottles sold in the American market in 1986. In the '80s, almost 50% of the white Bordeaux bottles sold worldwide were Mouton Cadet, and one bottle out of four red wines. Over the ten years following the creation of the Baron Philippe de Rothschild France distribution, sales of Mouton Cadet tripled in France, entering the mass retail market, while doubling in Germany. Mouton Cadet was also able to adjust to the evolution of the markets, further increasing its products range, with the creation of the label Réserve Mouton Cadet Médoc in 1996. The idea was to offer a red wine with greater aging potential. Later on, the label Réserve Mouton Cadet, which is targeted to wine merchants, retailers and restaurants, was complemented by additional wines: Réserve Mouton Cadet Saint-Émilion, Réserve Mouton Cadet Sauternes, and Réserve Mouton Cadet Graves (red and white).

MOUTON CADET IN THE 2000's & TODAY's TRADE ORGANIZATION

Mouton Cadet brand evolution continued in the 2000s with an exceptional year 2002, when sales reached fifteen million bottles worldwide. Afterwards, Mouton Cadet went through a more difficult phase, 2004 being a turning year. The branded wine underwent a slow-down phase. The fall of its sales, notably in the United States might be explained by a change in the customer's taste, as well as the generalization of an anti-French trend, but also mostly by dramatic changes and concentration of distributors. Figures showed a serious downgrade, from 6.5 million bottles sold in 1992 in the United States to 2.9 million in 2004. The brand reaction to this situation was backed by a broad market review in view of best responding to the evolution of the customers' demands and taste, and best adjusting to new trends applied to younger and urban customers. Mouton Cadet was able to proceed with such a comprehensive and accurate evaluation of its various markets, thanks to its large network abroad and its long-running commercial policy in the field. The company had indeed long developed and maintained a network of local partners in each of its subsidiaries or offices abroad, which among other activities permanently monitor, study and assess the changes in their respective market areas.

This resulted in two major changes related to Mouton Cadet blend and packaging. In 2004, a new blend was released. The new Mouton Cadet wine is rounder and fruitier, resulting from an adaptation to contemporary taste. It was nevertheless composed in compliance with Baron Philippe's genuine philosophy: developing a fine Bordeaux wine that is accessible to all. In addition, the bottle presentation and label also evolved toward greater simplicity. A brand icon was created, which shows a stylized sheep's head on a fleece shaped like a grape. This simple image perfectly embodies two of the brand constitutive elements: the sheep and the grape.

Finally, in 2005 Mouton Cadet signed a distribution agreement with North Lake Wines, a subsidiary of Constellation Brands, one of the world's largest wine distributors, which became its importer in the United States. Such international joint ventures have been core elements of Baron Philippe de Rothschild S.A. strategy. Initially, the joint ventures developed by the company concerned wine production, as with Opus One in California in 1980, or Concha y Toro in Chile in 1997, while the one with Constellation Brands was different since it was linked to distribution.

In terms of price, Mouton Cadet wines are situated from the middle to the high-end of the Bordeaux AOC wines price range. For instance, the price for a bottle of Mouton Cadet is a little less than €10, and between €12 and a little less than €20 for Réserve Mouton Cadet wines, while Bordeaux AOC wines are usually sold between €5 and €15.

The promotion of Mouton Cadet image has also been strongly encouraged by Baroness Philippine de Rothschild, notably through sponsoring operations and partnerships in the sport sector as well as with the fashion and movie industries. Mouton Cadet has sponsored many popular events such as the Calgary Olympic Games, Lancôme Golf Trophy, and many other international golf tournaments, as well as the French Open, and the Grand-Prix of Monaco. It has been the official supplier of Cannes Film Festival for more than twenty years. A Mouton Cadet Wine Bar was even created two years ago on the terrace of the Palais des festivals.

Mouton Cadet ended the first decade of the 21st century with the celebration of the 80th anniversary of its creation, and the organization of numerous events worldwide.

Mouton Cadet sells twelve million bottles each year. Seventy-two per cent of its production is exported, thanks to the brand presence in 150 countries, through 120 agents, importers and distributors. According to estimates, Baron Philippe de Rothschild S.A. earns each year between €2 and 4 million with Mouton Cadet.

Success of a Branded Wine, A Unique Case Among First Great Growths

Mouton Cadet is unique. No other Premiers Grands Crus have ever tried to develop a branded wine since such endeavor might jeopardize their excellence and scarcity, which are the strength and essence of these prestigious wines. Mouton Cadet's continued success certainly induces them to consider creating their own branded wines. But reproducing this outstanding story would not be easy given that it was the fruit of a combination of specific key factors—first of all, Baron Philippe's boldness, which led him to believe that a Grand Cru might produce more than one wine. Furthermore, he built the Mouton Cadet brand way before the general recognition of branding as an efficient business tool. Mouton Cadet also benefited from his creator's decision to handle the bottling of his own wine, rather than leaving it to the négociants as it was the usual and well-established practice. Baron Philippe made this revolutionary decision in order to be independent and cope with an increasing demand, while triggering discontent among the Bordeaux wine industry actors.

In order to insure a stable, high quality sourcing for Mouton Cadet wines, Baron

Philippe de Rothschild S.A. has established since 1992 close partnerships with more than 400 winemakers, which represent a large part of the Bordeaux wine industry. Mouton Cadet is success is also firmly rooted in the region and in the company involvement in the Bordeaux wine industry.

Above all, the greatest achievement of Mouton Cadet was to have succeeded on its own and written its own story without damaging the image of Château Mouton Rothschild, and maybe even contributing to the popularization of this Grand Cru name.

QUESTIONS

1. What can be said in terms of branding, especially for the wines of Bordeaux? In the case of Baron Philippe de Rothschild, is it a risky branding strategy?
2. Describe Mouton Cadet target marketing and comment on it.
3. How does the Baron Philippe de Rothschild distribution system operate? How is it connected and related with the local Bordeaux organization?

AUTHOR'S PERSPECTIVE

The case examines some marketing strategy aspects of a premium wine brand built upon a venerable history and the vision of Baron Philippe de Rothschild during the 1929 crisis. It pays specific attention to issues such as brand creation, notoriety, distribution channels strategy, and brand portfolio in a recently changing international market environment.

In addition, Mouton Cadet is of particular interest because of its specificity in Bordeaux landscape. The brand wine logic, which usually is the benchmark of New World countries, backed to a symbol of the selective classification of an Old World country makes it a fruitful, insightful and inspiring example for wine industry actors.

Beyond the unique organization of Bordeaux marketplace, as well as its specific channels in terms of wine trade, this case calls for reflection on three main questions:

Firstly, the brand related issue and its extension, notably in today's wine market, which increasingly involves greater and clearer visibility for consumers.

Then, we may question the opportunity for prestigious estates to engage in target marketing, allegedly with less risk, in the development of a consumer-brand. This underpins the question of positioning the branded wine accordingly with an important issue on brand portfolio management and the need not to confuse the consumers, with a clear distinction between first, second and sometimes third wines, and what is referred to as branded wine.

In consequence, thirdly, in case of a brand extension, what would be the appropriate distribution channels? Should they be dissociated, a the strategy chosen by Baron Philippe de Rothschild dictates, or linked as others recommend, in order to exert a greater pressure on first growth distributors who would desperately like to become allocators?

1. Brand and brand extension

Mouton Cadet is a good example of how a new brand (particularly in a traditional industry) adds dimensions differentiating the offering in some way from other offerings designed to satisfy the same need, e.g. wine and especially a wine from Mouton Rothschild.

Marketing activities throughout the organization as well as the value chain should be integrated to ensure consistency with the brand strategy.

It brings some elements to the decision maker when he/she has to devise a brand strategy, with the key question for the organization being first and foremost to decide whether "to brand" or "not to brand" a wine. If the organization decides to brand, it must choose which brand name to use, whether an individual name, château, varietal, region, family name, or corporate name combined with individual product name, etc.

This is a good example of brand extension, which consists in associating a new product with an existing brand, thereby extending the brand to cover the product. In the case of Mouton Cadet, this has increased the odds of success for the new branded wine. Here one of the key questions is the risk -with extensions- of diluting the brand. It happens when consumers can no longer associate a brand with a specific product or similar set of products, and start thinking less of the brand.

2. Target marketing and positioning

Target marketing is the decision to distinguish the different groups that make up a market to develop corresponding products and marketing mixes for each target market. Baron Philippe de Rothschild has created and implemented this "unknowingly." Nowadays, especially with the new competitive pressure from New World wines countries, wine operators (producers, wine merchants, etc.) are moving toward target marketing because it is often more efficient in spotting market opportunities and developing winning product marketing mixes. In that matter, Philippe de Rothschild was definitely a visionary.

By identifying and "profiling" a distinct group of buyers who may want Mouton wine at a lower price and on regular occasions, he identified a specific demand in a newly segmented market. Accordingly, Baron Philippe de Rothschild S.A. applies a different marketing mix, selecting different market segments to enter, and establishing and communicating the key distinctive benefits of the product or service to the target market (positioning).

3. Differentiating distribution channel

Marketing channel decisions are among the most complex and challenging decisions facing a firm, especially when one of your products is considered as a luxury good and/ or an icon. Channel choices must reflect the exclusive environment of your product. In addition, each channel system creates a different level of sales and costs. Once a firm selects a particular marketing channel, it usually must adhere to it for a substantial period of time. The chosen value network or channel will significantly affect and be affected by the other elements in the marketing mix.

Essentially, Premiers Grands Crus don't have their own channels, they all use the Bordeaux system for more than 90% of their production. In that matter Baron Philippe de Rothschild S.A., thanks to Mouton Cadet and other branded wines, is different, and has its own system. In the case of Bordeaux, the organization –which can be discussed with participants on its pros and cons- is very singular and powerful. Consequently, even if wine producers face many channel alternatives for reaching a market, they usually deal with local brokers and wine merchants.

For Mouton Cadet and branded wines, Baron Philippe de Rothschild S.A. has relevantly decided to distinguish channel distribution. Also, in line with its specific market approach, it has internalized specialized distribution business units for specific regional areas, as a vertical integration of its operations. This is also a clearly differentiated approach in the Bordeaux First Grands Crus world.

Last but surely not least, Mouton Cadet's overwhelming success notably raises the issue of the relevance for prestigious estates of developing branded wines, whose legitimacy and reputation will result from the château's long-established image. Nowadays it appears that the risk is limited for them, regarding profit at least. Given the very strong demand for premium wines, due to the high level of confidence placed in the château's wines production, the consumers' trust for its branded wine would initially be high.

The question not only concerns first growths, but second, third, fourth and fifth growths as well, which also enjoy a strong image and an important demand.

Another question regards these branded wines' identification, attributes and positioning within the château's products portfolio, or as in the concerned case for Baron Philippe de Rothschild S.A. Novice consumers often see Mouton Cadet as Château Mouton Rothschild's second wine. Somehow, Baron Philippe de Rothschild originally considered Mouton Cadet a second wine when he launched it in 1930. "Somehow" because at that time the production of a second wine neither existed nor corresponded to any established standard, except for Châteaux Margaux and other very rare estates. One of the reasons was that owners feared that the presence of a second wine might jeopardize the reputation of a whole estate.

READINGS

http://www.bpdr.com/fr

http://www.moutoncadet.com/

"Mouton Rothchild," by Jane Anson, Wine Business International, 2007

Union des grands crus classés de Bordeaux, http://ugcb.net/

Union des Maisons de Bordeaux, http://www.vins-bordeaux-negoce.com/

"Mouton Cadet, un pionnier à l'international," César Compadre, Sud Ouest, Nov 29, 2011, http://www.sudouest.fr/2012/11/27/mouton-cadet-un-pionniera-l-internation-al-891859-4964.php

"Médoc, second vin de cru classé : l'autre face du Château," Jacques Dupont, Le Point, Sep 02, 2004

"Les grands crus dégriffés," Eric Corian, L'Express, Jan 24, 2005
Kotler P, Keller K., Manceau D., Marketing Management, 14th edition, 2012

ENDNOTES

1. Or 294,055 acres.
2. Or 494 acres.
3. Mouton Cadet, Réserve Mouton Cadet, Les Cuvées Barons et Baronnes, Agneau/Berge Baron, La Bélière / Mise de la Baronnie made from the production of strictly selected wine-makers.
4. The Company's Pays d'Oc varietal wines are made from Cabernet Sauvignon, Merlot, Pinot Noir, Syrah, Chardonnay, Sauvignon Blanc and Viognier.
5. Spanish translation of red shield-Rothschild.

Bonnet-Gapenne

A BORDEAUX WINE MERCHANT EVALUATES FUTURE POSITIONING

Pierre Mora
KEDGE Business School, France

SUMMARY

Bonnet-Gapenne (B&G) is a Bordeaux-based wine merchant representing more than 400 producers. Although the Bordeaux region has not suffered the harsh weather conditions of other wine-growing areas, B&G still has had to reevaluate the nature of their market segments to help increase sales. Their past success has stemmed from maintaining frequent contact with their producers. By expanding an international sales presence, setting up international offices, and investing in storage facilities B&G can further increase their profitability.

INTRODUCTION

In July 2012, Bordeaux's three-day wine festival came to a close with a fireworks show celebrating an exceptional year that had brought 500,000 visitors to the city's waterside area. Fifty thousand tasting passes—twice as many as the year before—had been purchased by a public seeking to discover the region's many different appellations. Huge crowds largely composed of young people had come to meet with winegrowers and familiarize themselves with their products.

With more than 6,000 chateaux and estates operating in the region, 300 merchants with officers in the city, and 60,000 people employed directly by the sector (which sells 25% of its output in the export markets), the Gironde district's highly dynamic wine-growing sector continues to be a valuable part of France's economy and culture.

Figure 1: Simplified presentation of French wine-growing sector.

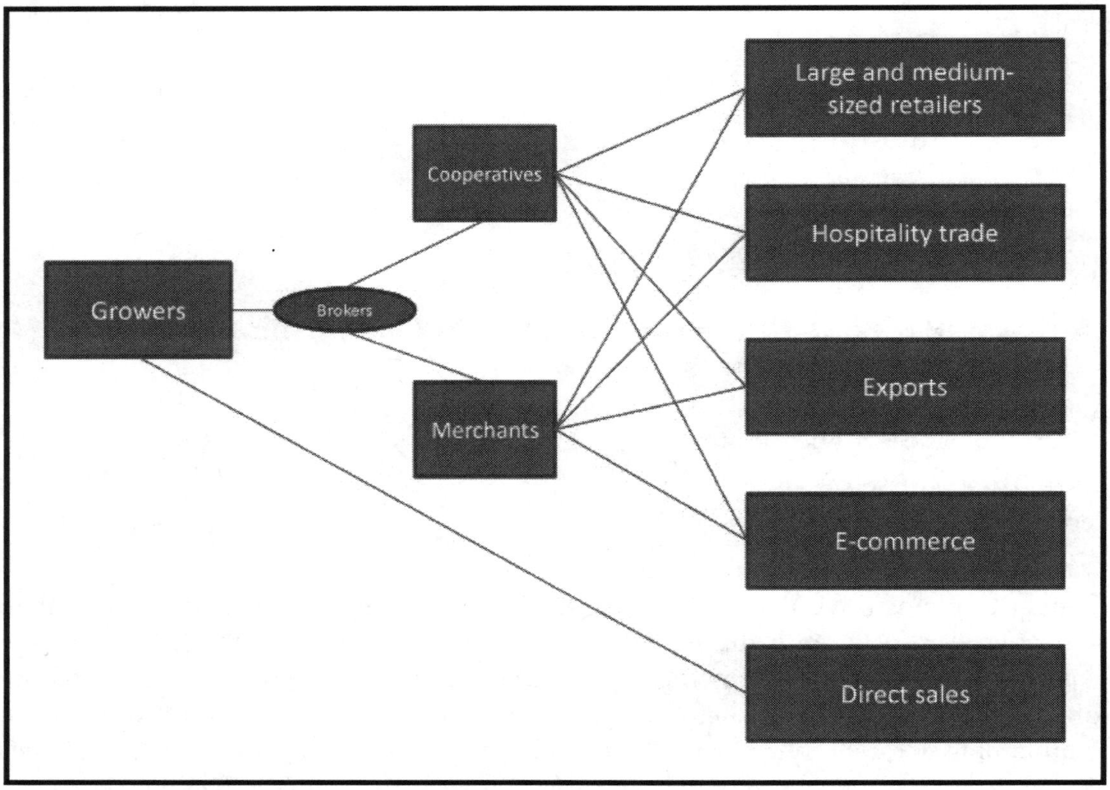

One of the event's organizers, Laurent Gapenne—joint CEO of Société Bonnet Gapenne (B&G) and vice president of the powerful CIVB (Comité Interprofessionnel des Vins de Bordeaux, "Interprofessional Committee for Bordeaux Wines") was gladdened by this show of enthusiasm, which had been surprising given the stagnation in wine consumption in France. Indeed, above and beyond organizing a festival, Bordeaux was already making a concerted effort to improve the quality of its wines as well as its communications at home and abroad.

Gapenne was also aware of the importance of considering the future of his company by grappling with strategic questions such as what kind of market demand was likely to arise over the medium term and how B&G should respond. Between stagnating domestic consumption, retailers' tendency to squeeze prices, sector's concentration in the hands of just a few growers and merchants, operatives' increased aggressiveness in the overseas markets, the unknown effects of e-business in the wine sector, and the business model's variable focus on "brand" and "land," Gapenne made the decision to review his strategic options—and to ask you what to do.

A Few Trends in the French Wine-Growing Sector (Source: France Agrimer)

"The global economic crisis has been a quiet interlude for the sector. French domestic consumption has continued to fall but the recovery in exports gives professionals a reason to hope."

From routine consumption to a moment of pleasure

France is still the world's leading consumer of wine, although per capita consumption has fallen since the 1960s, stabilizing at about 50 liters per annum per person. Today, most French wine purchases are from supermarkets, with 2010 volumes of 9.5 million hectoliters of still (non-sparkling) wine being comparable to 2009 levels but representing, in value terms, a 1.9% rise to €3.5 billion. With respect to the different product categories, the mass retail sector saw year-on-year AOP (appellation d'origine protégée, "protected appellation of origin") sales that were stable in volume (at 5 million hectoliters) but up 2.1% in value, reaching €2.6 billion. IGP (indication géographique protégée, "protected geographic reference") wine sales were 2.6% higher than 2009, coming in at 2.7 million hectoliters and generating revenues of €0.6 billion (+3.9%). However, non-IGP Vin de France wines (lacking any geographic references) fell by 7.3% in volume (0.9 million hectoliters) and by 6.4% in value (€170.3 million). The market share of bag-in-box wines (27.4% in 2010) continued to rise with volumes (2.6 million hectoliters) up 10.4% versus 2009 and turnover (€559.7 million) up 11.2%.

Recovery in imports and export

Whereas competition from so-called New World wines had had an effect on exports in 2009, the trend reversed the following year, with French wine exports up 7% in volume (13.5 million hectoliters) and 14% in value (€6.3 billion). Still wine exports recorded a small drop in volume (5.3 million hectoliters or −3% for AOPs; 6.7 million hectoliters or −6% for non-AOPs) but were up in value (€3.1 billion or +3% for AOPs; €1.1 billion or +10% for non-AOPs) thanks to higher average prices. Year after year Champagne exports were comparable in volume (1 million hectoliters) but fell slightly in value (€1.9 billion, or −3%). Other sparkling wines rose by an eye-catching 18% in volume (0.5 million hectoliters) and 25% in value (€0.2 billion).

Of 2010 French wine imports, 90% came from the European Union, particularly Spain (58%) and Italy (20%). Total volumes, slightly up to 5.9 million hectoliters, were composed of 70% IGP wines, 9% non-IGP wines, 18% AOP wines, and 3% sparkling wines.

Key figures

- 2010 wine exports: 6.33 billion (+ 14%)
- France is the third largest export sector and number one for agricultural products
- Number of growers: 95,000
- Thirty percent of all growers work on estates with an area exceeding 10 hectares, accounting for 79% of the total vineyard.

Table 1: Main target markets (Source: Vinexpo 2011)

Exports (in millions of 9 liter cases)	2010	2010/2005
Germany	26.245	-4%
United Kingdom	23.576	-27%
Belgium	17.610	-6%
Holland	13.134	-11%
United States	9.878	-9%
Canada	5.500	-10%
China	4.273	+134%
Note: In 2011 (and for the first time), non-European markets accounted for the majority of all sales.		

Table 2: Production and consumption forecasts (Source: Vinexpo 2011)

Billions of 9 liter cases	2005	2009	2012 (forecast)	2014 (forecast)
Production (vol.)	3091	3119	3049	3149
Consumption (vol.)	2513	2626	2645	2729
Consumption (value): $ billions	167	183	186	198

The role of merchants

Merchants' real business is worth exploring in greater detail. The Union des Maisons de Négoce de Bordeaux ("Union of Bordeaux Merchants"), the trade association to which B&G belongs, sees merchants as fulfilling five crucial functions that constitute their added value and make them central to the whole of the profession:

> **Selection:** Merchants choose which wines they want to sell. It is their knowledge that helps them respond to customer demand and satisfy consumer expectations.
>
> **Growing/blending:** Most Bordeaux wines are blended, coming from several growers and expressing sub-regional differences.
>
> **Bottling:** Wines are bottled by merchants or growers. The regulation applied to labels depends on the final destination. Bordeaux has a trading capacity of about 650 million bottles.
>
> **Promotions and sales:** These are key functions for merchants seeking to supply the French market, which accounts for two-thirds of total volume, as well as overseas markets. These tasks are carried out through merchants having a high-quality reference portfolio, imagining innovative packaging, coordinating their supply chains, and helping distributors through place-of-sale promotions.

Advice: Some merchants offer suppliers advice in vineyard management and vinification. Toward this end, they sometimes second their own technical teams. Further downstream, merchants will keep customers informed and help them make choices.

BONNET GAPENNE, THE COMPANY

B&G, a merchant company founded in 1981, is highly representative of the wine trade as it is practiced in France today.

The company recently expanded from sixteen to twenty staff members, reflecting market growth. It generates a turnover of around €8.4 million, with a supplier portfolio composed of something like 600 growers. Forty customers account for the lion's share of all sales. The activity is split 50–50 between the French and foreign markets. At home, 70% of all sales are done through large retail outlets and 30% in the hospitality sector. Seventy percent of the wine that the company sells in France comes from the Bordeaux region.

One of the company's key factors of success is the constant presence of four front-line officers who visit chateaux and other estates to increase their familiarity with wines by tasting them and gaining knowledge of conditions in which they are produced. Proximity to growers and responsiveness to opportunities are part of a merchant's added value. The French hospitality trade is currently experiencing strong growth in rosé wines. Conversely, bottles with screw-top capsules are not doing very well in the country. The same applies to white wine.

Globally, the company seems to typify the current situation in France, one marked by a return to normality with growers holding around sixteen months of stocks (less than in the early 2000s). In addition, the Bordeaux region has not suffered as badly as others from severe climate conditions: frost in the Loire and Burgundy regions; droughts in the south, Spain, and Australia. This seems to have reduced volumes, with the ensuing shortage benefiting Bordeaux in terms of selling its output and better remuneration for growers. As an example, the price of a 900-liter barrel of Bordeaux red went back up to about €1,000 in mid-2012.

B&G's organizational chart and financial data

Figure 2: The Bonnet Gapenne team (as of year-end 2011).

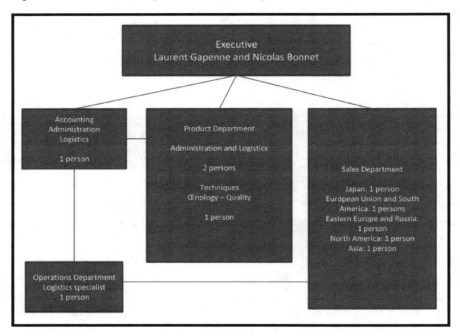

Table 3. Financial data (in euros).

	2009	2010	2011
Turnover	4,181,000	6,421,000	8,420,000
Net income	37,000	45,000	51,000
Staff numbers	10	12	16
Shareholder equity	30,000	30,000	30,000
Cash position	83,000	111,000	193,000

Factors of differentiation

Before knowing how to sell something, a trader must be a good buyer. Sourcing is a strategic activity in the wine trade, and with B&G's executive maintaining direct and permanent relationships with 600 growers, Gapenne believes that this upstream presence might be a factor differentiating it from the competition. To improve these relationships and lock in suppliers, B&G has recently invested in an application providing it with greater overview but also offering more information to growers. Lodged on a secure extranet, the application gives B&G a grower fact sheet for each of its partners, and as many product sheets as the number of references that it carries. Data includes ingredients, performance, availability, descriptions, and photos. The information is inputted and updated by the suppliers themselves, who verify data validity and help in this way to build up and maintain the database. Subsequently, the company can develop its product offers based on perceived customer demand. In return, growers receive information directly on how the products are selling and, ultimately, who the purchasers are.

Commercial activities

To describe changes in B&G's consumers and markets, Gapenne has started thinking according to a new segmentation suggested by CIVB.

Table 4: Segmentation of French market (Source: CIVB Bordeaux Demain ["Tomorrow"] Plan).

Segment	Description	Changes in company's customer base
Basic	Less than €2 (price in large retail outlets, ex-promotions) Men over the age of 50 Lower socio-professional categories Nutritional needs: routine	Progressively being eliminated by the company, to be replaced by non-IGP brands Launch of Bordeaux claret Development of a rosé that increasingly looks like a gateway product
Fun	€2 to €6 Women and men between the ages of 25 and 35 Middle socio-professional categories Style: importance of image, sharing, conviviality	Segment that is progressively expanding, thanks notably to exports USA and Japan characterize this trend. Positioned at $15 Opportunities for taking advantage of excellent recent vintages (2009 and 2010).
Exploration	€6 to €20 Women or men Higher socio-professional categories Autonomous, like experimenting Importance of relationship between price and enjoyment	Hardest segment to work Difficulty differentiating from fun segment Failure to extend familiar Cru Bourgeois term (which evokes "little local wonders") to whole of the Bordeaux district
Art	More than €20 Men over the age of 40 Hedonistic Significant perceived/real prestige	Great international enthusiasm Totally distinct market Marginal in terms of volume

In addition, Gapenne has noted a few positive trends that may turn into real opportunities for his company. One is the remarkable ongoing rise in 2012 of bag-in-box wines sold in large supermarkets. This format accounts for 25% of all sales volumes today and seems to reflect consumers' changing behavior at home, based on people drinking a glass here and there but not wanting to open a whole bottle because that makes it harder to keep the wine. In addition, two of the company's biggest customers—Carrefour (Prodis) and Géant Casino (Chais Beaucairois)—have indicated a rise in house brand sales.

Developments in the International market

Half of B&G's sales are overseas, meaning that the company does not suffer disproportionately from domestic or foreign competition. Different zones across the world have evolved in different ways, however. China, for instance, has witnessed strong growth of +93% in 2010 and +65% in 2011. The market is just starting to take shape, however, with local actors dividing various roles and product knowledge becoming increasingly important. French operatives will have to adjust their behavior to these changes. Japan is also a major growth market for the company. In North America, despite some difficult times, demand for $15 wine is on the rise, in competition with local wines (California) or South American products whose market share has also increased. Eastern Europe (notably Russia) is also experiencing an upturn, but has become quite unpredictable from year to year. Conditions in the European market are, however, less favorable, with demand remaining stable at best. England provides an interesting case with its alternating between demand geared some years toward branded wines (often based on a single grape) and other times returning to regional wines and "small French chateaux." What Gapenne has generally observed abroad is an alternation between people's desire to discover new products and seeking comfort in familiar ones. The first tendency makes small chateaux a differentiating factor for French growers. Conversely, the second strengthens branded wines that are more standardized. Here, the presence of powerful actors selling volumes and pursuing aggressive marketing techniques is a real problem for French companies. The challenge is figuring out when this trend might reverse. Toward that end, there needs to be an in-depth study of wine bars—which is where a great deal of after-work drinking takes place, thus, where people start to recommend certain wines, something that will often translate into future retail sales. It would appear that the quality of a particular vintage plays a major role in this respect.

Gapenne and the future of B&G

When asked about the future, Gapenne reasons like a chess player trying to calculate future moves. For the next three years, he is planning generally on maintaining volumes in the domestic market and increasing sales abroad. Profitability could be managed in two ways. B&G either keeps volume stable and increases margins (notably by intensifying the "exploration" segment, table 4) or increases volume by growing the size of the company, notably by hiring. In Gapenne's view, the latter option seems the best. Toward this end, three strategic maneuvers are being envisioned.

The first involves setting up offices in a few leading countries such as the United States, China, and/or Japan. Each would have one company employee whose goal would be to familiarize local customers with the company's culture and practices while also providing detailed descriptions of growers, chateaux, and the "wine-making stories" associated with their products.

This would be followed by the creation of a real sales force overseeing place-of-sales activities in mass retail outlets. Gapenne has often observed a gap between what is being referenced by his customers' purchasing combines and his products' actual presence on chains' shelves. To reduce this gap, he is thinking of putting together a sales force composed of four individuals covering the French market and running commercial events there.

Last, he might invest in storage facilities. For the moment, the company applies lean management principles and has one of the sector's lowest stock-to-turnover ratios. This can create a certain vulnerability, however, meaning that stock management has become a strategic consideration. Too many overseas clients have complained about Bordeaux companies' handling of top-quality grand cru wines, making sales conditional on the purchase of many other references that the customer does not necessarily want to buy. B&G does not practice this kind of sales approach and prefers letting customers freely put together their own orders.

Faced with these three orientations, the possibility of allying one day with another merchant should also be explored.

QUESTIONS

- Strategic marketing: What strategic orientations could B&G focus on for the next three years?
- Operational marketing: Given B&G's plans to build up its sales force, what advice would you give the company about how it might improve its sales force management?

AUTHOR'S PERSPECTIVE

B&G, a wine merchant working out of central Bordeaux, is highly representative of the French wine-growing economy. The case triggers two lines of questioning. The first relates to strategic development axes and long-term orientations (two). The second involves more operational, short-term marketing decisions (three). Before that, however, the identity and culture of this kind of company, operating as it does in France's wine-growing sector, needs to be specified (one).

A. STRATEGIC MARKETING
One: corporate identity and culture

B&G's corporate brand identity can be identified using McKinsey's "7S" model:

- Structure: Responsive organization with few staff members, a flat management structure, and high per capita turnover. In France, the sector is highly fragmented and broken up into a multitude of interests (more than 300 operatives in Bordeaux alone), often family-run companies with little equity capital.

- System: Traditional French business model in which tasks are split between two activities and merchants get involved: direct relationships with more than 600 growers (diversification of supply portfolio), all of whom are closely monitored nowadays thanks to new IT applications, and a balance between the domestic market (notably relationships with mass retailers) and exports.

- Strategy: The company's positioning outside of the world of grand cru top-quality wines is finely balanced between a very safe domestic market that is at best expanding slowly and export markets where the company, despite being at an early learning phase, is taking advantage of strong global growth.

- Shared values: Expertise, direct relations with growers, focus on adapting to consumers or new forms of market segmentation—all of this shows that B&G is market-oriented. In management terms, the corporate culture is characterized by a closely knit team built by senior management.

- Know-how: In terms of factors of differentiation, it is worth mentioning the diversified supplier portfolio (and the decision to entertain direct contacts with each) as well as real merchant know-how about the highly demanding mass retail market (exclusive offers, innovations). In the export markets, after the establishment of a few "bridgeheads," what is noteworthy is the company's willingness to secure its outlets.

- Staffing: The company's growth has given birth to new lines of business, notably international logistics and export sales. These are areas in which the company is understaffed and will have to invest.

Figure 3: The "7s" model

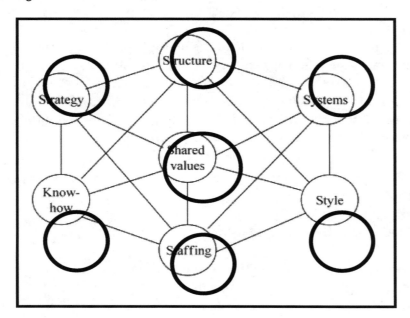

Two: strategic development

A DAS (Domaines d'Activités Stratégiques, "Areas of Strategic Activity") analytical tool provides enhanced understanding of the logic underlying B&G's product offer.

Figure 4: Areas of strategic activity

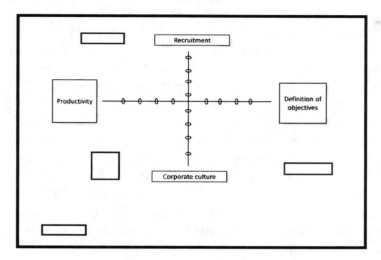

B&G's product offer is structured along three lines:

- Needs (French market): divided into three segments, with "fun" and "exploration" being the only ones that seem crucial at B&G. This appears to be a judicious choice because the "art" sector, which corresponds to top-quality grand cru, is rationed and associated with speculative and unpredictable behaviors. For storage volume reasons, the low-value "basic" segment is not really part of the company's mission, thus not viewed as a growth driver at present.

- Products: The company emphasizes traditional product offers (small French chateaux) composed of mixed wine brands that can vary depending on international demand. It is basically impossible, at this level, to determine an invariable product offer. Quite the contrary, ongoing adaptation to new trends is the rule. Otherwise, the growing bag-in-box market does not seem to be either a competitive advantage or a key factor of success for the company (volume logic). Having said that, B&G's ability to come up with special offers sold through mass retail outlets is a competency that should be accentuated (large accounts strategy, starting with Carrefour and Casino).

- Markets: Gapenne's relative disinterest in traditional markets is counterbalanced by his sense of the need for a greater frontline presence in mass retail channels and a few key overseas markets. This orientation consists of relying on a human presence to advise foreign importers or retailers and to help wine section point-of-sales managers. This makes face-to-face sales and advice a strategic priority for B&G and requires investment in sales force management, notably involving recruitment and training, network oversight, and the evaluation of frontline sales specialists.

B. Operational marketing

Similar to all companies, B&G's operational marketing relies on the coherency of the mix. In Gapenne's view, there is no real problem with B&G's product portfolios, advice, or price competitiveness. Similarly, communications are not very developed here, but this does not appear to be a key factor of success for an SME that has no ambition to grow globally but intends instead to target and lock in certain customers. After the recent major investment in a CRM (customer relationship management) application, there are still issues with the distribution channels and B&G's relations with partners at home and abroad.

The French wine-growing sector is very specific. Traditionally (and above and beyond the cooperative system), it has been characterized by a very strict rules-based system distinguishing between chateaux and other estates that account for most of the production versus merchants who are responsible for blending wines from different sources, developing product lines or brands, and marketing them. Things have also changed recently in France due to the actions of two new categories of market participants: the mass retail sector, which is in the hands of five big players (Carrefour, Auchan, Casino, Intermarché, and Leclerc) that account for 80% of total annual wine sales, and Internet and e-business channels, both of which constitute an argument for dealing directly with end users.

B&G does not really have any differentiating features online aside from its customers' greater familiarity with suppliers due to the secure extranet. However, its strong relationship with two mass retailers (Carrefour and Casino) is a key success factor. Despite being smaller than other top merchants (Castel, Grands Wine de France, GVG, CVBG, Ginestet, Mau, etc.) B&G has specific and exclusive product offers that the big retailers appreciate for category management reasons.

Behind this distribution of roles lies the whole issue of who in the French wine-growing sector captures whatever added value is being created. The battle here is between chateaux and other estates in certain districts (such as Saint Emilion, Médoc, Graves, or Côtes de Bordeaux) that make unique products and benefit from personal fame, thanks notably to direct sales or because they are part of a prestigious region—versus merchants who offer consumers their own added value by blending wines from rigorously selected sources. Last, the ability to work with large retailers is also paramount at a time when shelf space has become increasingly expensive. Value-added issues have long been a topic of debate, with answers generally depending on the circumstances at a given moment in time.

What is clear is that chateaux and other estates generally lack a sales culture. They have little knowledge of end users and few salespersons. They prospect rarely and have limited marketing resources. This explains why it is so important for a merchant like B&G to invest in sales. In France, the real mission for this kind of company is to blend wines and regulate the market by adjusting stock levels.

B&G is looking for two sales professionals: one specialized in the international market and the other in the mass retail sector.

Figure 5 shows the four parameters determining the efficient management of a sales force. We will be adapting it to B&G, an SME operating within the very specific context of the French wine-growing sector.

Figure 5. Evaluating sales force management.

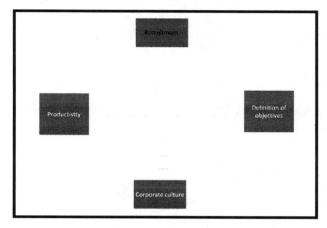

- Recruitment: Two kinds of competency are necessary at this level. Wines are complex products and retailers and consumers are afraid to make the wrong choice. They also require a significant amount of involvement as well as commitment to the purchasing act. We will therefore recommend a selection of applicants possessing basic technical training (undergraduate level) supplemented by graduate-level business studies. Salespersons working with large chains, which remain B&G's main commercial investment, will be asked to promote their wines to potential customers who are relatively knowledgeable, possess a great deal of information, and really only want to speak with a specialist.

- Productivity: International professionals must be fluent in English and familiar with distribution channels in the countries concerned (notably the United States). This would also be a new investment for B&G in an area that is less familiar to the company. The question here is the productivity of a new overseas sales force that is expensive and would not necessarily offer a good short-term return on investment. Penetrating a network composed of foreign importers and retailers requires understanding the local culture and knowledge of the state of international competition, which can be very different from the highly protected French market, where foreign wines have a market share of only 5%.

- Definition of objectives: Although managing this expanded sales force, B&G will have to distinguish between the objectives that everyone is being allocated. Some new recruits will work on prospecting, others on locking in customers, a third category will seek returns on promotional operations, and the final group of "ambassadors" will try to educate the markets in a top-of-the-range niche.

Through these four criteria, what becomes clear is how hard it is to accurately define the management of a sales team in a wine world that has become very heterogeneous in terms of culture and behavior.

READINGS

Davis, Timothy R., Ahmadi-Esfahani, Fredoun Z., and Iranzo, Susana, (2008), "Demand under differentiation: An empirical analysis of the US wine market," *The Australian Journal of Agriculture and Resources Economics*, 52, pp. 401–417.

Mora, P. (2006), "Key factors of success in the today's wine industry," *International Journal of Wine Marketing*, 18(2), pp. 139–149.

Mora, P., & Akhter, M. (2102), "Why and how some wine SME's resist to the crisis," *International Journal of Business and Globalization*, 8(1), pp. 95–111

Stanley, F., et al. (2000), "Strategic type and performance: The influence of sales force management," *Strategic Management Journal*, 21(8), pp. 813–829.

Wine Business Books From the Wine Appreciation Guild

Wine Marketing Online

How to use the newest tools of marketing to boost profits and build brands

Brue McGechan

The whole wired realm of wine marketing revealed in this encyclopedic yet readable and easy-to-follow guide.

- Discover the secrets that successful wine businesses use to market their wines online.
- Learn how to increase your credibility and be seen as an expert by your local customers.
- Generate Traffic to your website using Google.
- Convert that traffic into sales through fine-tuned content and a positive user shopping experience.
- Utilize social media to effectively engage with new and existing customers on your blog, Facebook, and Twitter.
- Ride the coming wave of mobile websites, apps, advertising and location based services like Foursquare and Yelp.
- Analyze your wine eCommerce software options.
- 'Finally' turn one-off orders into repeat loyal customers.
- and last but not least share your enthusiasm for wine and really enjoy your business

Wine Marketing Online includes a winery internet marketing and brand plan, wine store internet marketing plan, wine store financial model and wine competitor and customer research.

Paperback, 6 x 9 inches, 418 pages
Illustrations
Fully indexed
$29.95.
ISBN 978-1-935879-87-9

Wine Marketing & Sales: Success Strategies for a Saturated Market 2nd Edition

Paul Wagner
Liz Thach, Ph.D.
Janeen Olsen, Ph.D.

This completely revised and updated edition of the bestselling book by three of the industry's most connected insiders puts new, practical and powerful strategies into the hands of veteran brand managers and marketing professionals, and the vast bank of wine marketing knowledge within reach of the nascent winery owner.

"It's crucial to understand how to make a winery stand out from the crowd and yet fit into people's lifestyles in an enjoyable, meaningful way. This book does all of that and more. It is both credible and authoritative and very, very useful."
—**Robert Mondavi**

Hardcover, 7 x 10 inches, 400 pages,
Illustrated
Fully indexed
$75.00
SKU 7617-2ND
ISBN 978-1-934259-25-2